European Union Foreign Policy

What it Is and What it Does

Hazel Smith

Pluto Press

LONDON • STERLING, VIRGINIA

First published 2002 by Pluto Press
345 Archway Road, London N6 5AA
and 22883 Quicksilver Drive,
Sterling, VA 20166–2012, USA

www.plutobooks.com

British Library Cataloguing in Publication Data
A catalogue record for this book is available from the British Library

ISBN 0 7453 1870 3 hardback
ISBN 0 7453 1869 X paperback

Library of Congress Cataloging in Publication Data
Smith, Hazel, 1954–
  European Union foreign policy : what it is and what it does / Hazel
Smith.
    p. cm.
Includes bibliographical references and index.
  ISBN 0–7453–1870–3 (hardback) — ISBN 0–7453–1869–X (pbk.)
  1. European Union. 2. European Union countries—Foreign economic
relations. 3. European Union countries—Foreign relations. 4.
Europe—Foreign relations—1989– 5. International economic relations.
I. Title.
  D1060 .S58 2002
  341.7'094—dc21
                                                          2001005310

10   9   8   7   6   5   4   3   2   1

Designed and produced for Pluto Press by
Chase Publishing Services, Fortescue, Sidmouth EX10 9QG
Typeset from disk by Stanford DTP Services, Towcester
Printed in the European Union by Antony Rowe, Chippenham, England

To my three wonderful sisters – Yvonne, Helen
and Stephanie – with love and respect

Contents

Abbreviations and Acronyms

ACP	African, Caribbean and Pacific countries
AIPO	ASEAN Interparliamentary Organisation
ALA	Asian and Latin American countries
ALADI	Latin American Integration Association
AMU	Arab Maghreb Union
APEC	Asia-Pacific Economic Cooperation Forum
ARF	ASEAN Regional Forum
ASEAN	Association of South-East Asian Nations
ASEM	Asia-Europe Meeting
BFTA	Baltic Free Trade Area
CACM	Central American Common Market
CAP	common agricultural policy
CCP	common commercial policy
CEEC	Committee on European Economic Cooperation
CEFTA	Central European Free Trade Area
CET	common external tariff
CFSP	Common Foreign and Security Policy
CIS	Commonwealth of Independent States
CJTF	Combined Joint Task Force
CMEA	Council for Mutual Economic Assistance
COMECOM	Council of Mutual Economic Assistance
COREPER	Committee of Permanent Representatives
Cost	Cooperation in Science and Technology with Central and East European Countries
CSCE	Conference on Security and Cooperation in Europe
CSCM	Conference on Security and Cooperation in the Mediterranean
DG	Directorate-General
DPRK	Democratic People's Republic of Korea
EAD	Euro-Arab Dialogue
EAPC	Euro-Atlantic Partnership Council
EBRD	European Bank for Reconstruction and Development
ECHO	European Community Humanitarian Office
ECSC	European Coal and Steel Community
EDC	European Defence Community

EDF	European Development Fund
EEA	European Economic Area
EEC	European Economic Community
EFTA	European Free Trade Association
EIB	European Investment Bank
EJC	European Court of Justice
EMU	European Monetary Union
EP	European Parliament
EPC	European Political Cooperation
EPRD	European Programme for Reconstruction and Development
EPU	European Payments Union
ERASMUS	European Action Scheme for the Mobility of University Students
ERP	European Recovery Programme
ESDI	European Security and Defence Identity
ESDP	European Security and Defence Policy
Euratom	European Atomic Energy Community
EUREKA	European Research Coordination Agency
FDI	foreign direct investment
FPA	Framework Partnership Agreement
FRG	Federal Republic of Germany
Fritalux	French/Italian/Benelux tariff agreement
FSU	Former Soviet Union
FTA	free trade agreement
FYR	Former Yugoslav Republic
GATT	General Agreement on Tariffs and Trade
GCC	Gulf Cooperation Council
GRULA	Group of Latin American Ambassadors
GSP	Generalised System of Preferences
HSG	Heads of State and Government
IEPG	Independent European Programme Group
IFOR	Implementation force for Bosnia
IGC	Intergovernmental conference
IMF	International Monetary Fund
INOGATE	Inter-State Oil and Gas to Europe
JHA	Justice and Home Affairs
JOPP	Joint Venture Support Programme
KEDO	Korean Energy Development Organisation
KFOR	United Nations forces in Kosovo
LDC	less-economically developed country

MECU	million ECU
MEDA	financial and technical measures to accompany the reform of social and economic structures in the Mediterranean non-member countries
MERCOSUR	Common Market of the Southern Cone [of Latin America]
MFN	most favoured nation
NAFTA	North American Free Trade Area
NATO	North Atlantic Treaty Organisation
NGO	non-governmental organisation
NIS	Newly Independent States – normally referring to Russia and the successor states of the Soviet Union but excluding Estonia, Latvia and Lithuania
OAU	Organisation of African Unity
OECD	Organisation for Economic Cooperation and Development
OEEC	Organisation for European Economic Cooperation
OSCE	Organisation for Security and Cooperation in Europe
Overture	The Programme of Local Government Cooperation East–West
PCA	Partnership and Cooperation Agreement
PHARE	Poland and Hungary: Aid for Economic Reconstruction – the acronym comes from the French. The term now covers aid to all the countries of East and Central Europe
PLO	Palestinian Liberation Organisation
PPEWU	Policy Planning and Early Warning Unit
QMV	Qualified Majority Voting
ROK	Republic of Korea (south Korea)
SAA	Stabilisation and Association Agreement
SAARC	South Asian Association for Regional Cooperation
SACB	Somalia Aid Coodination Body
SDI	Strategic Defence Initiative
SEA	Single European Act
SELA	Latin America Economic System
SFOR	Stabilisation Force for Bosnia
SME	small and medium sized enterprise
STABEX	stability in export earnings
SYSMIN	support for mining sectors
TACIS	Technical Assistance for the CIS
TEMPUS	Trans-European Mobility Scheme for Universities

TEU	Treaty on European Union
TRACECA	Transport Corridor Caucasus Europe Asia
UNHCR	United Nations High Commissioner for Refugees
UNMIK	United Nations Mission in Kosovo
UNPROFOR	United Nations protection force for Bosnia
UNRWA	United Nations Relief and Works Agency
WEU	Western European Union
WTO	World Trade Organisation

Preface

European Union foreign policy is a moveable feast. The scope of activities and even its constituent territory and basic administrative apparatus are in a state of constant flux. When I started this book, however, while a Fulbright scholar at Stanford in 1994/95, it wasn't very fashionable to conceive of the EU as possessing a foreign policy. By the time I had finished it, while I was working with the UN World Food Programme in the DPR Korea (north Korea) in 2000/01, it was much more acceptable to talk about the Union as foreign policy actor – albeit a peculiar one. Today there seems a general acceptance that the Union is more than the sum of its parts when it acts abroad. Certainly for its many partners and competitors, its allies and adversaries, it is an international actor that has to be taken into account – and therefore understood – when considering strategies to manage international affairs. How to explain what the Union has done and is capable of doing abroad – what its priorities are and how it handles them – is the theme of this book.

Unfortunately the debates around EU foreign policy have too often been caught in the awful institutional cul de sac as to whether or not the Common Foreign and Security Policy (CFSP) should be considered as a 'fully-fledged' foreign policy. As the CFSP remains small in scope and based solely around what is discussed within certain (CFSP) procedures, it is self-evident that if the CFSP is taken as synonymous with European Union foreign policy, the Union has little to boast about in terms of its foreign policy activities. If foreign policy is understood, however, as something which includes all the Union's activities abroad, we can suddenly start to see a whole array of sometimes very important activities which, if carried out by a state, observers would have no difficulty identifying as part of that state's foreign policy (offering trade concessions to poor countries to discourage uncontrolled immigration for instance).

This book then is an attempt to chart the development of a Union foreign policy that is much more than that which happens to fall within the treaty provisions relating to the procedures of the CFSP. The book justifies this approach both analytically and empirically. In so doing the book also gives an account of what the Union has been up to throughout the world in its 50 years or so history. That this is necessary is testament to how much of the literature has been side-tracked into institutionalist scholasticism at the expense of trying to relate to students, scholars, practitioners and the general public just what the Union has achieved and where it has failed abroad and why that might be so.

I want to thank Jean Grugel, Fred Halliday, Chris Hill, Margot Light, Michael Nicholson, Jenny Pearce and Paul Taylor for their constant support, which I have greatly valued. Their high scholarly and ethical standards continue to provide an example to the profession. In this respect I want to again mention John Vincent, former professor at the London School of Economics who is still missed – not just for his out-standing work but also because of his humanity.

Finally, a special mention of Peter Burnham, Shirin Rai and Mark Rupert – fine and ethical scholars – and friends. Many thanks and much appreciation.

1 Does the European Union Have a Foreign Policy?

It seems an odd question to ask, if the European Union has a foreign policy. After all the title of this book presumes it has one and the contents list of this book shows a list of areas of discussion in relationship to that foreign policy. The reason we need to start with the question, however, is that it is by no means accepted as 'common sense' by policymakers, academics or students that the Union has a foreign policy as do states – for example, Britain or France or the United States. This chapter therefore sets out to show that the European Union does indeed have a foreign policy and that it can be analysed in pretty much the same way as we can analyse that of any nation-state. This chapter also presents a framework for analysis – a framework that is further developed in Chapter 4 – and which is used throughout the book to help us understand the scope and scale of the European Union's policies and activities abroad – its foreign policy. First of all, however, we need to look at and dispose of the objections to the *idea* of a European Union foreign policy.

SIX OBJECTIONS TO THE IDEA OF A EUROPEAN UNION
FOREIGN POLICY

Criticisms of the concept (the idea) of European Union foreign policy are both structural/institutional and capacity related. Structural/institutional critiques argue that the European Union is so deficient structurally or institutionally that it cannot take and implement foreign policy decisions. Capacity critiques argue that the Union may make decisions but its weak capacities prevent effective implementation and therefore the Union cannot be considered a foreign policy actor in the way that a nation-state can be considered so. The main structural/institutional critiques are that the Union is not a sovereign entity, it is subordinate to the wishes of the 15 member states and it does not have a centralised decision-making authority with a single executive. The three main capacity critiques are that the Union does not have a direct military capacity, that there is a significant capability–expectations gap and that it is not very effective in international crises. These are not mutually exclusive criticisms but it is useful to deal with them one by one – and then decide whether individually or in aggregate terms they amount to a compelling refutation of the idea of a European Union foreign policy.

The European Union is Not a Sovereign Entity

The European Union comprises 15 sovereign states. It has neither legal sovereignty nor international legal personality. Of the various institutions that together make up the Union only the European Community possesses legal personality and can therefore sign international legal agreements. Yet the Union, as represented by the European Council and the subsidiary Councils which preside over the Union, regularly takes decisions which are then implemented by the Community and a number of different actors. In other words it behaves *as if it were* sovereign. Certainly its partners – both allies and adversaries – negotiate and react to the Union as if it were a sovereign actor. This is because the Union has an impact on both the domestic and international affairs of partner countries such that it cannot be ignored. This is only partly because the member states have given up sovereignty to the Community (as part of the Union) on external trade.

Most importantly, however, the European Union is treated as if it were sovereign because even where the member states have not formally abrogated sovereignty they have allowed the Union, on many issues and with their participation, to take and implement decisions on their behalf. The Union therefore exercises sovereignty, not as something separate from the member states but as something that provides an addition to member state activities in international affairs. This does not mean that the European Union is a simple instrument of member states. Instead its decision-making structures allow for a process of negotiation so that a European Union commonality of foreign policy interest can be achieved. This commonality of foreign policy interest is not a simple aggregation of individual member states interest. It is also sometimes hotly contested by individual member states. On some foreign policy issues members states even accept 'losing out' because their overall view is that a commonality of European Union foreign policy provides more advantages than disadvantages. In other words the individual member states become more powerful in world affairs to the extent that they can regularly 'speak with one voice' on the world stage.

The European Union as such is not a sovereign international actor. Lack of formal sovereignty, however, has never stopped the Union from taking and implementing foreign policy decisions. Neither has the worry about giving up sovereignty to the European Union in practice affected member states' decisions to allow the European Union a very large degree of autonomy in a number of different areas – most noticeably in foreign trade. This should come as no surprise. After all many of the states of the European Union have already permitted a derogation of sovereignty on much more sensitive issues. The European Union member states that are also member states of NATO agreed when they joined that organisation that a United States supreme commander should take control over national military forces in times of crisis.

The European Union is a Subordinate Actor to the Member States

This objection is a variant of the lack of sovereignty thesis but emphasises that the Union is merely an instrument of the member states. For this criticism to make some sort of conceptual sense, it would have to take into account how the European Union manages to develop and implement foreign policy that somehow ends up serving the national interests of 15 different member states with 15 different foreign policies. Instead this argument seems to presume what it wishes to deny – which is that the European Union is a strong sovereign actor – so strong that it can transform 15 member states' foreign policies into a homogeneous single approach. Instead the answer is more complex.

In practical terms, the European Union does not act independently of the member states but neither is it either instrument of or subordinate to member states. Instead the various interests of the various actors involved in the Union are negotiated so as to find commonality of interests. The evidence for this is provided by the sometimes tortuous decision-making – involving trade-offs across policy areas – that accompanies the development of European Union foreign policy. It is also clear in foreign policy outcomes – for instance in the now notorious decision of the Union to recognise Croatia and Slovenia at the beginning of the Yugoslav wars (see Chapter 8), despite the major doubts of key member states.

In both conceptual and practical terms therefore it does not make much sense to conceive of the European Union as a subordinate actor to or mere instrument of the member states.

Lack of a Centralised Decision-making Capacity with a Single Executive

Another objection to the idea of the European Union possessing a foreign policy is that, because it does not have a centralised decision-making capacity with a single executive power such as a president or a prime minister, it cannot develop and implement foreign policy. The Union has a complex set of decision-making procedures with a central executive that is not one person but rather a group of people – the European Council. Decision-making procedures are clearly spelt out in the various legislation that underpins the Union in which the powers of the executive authority of the Union are also recognised.

What this criticism does is to confuse speed and alleged effectiveness with capacity. Decision-making processes are slower than in most national states and it is difficult to find a commonality of interests on every issue. These are, however, practical difficulties – sometimes very important practical difficulties – but they do not constitute a conceptual difficulty in the notion of a European Union foreign policy. Many states, particularly democratic states that are built upon a separation of governmental powers, are vulnerable to conflicting interest groups demanding different foreign policies in response to those different interests. The United States provides the best example of where conflicts over foreign policy result in inability of the central government to carry out its preferred policies. The unpopularity of President Reagan's policy towards Central America in the 1980s for instance forced the administration to 'go underground' – resulting in the illegal arms for hostages, the 'Irangate scandal' – which severely damaged the Reagan presidency. On the whole though the United States does not face such stark conflicts of foreign policy priorities such as to prevent its administration from carrying out foreign policies in areas which it considers vital to its national interests. Neither in practice has the Union been prevented from developing and implementing policies that serve the commonality of European Union foreign policy interest.

The most significant aspect of the criticism that the European Union does not possess a single executive capable of taking centralised decisions is the practical question of the time decisions take to be made. By itself this would not be a substantial criticism – after all the most efficient decision-makers are dictators given that, by definition, they do not have to consult at all prior to deciding policy. This criticism would be valid, however, if consistent delays meant that the European Union was unable systematically to develop and carry out its foreign policies. The rest of this book will show that this has occasionally been a problem for the European Union but not as much as it has sometimes been alleged – and not such as to prevent it from carrying on to develop policy where it wishes to sustain its interests and activities.

Lack of a Military Capacity

The European Union does not possess its own military forces although it is moving to develop a rapid reaction force so that it can respond more effectively to international emergencies. It can, however, call on the military resources of member states and has in fact worked closely with member state peace-keeping forces in international crises, for instance in former Yugoslavia. Like the member states, the European Union prioritises NATO as providing the defence mechanism for Western Europe. Indeed, many states throughout the world do not possess effective military forces yet most analysts and policymakers would accept that such states possess foreign policies. Costa Rica, which abolished its army in 1948, provides the extreme version of this thesis. Yet other states like Luxembourg for example do not have the capacity for either aggressive or defensive military activity. This does not prevent Luxembourg from possessing and implementing an active foreign policy. Neither does the absence of direct control over military resources prevent the European Union from pursuing and implementing foreign policy.

The Capability–Expectations Gap

The simplest version of this thesis is that the Union generates expectations that it simply cannot deliver on. The argument is that the Union puts out large numbers of statements on every conceivable foreign policy issue and yet is able to act effectively in very few areas. This can be for a number of reasons. It can be because of dissension between the member states, because the Union does not have appropriate instruments at its disposal – particularly military force – or simply because it was not designed to be a foreign policy actor and so finds it too difficult to respond effectively.

This argument has some merit as the Union clearly finds that it sometimes cannot operate as effectively as it might wish in international affairs despite the fact that it may have generated high expectations of its potential input. The classic example was the Union's early activity in Bosnia when it was hoped that 'Europe' would be able to settle matters without United States assistance (see Chapter 8). That this was a false hope caused some reconsideration of the Union's foreign policy capacity – resulting in the eventual moves to create a European Security and Defence Identity (see Chapter 3).

The error of this argument, however, is to infer that a capability–expectations gap is singular for the European Union. Many states – large and small – cannot put into practice foreign policy ambitions and when they do, sometimes fail to achieve their goals. China is a case in point in that during the Cold War China generated huge expectations from independence and revolutionary movements globally that it would be able to offer effective support. These expectations were not met. The United States, the world's only superpower, provides another salutary example. It was not able to achieve its war aims in Korea (1950–53), lost the war against tiny Vietnam (1975) and in the early twenty-first century is spending billions of dollars in an unsuccessful drive to eradicate narco-trafficking and anti-governmental guerrillas in Colombia.

The point is not then that the argument does not have merit but that it is an argument that is also applicable to the activities of most states as they try to achieve foreign policy objectives. The argument would have more merit if the Union could be shown as systematically not achieving objectives through lack of capabilities – more so than in the case of most nation-states. The chapters in this book which evaluate the foreign policy activities of the Union in practice – the empirical material – indicate, however, that the Union has achieved a large number of objectives and engaged in significant (and not so significant) foreign policy activities abroad (see Chapters 5, 6, 7 and 8).

The Union is Not Very Effective in International Crises

This effectiveness argument is a variant of the capability–expectations gap thesis except that it accepts that the Union can be an important foreign policy actor in, say, foreign trade or development issues, but argues instead that the Union cannot respond rapidly enough to international crises and its lack of a military capacity is fundamentally debilitating for its foreign policy ambitions. This argument certainly has plausibility in that the Union has been exposed as wanting in crises. Its structure means that it must achieve consensus on major issues and it simply does not have the power or the instruments to engage in crises at very short notice. On the whole though this does not provide a telling critique against the idea of a European Union foreign policy. It is not just that many states do not have the military power to intervene effectively in international crises. It is rather that even if the Union has difficulties in achieving short-term interventions, what it has shown is that it is particularly suited for more long-term interventions in crises. The Union's capacity to mobilise its own resources as well as to coordinate the activities of member states and other international organisations provides perhaps stronger guarantees for long-term sustained involvement in post-conflict reconstruction than promises by an individual state that may have to bend to domestic exigencies. In other words there is some argument that the Union may be uniquely well suited to manage more long-term involvement in what are increasingly the foreign policy tasks of the post-Cold War era – peace building and economic and political reconstruction.

In some ways the effectiveness argument is not predicated at all on the Union's lack of prowess as compared to the nation-state in general. What the argument rather presupposes is that the Union is not as effective in international crises as the United States. This is most of all an argument about power politics and relative capability of important political and economic entities. It is not about the theoretical possibility or not for the European Union to possess a foreign policy.

A EUROPEAN UNION FOREIGN POLICY

There are, therefore, no conceptual difficulties and few practical difficulties to the idea of the European Union possessing a foreign policy much the same as that of the nation-state. By foreign policy we mean the 'capacity to make and implement policies abroad which promote the domestic values, interests and policies of the actor in question'. This is not a catch-all definition which would permit an intergovernmental organisation like NATO or the Organisation for Security and Cooperation in Europe (OSCE) to claim foreign policy attributes. Instead this definition assumes an entity with a more or less coherent set of domestic values, interests and policies. This is certainly so for the European Union with its developed philosophy based on liberal capitalist democracy, and its panoply of domestic competencies and policies on issues ranging from the common market to cooperation in policing and judicial matters. *The foreign policy of the European Union is the capacity to make and implement policies abroad that promote the domestic values, interests and policies of the European Union.*

Common Ways of Understanding the European Union Foreign Policy

The most common ways of understanding (or theorising about) the foreign policy of the Union have been through procedural analysis. Some attempts have been made to theorise about the nature of the European Union as a foreign policy actor (its ontology). Less common have been empirical accounts of European Union activities abroad. One or two analysts have located the empirical material in analytical frameworks that consider the entirety of European Union foreign policy. These have been generally structured around a geographical or an issue-based approach.

Procedural or institutional analysis is that approach which examines the foreign policy of the European Union by taking the procedural and institutional competencies of the European Union as the primary level of analysis. It takes as central the legal division of international competencies into those derived from the treaties establishing the Communities and the Treaty on European Union. The treaties establishing the European Communities cover specified areas such as foreign trade and development and give the Commission a relatively large amount of authority and provide the Union with a wide variety of instruments with which to implement policy. By contrast the 'Common Foreign and Security Policy' provisions of the Treaty on European Union give the member states a predominant say in decision-making on every aspect of foreign policy that they should choose to discuss but offer few instruments for implementation of policy. Instruments are indirect – belonging either to the member states or deriving from the competencies allocated by the treaties for implementation through Commission-led procedures.

Procedural analysis equates the foreign policy of the European Union with that which emanates from the procedures of the Common Foreign and Security Policy. The effect of this conceptual error – the elision of 'European Union foreign policy' with 'the Common Foreign and Security Policy' – is to minimise and downgrade the foreign policy activities of the Union. First, as the CFSP has few instruments and is structurally unable to implement policy of itself, the impact is to argue that European Union foreign policy has little or no implementation capacity and therefore is inherently likely to be ineffective. Second, such an analytical strategy simply ignores the vast amount of external activity implemented through the legal competencies of the treaties establishing the European communities – on the grounds that this is not foreign policy 'proper'. The staggering effect is to rule out consideration of, for instance, many cases of sanctions or democracy promotion or the large-scale attempts to help create market economies and liberal democracies in Eastern and Central Europe – all of which are implemented through Community procedures – as foreign policy.

Procedural analysis is also misleading in that it underestimates the significant interplay between legally differentiated procedures. The General Affairs Council of the European Union discusses strategic foreign policy and then finds ways to implement policy – using either Community or 'Union' procedures in a fairly pragmatic manner. This approach also leads to an over-concentration in analysis on how decisions are made, at the expense of the study of what the European Union has actually been engaged in abroad. Compared to the evaluations of decision-making and procedures, there are relatively few case studies of European Union foreign policy to be found in the literature.

The procedural or institutional approach is enormously influential and is so pervasive that it shapes most evaluations of the foreign policy of the European Union. Exceptions include those that have tried to conceive of the nature of the European Union as a foreign policy actor as either a 'presence' in international affairs or in some ways a *sui generis* actor. Whether the European Union can best be conceived of as presence, quasi-state or some form of unique political entity does not, however, necessarily help in the evaluation of the scope and scale of that entity's foreign policy activities.

THE GEO-ISSUE-AREA APPROACH

The most useful ways of thinking about the foreign policy of the European Union have been those which engage with either the geographical reach of the Union abroad or which attempt to evaluate the various issues with which the Union has involved itself abroad. Both these approaches treat the European Union as a conglomerate actor. In other words they reject a one-sided analysis that treats

European Union foreign policy as only that which is operationalised through the mechanisms of the Common Foreign and Security Policy. These approaches avoid the error of only considering as important that which falls under the legal competence of the Common Foreign and Security Policy mechanisms. They are therefore able to offer a balanced appraisal of the various policies and activities that together comprise the foreign policy of the European Union.

This book combines both the geographical and the issue-area approach to explain and interpret European Union foreign policy. It takes as its premise that the European Union is an important actor in world affairs and that it makes and implements foreign policy and that it does this as a complex but relatively cohesive actor. The European Union engages in policy internationally although not in every area of the globe to the same extent. Like most nation-states, it has geographically different and distinct interests. It is also involved in different issue-areas to a greater or lesser extent – an issue-area being a complex body of policies related to one core theme.

The book does not suggest – far from it – that geographical areas of interest or issue-areas do not in practice overlap with each other in a sometimes messy and sometimes hard to discern separateness. The broad analytical structure presented here that argues for policy to be understood as operating more or less through the discernible analytical prism of the geographical categories suggested and the issue-areas identified can, however, be justified as the reflection of how EU policymakers seem to organise and see their subject matter. EU policymakers (and most observers) recognise the real life porousness of such categories but also recognise the real life necessity to delineate the categories to make them manageable.

GEOGRAPHICAL DEMARCATION

Broadly speaking the Union divides its attentions in the early twenty-first century into three broad areas of geographical and political interest. These are the rich members of the OECD, identified in this book as the 'North', the poorer countries of the 'South' and, third, the rest of Europe – termed here as the 'New Europe'. These are broad characterisations and there are clearly overlaps between groups. The Union for instance tends to deal with Russia as a European state – even though large parts of both the former Soviet Union and the current Russian states are by any definition part of the Asian landmass. In this book the North is understood as comprising most of the non-European Organisation of Economic Cooperation and Development (OECD) countries, the 'neighbouring South', the Mediterranean neighbours and the Arab world, and the distant South – the African, Caribbean and Pacific (ACP) countries, Asia and Latin America. The 'New Europe' comprises post-Cold War Europe – including the non-EU Scandinavian states, Russia and the Newly Independent States of the former Soviet Union, the East and Central European states, the South-eastern European states and the three Mediterranean applicants (Cyprus, Malta and Turkey).

The South is clearly itself a very heterogeneous grouping of countries indeed – ranging from the micro-states of Polynesia to the immensely large countries of China, India and Brazil. One way that the EU has dealt with the necessity to differentiate within the South has been to concern itself more directly with Southern states that are contiguous to its landmass and therefore of more direct security and economic concern – and, conversely, to involve itself in a much more diffuse manner with states that are geographically distant. We can think of Union foreign policy towards the South, therefore, as being divided into that directed towards the 'neighbouring South' and the 'distant South'. This again is not a hard and fast definition. During the 1980s for instance the European Union became politically and economically involved in the faraway Central American crisis in a sustained and important manner – helping to resolve the conflicts that had caused massive loss of life and economic destruction during the 1970s and 1980s (see Chapter 7).

The analytical framework for the empirical Chapters 5, 6, 7 and 8 is shaped by the Union's geographical demarcation of foreign policy. Chapter 5 considers EU relations with the North, Chapter 6 the neighbouring South, Chapter 7 the distant South, and Chapter 8 reviews the European Union in the New Europe. In terms of balance, the book has less to say on relations with the North, partly because the volume of activities in relation to the South and, since the early 1990s, the East is relatively larger – the Northern countries, after all, forming only a very small percentage of the world's states.

The North

For the European Union, the OECD states, with some exceptions, constitute the North. Mexico and the Republic of Korea have joined the OECD but it will probably take some time before the European Union shifts from its primary orientation towards these states as within the context of an Asian and Latin American focus. In addition, European Union foreign policy towards the OECD, extra-EU European states, including Norway and Switzerland, is assessed in Chapter 8 in the context of EU policy towards the New Europe. In Chapter 5, therefore, it is the non-European OECD states that are discussed – that is the United States, Japan, Canada, Australia and New Zealand. European Union foreign policy towards the North is focused on trade – although security differences have sometimes caused rifts between the Union and its major OECD partner, the United States. European Union foreign policy towards the North has been absolutely dominated by its concern with relations with the United States and these relations, which are documented in Chapter 5, have not always been harmonious.

The South

The European Union of the early twenty-first century has no formal hierarchy of commitments in its relations with the countries of the South and has a range of different, sometimes competing and conflicting, political and economic objectives in respect of its Southern partners. Policies towards the South are in a state of flux, as indeed are the instruments used to implement those policies such as the different types of association, cooperation and trade agreements. Internal and external pressures have combined to force the EU to review both policies and instruments. The successful conclusion of the Uruguay Round of the General Agreement on Tariffs and Trade (GATT) in December 1993 meant that the EU had to review all its trade agreements with third states and regional groupings, particularly those with which it has had some form of protected or specially regulated arrangements. But probably the most important of the external pressures forcing a review of policy were the enormous political and economic changes in Eastern Europe in the 1990s which sharply focused EU foreign policy attention on pan-European politics and, some would argue, away from its broader global commitments.

Change in Union foreign policy towards the South

When the EC was established, policy towards the South was relatively uncomplicated. Clear priorities were to forge mutually beneficial trade and aid links with ex-colonies and overseas territories of the member states. From the 1950s up until the early 1970s, the EC emphasised its special relationships with ex-colonies and overseas territories – relationships which were managed by first the Yaoundé (see Chapter 2) and, from 1975, the Lomé conventions.

The oil crisis of 1973, however, forced a reconsideration of the EC's Southern priorities, ensuring that the EC and its mainly oil-importing member states would have to take seriously the claims of oil-producing states – predominately from the Arab world. The second Cold War of the 1980s further pushed small poor countries on to world agendas as the bellicose Reagan administration in the United States engaged itself in a worldwide fight against the Communist Soviet Union that was mainly fought out in what was commonly called the 'Third World'. The European Community as an ever stronger international actor with interests and objectives of its own which were sometimes at variance with those of the United States found itself acting as participant and occasional mediator in some of these conflicts (see Chapter 5) and inclined to use its increasingly more powerful instruments (economic aid, sanctions and diplomacy) to intervene to defend its own interests. The 1981 and 1986 enlargement of the Community to include the Mediterranean states of Greece, Portugal and Spain, also brought new issues on to the foreign policy agenda. The EC's new neighbours in northern Africa demanded new deals in terms of economic assistance and trade agreements, while the EC was anxious to secure arrangements that would help it to forestall political and economic instability on its southern flank.

By the early 1990s, however, the EC/EU was chastened in its attempted international role towards the South by its inability to act as anything other than junior partner to the United States in the Gulf War of 1990/91 and the subsequent Middle East peace process. Yet the EU also wanted to promote its specific interests in the context of increasing worldwide economic interdependence through trying to forge new relationships with Asia and Latin America, the southern pacemakers in the world's globalising economy. The EU recognised the rise in international importance of the 'emerging' Asian polities and economies, particularly China and South Korea but also the Association of South East Asian (ASEAN) countries and tried to develop new forms of partnership with these states (see Chapter 7). Similarly the EU attempted to rework its relationships with Latin American states which, in the 1990s, began to play a more significant role in the international political economy. Mexico was important because of its institutional link to the United States and Canada in the North American Free Trade Area (NAFTA) and MERCOSUR (the southern common market of Latin America comprising Argentina, Brazil, Paraguay and Uruguay) because of its economic weight and potential (see Chapter 7).

The foreign policy constants

The EU has had two constants in its foreign policy towards the South. The first was the concern to manage relations effectively with its southern neighbours to avoid 'spill-over' of instability and violence into its territory. The second was to continue to deliver on its historic commitments to ex-colonies and overseas territories and dependencies. The EU attempted to integrate these commitments into a global foreign policy towards the South in the context of the evolution of what is by now an extensive network of international relations. Much of this network is institutionalised in formal agreements and many of these agreements are incorporated into what has become the EU's characteristic regional approach to foreign policy. The EU prefers to negotiate region to region agreements and to encourage regional associations with its partners where this is possible. This regionalisation strategy is not confined to relations with the South but this approach is particularly manifest there, in the number, duration and visibility of interregional arrangements – most clearly with the long-lasting association with the African, Caribbean and Pacific states via the Lomé, now the Cotonou, agreements.

The EU boasts that it is the developing world's major trading and development aid partner. In 1999, Development Commissioner Poul Nielson announced that the Union constituted the developing countries' first trade partner – providing around 22 per cent of their exports and imports. In 1998 the European Union and the member states provided nearly 50 per cent of the world's official development assistance. In 1997, the EC alone was the world's fifth largest aid donor. It has cooperation agreements of various sorts with around 120 Southern states and by 1998 was funding development projects in over 170 states and dependent territories. Aid priorities have changed such that Russia, Eastern and Central Europe, the Mediterranean and the Middle Eastern states have assumed more prominence – at the expense of the poorer African, Caribbean and Pacific states. Actual disbursements of aid in 1998 for instance gave 1,958 million Euros to the East and Central European states and the Newly Independent States of the former Soviet Union, compared to 1,711 million Euros to sub-Saharan Africa and 438 million Euros to south and central Asia. Between 1986 and 1998 the sectoral breakdown of EU aid also changed from around 45 per cent to 65 per cent for long-term development projects. In the same period food aid decreased from just under 40 per cent to around 10 per cent of all EU aid. The rest has been allocated to areas ranging from humanitarian aid for refugees and victims of natural disasters through to assistance for trade expansion schemes and structural adjustment support.

Two different emphases

The European Union's foreign policy to its nearest Southern neighbours has been shaped by its broad security concerns. Its approach to the more distant South has, by contrast, been framed within the context of straightforward trade and development cooperation concerns – and very infrequently by security issues. The two chapters on foreign policy towards the South follow, therefore, these demarcation lines. Chapter 6 analyses foreign policy towards the Mediterranean, including the Maghreb, Mashreq and the Middle East sub-regions and the Gulf states. Chapter 7 reviews policy and practice towards Africa, the Caribbean and the Pacific (the ACP); Asia; and Latin America.

THE NEW EUROPE

The foreign policy of the European Union towards the rest of Europe has been transformed from something almost peripheral to its external concerns to the centre of its foreign policies and activities. This change has occurred in a very short period of time – beginning at the end of the Cold War in the late 1980s. At the same time, EU policies towards the rest of Europe have assumed an interchangeable internal/external relation as Austria, Finland and Sweden joined in 1995 and most of the rest of the continent is either engaged in active negotiations to join or planning how it can enter into that process. There is a huge variety of EU concerns in the New Europe at the turn of the twenty-first century. These range from preventing further killing and violence in South-East Europe and Turkey to managing trade and cooperative relations with nations like Norway and Switzerland which, although non-members, are extraordinarily close to the EU in terms of harmonisation of domestic and external policies.

Europe or Asia?

There is a geographical overlap between Europe and Asia – and this book includes as European states those which have both identities – most notably Russia and Turkey. The analytical reasons for treating these regions as part of 'Europe' reflect the political concerns of Union leaders. Core European Union security concerns depend upon and are directly tied up with Russian and Turkish policies and activities in Europe. It is inconceivable, for instance, that a resolution to the conflicts in South-East Europe could be resolved without some form of Russian participation. In addition, there will be continuing Russian sensitivities in terms of any build-up of military capacities and/or political systems which could provide perceived threats to Russian security from the East and Central European border states to Russia. Apart from the fact that the EU recognised that Turkey was 'European' enough to join the then EC when it accepted Turkish candidature for membership as far back as 1963, Turkey is also important as a security actor in European Union affairs. It is not just a key player in the resolution of the Cyprus problem but also provides a potential EU 'gateway' to the former states of the Soviet Union in Central Asia.

For the European Union, the Former Soviet Union (FSU) states of Central Asia and the Caucasus are often referred to in the context of discussions about the New Europe. This 'European' status partly reflects Organisation for Security and Cooperation in Europe (OSCE) policy to allow these states membership of the pan-European organisation in recognition of their position as successor entities to the former Soviet Union.

The Sub-regional Divisions

In Chapter 8, EU foreign policy towards the rest of Europe is analysed in respect of five sub-regions. These are Northern Europe, Russia and the Commonwealth of Independent States (CIS), East and Central Europe (ECE), South-East Europe (SEE) and the three remaining southern Mediterranean applicant states – Turkey, Cyprus and Malta.

The European Union has treated the Baltic states as 'East and Central European countries' – not states of the FSU – since 1991 after it considered them eligible for EU economic reconstruction funding for East and Central Europe – the PHARE facility. This compares with the EU categorisation of Russia and the CIS states or the 'Newly Independent States' (NIS) as a coherent group. This group of states is treated differently from the ECE states in that their primary source of Union development assistance is from the TACIS funding mechanism – not the PHARE facility. In addition the European Union has increasingly categorised states which it foresees it may accept into Union membership as ECE states. The designation of NIS is partially designed to differentiate applicant states from those whose candidature would be a very distant prospect.

ISSUE-AREAS

The European Union, like most states, is involved in a whole number of foreign policy issues – some of which are little more than uncontroversial day-to-day interchanges with persons, entities and countries outside its borders. Other issues, however, can assume grave political importance and these issues are only sometimes confined to the classical issues of high politics or military security. For example, the European Union's unwavering commitment to help redemocratise the states of Eastern and Central Europe has little to do with a potential military attack on EU territory but everything to do with political security and stability for EU states that want to protect themselves against any future Communist threat to EU governing regimes. An issue-area perspective allows for an interrogation of foreign policy areas so as to determine when low politics becomes high politics – and allows us to keep on the analytical agenda all the issues which the EU has been concerned with abroad in its mission to protect its domestic interests and values at home. An issue-area is constituted by a complex body of policies related to a core central theme.

The classical themes of foreign policy analysis are security and defence. Since the ratification of the Maastricht Treaty in November 1993, with its consolidation in the Amsterdam Treaty of 1999, the EU is now in official possession of a common foreign and *security* policy – a recognition that the classic concerns of the foreign policy of states are also central to the foreign policy of the EU. There are also other issues, however, which are important for foreign policy-makers and hence foreign policy analysts. The international politics of trade and money are key concerns of any contemporary government – as are less controversial areas such as overseas aid. And the European Union, like national governments, has a wide variety of foreign policy concerns in different issue-areas, including security. In the early twenty-first century, the most important of EU foreign policy issue-areas are *security and defence, external trade, development aid, interregional cooperation and enlargement.*

EU foreign policy is implemented by various key actors, underpinned by differing legal foundations, and characterised by different decision-making procedures depending on the issue and the policy. In addition, the European Union implements policy in each issue-area using a variety of different instruments. This section outlines these core issue-areas and indicates some of the actors, instruments, legal bases and decision-making procedures utilised by the European Union within these issue-areas. One word of warning is warranted, however. The organisation of the material in terms of 'issue-areas' is only an analytical device that is meant to help elucidate the relevant dynamics of Community/Union foreign policy. Such an organisation of the material does not imply that there ever was not or is not, in practice, a great deal of overlap and trade-off between issue-areas.

Security and Defence

In the classical sense of a security policy that is based on military policy and practice, the European Union has only a weak interest in this issue-area and few direct capabilities. Security in the post-Cold War world, and arguably before, means much more to the Union, however, than military defence. Security, for the Union, includes political stability that in turn involves, among other things, reduction of crime, control of the narcotics trade, migration control, environmental protection and the maintenance of liberal democratic systems. These 'new' areas of security are of direct concern to the Union, which engages in a wide variety of policies in order to respond to changing threats to stability worldwide.

The idea of the EU engaging in security-related issues has, however, been controversial given that the member states regard this issue-area as at the core of their national prerogatives – particularly in the military arena. It was only as recently as 1983 that the EC had been first permitted to discuss 'the political and economic aspects' of security. No further authorisation was given in the 1987 Single European Act (SEA). If anything the SEA reinforced the separation of security institutions from politico-economic institutions in Western Europe – insisting that those states which wished to form closer security links should do so via the Western European Union or NATO. The ratification of the Maastricht Treaty on European Union (TEU) in 1993 brought quite an innovation in that it recognised that the Union had developed cooperation between its member states to such an extent that security cooperation was politically feasible. Although the TEU did not identify areas in which security cooperation might be immediately possible, discussions did take place during the treaty negotiations which resulted in an agreement that four areas would be priorities for EU action. These were the Conference on Security and Cooperation in Europe (which changed its name in January 1995 to the Organisation for Security and Cooperation in Europe – OSCE); disarmament and control of arms in Europe; nuclear non-proliferation; and the economic aspects of security – particularly the transfer of military technology to third countries and arms export controls.

The EU has not managed to move along the continuum from discussion of security-related issues to organisation of a common defence policy and is certainly not in a position to offer a common defence of the Union. This was particularly evident in the mid-1990s in the former Yugoslavia crisis as the United States resumed its leadership role in the Western alliance in respect of European security. Implementation of any security policy that is discussed within the framework of the CFSP remains, therefore, with a number of different actors – within and without the EU. On issues that involve the deployment of military forces it is NATO that remains the core actor. The WEU has extended its capacities and engaged in actions on the ground – for instance it provided police forces for the EU administered town of Mostar in Bosnia – but it has not evolved in any way as a comparable security instrument to NATO. The Amsterdam Treaty bolstered this cautious approach to allocating security responsibilities to the European Union. The Union was now permitted to 'avail itself' of Western European Union capabilities and some possibility was allowed for merger of the WEU and the EU should the two organisations consider this fruitful in the future. Procedures were improved and clarified (see Chapter 3) but considerable autonomy was left to member states to decide on whether or not to engage in Union-led collective security ventures.

Further attempts to create what has become known as the European Security and Defence Policy (ESDP) materialised at the 1999 European Council in Cologne which announced that it intended to develop a military capacity in the context of member states' commitments to NATO. The intention was, 'where NATO as a whole is not engaged', to be able to deploy European Union military forces where necessary – particularly to respond to the exigencies of crisis management. To this end the Union committed itself to creating a 50,000 to 60,000-strong Rapid Reaction Force by 2003. The Union was very careful to spell out its primary commitment to NATO, however, and it remains to be seen as to whether the force envisaged will become operational and, if it does, whether it will be of significance in helping the Union achieve foreign policy goals.

Actors, instruments, legal bases and decision-making procedures

The key actors on security and defence issues continue to be the member states. The European Council therefore provides a significant forum in respect of developing common positions on security issues. The importance of the Council has been magnified since the 1993 Treaty on European Union (TEU). This is partly because it contains two states – Britain and France – that are permanent members of the UN Security Council and that are now bound by the TEU to coordinate with the other 13 member states on issues that concern them all. The Council is also a significant actor for coordinating European security positions given that not all EU member states are NATO members, but NATO has proved itself the key actor in pan-European security in the 1990s and early 2000s. EU non-NATO members have a potentially significant part to play in helping shape policies of EU states that are also members of NATO. The TEU committed the EU to work in harmony with NATO and the Council's coordinating role is therefore potentially significant. Military force, trade sanctions and aid, development aid and diplomatic intervention provide the potential armoury of EU security potential. The instruments at the disposal of the EU, in theory, include the whole gamut of EU and member state foreign policy capabilities. The legal foundations for security cooperation can be found in Title V of the 1999 Amsterdam Treaty. The decision-making procedures are intergovernmental.

Trade

The European Community assumed supranational capacities in respect of member state domestic and external trade policy in the Treaty of Rome. The various treaties signed since 1957 have tended to diminish the Commission's autonomy in trade matters but it is still the policy area in which the Union (through the Community pillar) has powers over and above those of the member states. Trade-based relationships often form the foundation of EU foreign relations and the Union has trade-based relationships with over 150 states and international organisations. Some agreements are extensive – for instance the comprehensive agreement negotiated within the GATT at the end of the most recent round of multilateral trade bargaining – the Uruguay Round. Others can involve just one product and involve an agreement with one state.

Some trade agreements have very little directly to do with major foreign policy concerns. These contrast with those such as the GATT negotiations that involved friction with the EU's most important ally, the United States, and were of foreign policy consequence. However, even trade policies in respect of just one product can have foreign policy ramifications. A very visible manifestation of this was the row over the EC/EU's banana imports in which African, Caribbean and Pacific (ACP) banana producers were in conflict with Central American banana producers for European markets. For small states that rely on one or two crops like bananas to provide vital revenues, EU trade decisions are more than economic and can involve the EU in diplomatic efforts to avoid conflict. The most high-profile aspect of the EU's trade competencies in foreign policy terms, however, is the Union's power to impose sanctions on a third state. The Maastricht Treaty recognised this capability in Article 228a (since the Amsterdam Treaty Article 301) when the Union explicitly accepted linkage between this feature of EU trade policy and the common foreign and security policy.

The Union's trade links have had a dual impact on the development of a Union foreign policy. On the one hand EC/EU trade policies and instruments enabled it to operationalise its foreign policy goals. Trade incentives, for instance, are an important instrument in the pursuit of foreign policy objectives such as stability in the Mediterranean and democratisation in Central and Eastern Europe. On the other hand the fact that the EU is the world's largest trading bloc elicits a foreign policy momentum of its own. Trading partners do not separate EU trading policies from a composite assessment of EU and member states' foreign policies – and thus pressure remains on the EU to maintain consistency in its external relations. Over the years this need for consistency between all aspects of EC/EU policies has been recognised as a major aim. The Treaty on European Union laid an obligation on the Council to 'ensure the unity, consistency and effectiveness of action by the Union'. The Amsterdam Treaty also attempted to tighten coordination so as to have a more efficient and effective foreign policy.

Actors, instruments, legal bases and decision-making procedures

The Council and the Commission are the key players in the trade aspects of EU foreign policy. The Parliament's role has increased in recent years so that it can now hold hearings and adopt resolutions on trade issues which come under Article 133 (ex 113) of the treaties.

It is the Commission's responsibility, however, to bring proposals forward on the common commercial policy (CCP) although the Council must authorise the Commission to open negotiations with third states or international organisations. The Council is also involved in CCP decision-making through the Article 133 (ex 113) committee, which is a Council-appointed committee designed to ensure that the member states' interests are taken into account. The Parliament has an important input into association agreements, which are always a mix of trade and other provisions. Under Article 310 (ex 238) the Parliament must give its assent to the agreement. The instruments at the Union's disposal are diverse and include simple tariff agreements, the GSP, trade, cooperation and association treaties, and diverse economic sanctions.

The legal bases for Union decision-making vis-à-vis trade are founded in the Treaty of Rome provisions and brought up to date in the 1999 Treaty of Amsterdam. Trade competencies are subject to European Court of Justice jurisdiction and 'Community procedures' and in this sense there are elements of supranationality in the decision-making process. Another supranational element is in the system of qualified majority voting used by the Council to decide on issues relating to the common commercial policy.

Development Cooperation

The Amsterdam Treaty did not alter the changes effected by the 1993 Treaty on European Union that consolidated custom and practice of EC/EU development cooperation. It had done so by both adding new treaty provisions and by retaining relevant parts of the 1957 Rome Treaty. The founding treaty had specifically included provisions for association with countries and territories that had 'special relations' with member states. These 'special relations' referred to the dependent status of colonies or overseas territories and the purpose of such association was to assist both in economic and social development of those countries and to strengthen economic relations between them and the then EEC. As ex-colonies became independent, their association with the EC was institutionalised in the treaty framework of the four Lomé conventions of 1975, 1979, 1984 and 1989 – now bringing together 71 African, Caribbean and Pacific states in association with the EU (Lomé being replaced by the Cotonou agreement in 2000).

The Maastricht provisions went further than the original Rome Treaty intentions by allowing the Union a capacity to enter into development cooperation with *all* less-economically developed states – although it still acknowledged the special status of its relations with the ACP states and with the remaining dependent territories. Developing countries are divided into two categories for EU purposes. The first is that of the 'associated' countries and, as the term suggests, includes all those developing countries that had some form of association agreement with the Union. Conversely, 'non-associated' developing states are those less-economically developed states that had agreements – some of which are institutionalised, such as the San José process of negotiations with the Central American Common Market (CACM) states – but which were less comprehensive and substantial than the 'association' agreements. The non-associated states are predominately situated in Latin America and Asia.

The Maastricht Treaty provisions on development cooperation had increased the Union's competencies in respect of development cooperation but also stressed that the Community's aid should be complementary – not a substitute – for member state aid. The Treaty correspondingly insisted on the importance of close coordination between the Community and the member states on their aid programmes, in international organisations and in international conferences. The Commission was permitted to take initiatives to bring about any necessary cooperation although the Treaty emphasised that provisions on development aid could not override member states' competencies in this area. In practice the TEU codified the actual evolution of EU aid-giving and did not offer substantial new powers to the Union.

The most obvious link between development policy provisions and the foreign policy of the Union was the reference in Article 177 (ex Article 130u) to the objectives of policy, which 'shall contribute to the general objective of developing and consolidating democracy and the rule of law, and to that of respecting human rights and fundamental freedoms'. This sentence replicated, almost word for word, one of the objectives of the CFSP, as set out in Article 11 (ex article J.1) of Title V of the TEU. Thus development cooperation was very specifically intended to assist achieve the overall foreign policy aims of the Union. This represented a change from earlier EC development cooperation policy, which was to develop 'partnerships of equals'. Since Maastricht, the emphasis has been on conditionality in EU development policy.

In this book development cooperation includes long-term aid – and humanitarian and emergency support, including food aid. In short, development cooperation includes grant or loan assistance in the form of cash or kind which is offered to partner countries on non-commercial criteria.

Actors, instruments, legal bases and decision-making procedures

The Council, Commission and Parliament have input into development policymaking. Implementation is by a number of actors including directly by the Commission and the European Investment Bank and indirectly by non-governmental organisations. The EU also works closely with other international organisations such as the UNHCR, the World Health Organisation (WHO), UNICEF and the World Food Programme (WFP) – in particular in the joint-funding and management of humanitarian operations.

The Union is able to use at least three different sources of finance to pursue its development cooperation objectives – and therefore its foreign policy objectives. These sources are the EU's own budget, the European Development Fund (EDF) and the European Investment Bank. Between 1986 and 1988 the percentage of resources from the budget that were spent on external cooperation was only 36 per cent; between 1996 and 1998 this percentage had rocketed to 75 per cent. This increase is largely due to commitments to support East and Central Europe and the Newly Independent States of the former Soviet Union. In parallel, the percentage of external cooperation funded from the EDF has decreased from 57 per cent to 18 per cent in the same period and EIB resources have remained at a steady state of 7 per cent. The 1999 financial framework for EU spending increased projected external cooperation spending so that between 4½ and 6 billion Euros a year will be spent on external action. These sums still remain very small compared to, for instance, the major areas of Community expenditure which are on agricultural support (some 40 billion Euros in 2000) and structural funds (around 30 billion Euros in 2000).

Additional aid to the ACP countries came from the EDF – funded by EU member states separately from the EU's budget but managed by the Commission. A third source of funding for developing countries is the EIB whose loans are available to ACP and non-ACP states that meet the criteria for EU assistance (including those located in Central and Eastern Europe). Apart from EIB funding, most EU aid is disbursed in the form of grants – not loans. Development cooperation funding may be disbursed within the context of different programmes, ranging from that of emergency aid to aid allocated within the context of long-term, comprehensive partnership agreements – such as the Cotonou agreement.

The legal basis for funding development cooperation is institutionalised in Article 177 (ex Article 130u) to Article 181 (ex Article 130y) of the treaty. Part Four of the Rome Treaty remained as Articles 182 to 188 in the revised treaty establishing the European Communities and this allowed for continued 'association' of still dependent territories with the Union. 'Association' of the *independent* lesser developed countries (LDCs) – for instance the ACP states and the Mediterranean countries – operates on the basis of a different part of the amended Rome Treaty – Article 310 (ex Article 238).

The decision-making procedure on the making of development cooperation policy is governed by the Union's interinstitutional cooperation procedure (set out in Article 252 – ex Article 189c) which permits the Parliament to offer opinions and propose amendments to Commission-initiated legislation. There is a further element of supranationality involved in that where the Parliament approves or does not comment on a Commission proposal, the Council may agree the proposed legislation by qualified majority (should the Parliament reject the proposal the Council is required to reach unanimity).

Interregional Cooperation

The EU has developed political and economic relations with over 20 groups of states. These 'group-to-group dialogues' as they are sometimes called, bring the Union into institutionalised relationships with regional associations of states from both the industrialised world – as with the European Free Trade Association link – and the South. The largest of the latter links is the ACP–EU relationship but others include the links with the Association of South-East Asian nations (ASEAN), the Gulf Cooperation Council (GCC), the Rio Group and the Common Market of the Southern Cone of Latin America (MERCOSUR) – to name but a few. These institutionalised links have grown in scope and importance so that, at the beginning of the twenty-first century, European Union interregional cooperation covers much of the world and coordinates aid, trade and sometimes political dialogue in these multilateral relationships. This aspect of EU foreign policy developed through a combination of a philosophical bias towards interregional cooperation and pragmatic responses to events.

An EU bias towards interregional cooperation and the encouragement of regional cooperation and integration elsewhere in the world is a result of a philosophy which argues that the postwar creation of the EC helped not just to create a more prosperous Europe but also, through integration, to create the conditions where war, especially between the historic enemies of France and Germany, could not take place again. Thus, the reasoning goes, if states elsewhere learned to resolve their disputes peacefully, as had the EC, the prospects for a peaceful world might improve. Given this philosophy, when the EU engages in *inter*regional cooperation, it almost always, at the same time, supports *intra*regional cooperation.

Interregional relationships were established out of both economic and political motivations. The Euro–Arab dialogue (founded in 1973), for instance, was intended to form part of a European Community strategy to both safeguard oil supplies and to work out ways of assisting in bringing stability to the Middle East. The dialogue with the Central American Common Market (established in 1984) was almost entirely designed to find ways to assist the peace process in the then Central American conflicts. Relations with ASEAN, although ostensibly economic in nature, were motivated by the ASEAN nations' fear of communism and their perception that EC links would assist their consolidation into the Western camp (during the Cold War). For the Union, the links with ASEAN give the Europeans a 'bridge' into Asia. Interregional cooperation remains a preferred option for the EU – as is evident by its initial attempts to build multilateral agreements with the former Communist states of Eastern Europe.

Actors, instruments, legal bases and decision-making procedures

The Council, Commission and Parliament play a role in the development of group-to-group dialogues and it is difficult to generalise about their activities as each case of interregional cooperation has evolved in a different manner – in response to the different characteristics and requirements of each separate relationship. There is no specific discussion in the treaties of interregional cooperation even though this has become an important aspect of EU foreign policy. The association agreements are themselves instruments of policy in that trade, aid and political protocols are coordinated within the cooperation framework established by agreement.

Article 310 (ex Article 238) specifically permits the EU to enter into association with 'one or more states or international organisations'. Article 308 (ex Article 235 of the Treaty of Rome), which permits the Council to take action even if the treaties do not provide explicit competence, and which prior to the TEU sometimes served as a legal base for interregional cooperation, remains in force. The decision-making procedures in respect of agreements set up under Article 310 (ex Article 238) relating to association with one or more states are set out in Article 300 (ex Article 228). Parliament must be consulted and must give its assent to all association agreements that either establish institutional frameworks for organising cooperation or 'having important budgetary implications'. This process of consultation must follow the new conciliation procedure established by Article 251 (Article 189b) of the Treaty on European Union. In this procedure the Commission proposes and both the Council and the Parliament, through a complicated legislative procedure, consider the proposal. Effectively, the Parliament has a strong input in region-to-region cooperation as it may, in the last instance, veto any proposal.

Enlargement

The impact of the various stages of enlargement has had two sorts of foreign policy implications for the Union. The first concerns how the EC/EU has used the prospects of membership to further its own foreign policy interests. The second is how the foreign policies of the applicant states have changed EC/EU foreign policy.

In the first enlargement in 1973, when Britain, Denmark and Ireland joined the then Community, the Community's goals were primarily economic and 'domestic' in the sense of being concerned primarily with intra-EC affairs. Neither Britain's residual global relationship with the Commonwealth, nor Denmark's links with the Nordic countries, nor Ireland's neutrality were seen as insuperable obstacles to membership or as aspects of those countries' policies that had much to do with EC negotiations. By contrast, in 1981 and in 1986, when respectively Greece, and Spain and Portugal joined, the EC's foreign policy interests were significant. In the midst of the Cold War, EC member states were anxious to reduce the possibilities of political instability in their Mediterranean border area by incorporating these three countries into the Community as part of the 'West' – contra the Soviet Union and the Warsaw Pact. The Community also wanted to encourage capitalist economic development, political pluralism, representative democracy and respect for human rights in these post-fascist states. The northern European expansion of 1995 – to include Sweden, Finland and Austria – was motivated by both economic and political rationales. These three prosperous states would provide a net economic benefit and, by doing so, they would assist the Union in its objective of gradually assimilating Central and Eastern Europe into Western levels of economic development and political mores as part of a strategy to provide stability to post-Cold War Europe.

The foreign policy agenda of the Union has been surprisingly unaffected by changes to its membership. Perhaps the greatest, though probably the least publicised, effect was the impact of Britain's membership, which resulted in the EC becoming the centre of a vast network of trade and aid with ex-British colonies as well as the former and current dependencies of the original six member states. Greek membership is often considered as having produced a foreign policy inclination which leans more towards 'radicalism' – in particular in its support of the Arab side of the Arab–Israeli conflict – although, in actuality, well before Greek accession, the EC developed a policy that attempted to reflect the aspirations of both Arabs and Israelis. Spain and Portugal, likewise, were expected to bring a more Latin American slant towards Community policies but in practice, have been more concerned with issues closer to home, in particular Mediterranean security issues. It was also initially expected that the last three northern European members would bring a more liberal slant towards EU development aid policies but changes in development policy orientation have not proved significant for overall foreign policy alignments.

In summary, enlargement has proved useful as an instrument of Union foreign policy. By promising the opportunity of economic development through membership the Union can insist that applicant states shift their polities in the direction of the EU model which is explicitly based on, among other things, market economies, pluralist democracy, respect for human rights and adherence to the rule of law. The promise of future accession to Central and East European countries is an example of enlargement as an instrument of foreign policy. In contrast, the consequences of previous enlargements have not had an appreciable impact on the direction of EU foreign policy – instead serving to consolidate the EU's liberal vocation in world affairs.

Actors, instruments, legal bases and decision-making procedures

The European Council is the single most important actor in the initial stages of the enlargement process but the Commission's role as chief negotiator is crucial throughout the various stages prior to accession. The Parliament has a significant input into the enlargement process, as it must assent to accession before any new member state may be admitted to the Union. Finally, the member states must ratify any new membership via their own national procedures. The instruments available to the Union to encourage and facilitate the smooth transition to membership include financial aid and trade preferences – all of which are regulated by agreements drawn up with the applicant country in the pre-accession stages. The legal foundation for enlargement can be found in Article 49 (ex Article O) which states that 'any European state may apply to become a member of the Union'. The emphasis within the decision-making process is on consensus as no successful accession can take place without every member state being in agreement.

EUROPEAN UNION FOREIGN POLICY THROUGH THE GEO-ISSUE-AREA LENS

This book shows that the European Union has involved itself in a number of foreign policy issues with the scope and scale of involvement varying according to the countries and regions with which the European Union has had contact. It argues that this involvement can best be understood through the prism of a geo-issue-area perspective. This book has chosen to identify five areas as key issue-areas for European Union foreign policy. These are security, trade, development cooperation, interregional cooperation and enlargement. It is a matter of debate and constant empirical reflection, however, as to which issue-areas are important for European Union foreign policy at particular points in time. It is likely in the future, for instance, that the issue-area of money will assume importance. Some have already argued for the environment as a policy-salient issue. It is also not inconceivable that democracy and human rights promotion, two increasingly significant policy areas, could merit attention of their own – as opposed to their incorporation in the security issue-area that is the choice of this book.

The book provides both an analytic framework for the better understanding of European Union foreign policy and at the same time provides empirical coverage of the vast array of European

Union foreign policies abroad. This latter objective of the book is partly to counter the lack of empirical studies of European Union foreign policy. Although it is fairly straightforward, for instance, to find material on how the Union carries out policy and through what treaty provisions, the lack of information on what the Union has actually achieved in its foreign policy has contributed to the downplaying and minimising of the scope and scale of European Union foreign policy.

STRUCTURE OF THE BOOK

The book takes what the European Union has done and why as the primary level of analysis. The question of how European Union foreign policy is made and implemented – the procedural and institutional evaluation – is viewed as a secondary level of analysis. This book outlines the first efforts at foreign policy cooperation in Chapter 2. It then demonstrates in Chapter 3 the efforts made by decision-makers – sometimes mirrored by academic studies – to separate out the practice of high from low politics in foreign policy – crudely speaking the efforts made to separate the politics from the economics of the foreign policy of the European Union. In Chapter 4 the book further elaborates the geo-issue-area framework – contrasting the pragmatic development of foreign policy competencies 'in real life' with the theoretical split of competencies discussed in Chapter 3. This chapter also specifies the key actors and instruments available to the European Union for use in the various issue-areas. Chapters 5, 6, 7 and 8 follow the framework established in Chapters 1 and 4 so that Chapter 5 discusses policy to the North, Chapter 6 to the neighbouring South, Chapter 7 to the distant South and Chapter 8 evaluates the European Union's approach to the 'New Europe'. Policy within issue-areas can be very different according to the geographical region with which the Union is working. For this reason each of Chapters 5 to 8 first delineates the geographical areas into which the Union has broadly targeted its interventions, before going on to evaluate the nature of the concerns that comprise each of the specified issue-areas. The final chapter provides a brief overview of the argument before demonstrating that there are no theoretical obstacles to the approach. The chapter concludes by briefly considering the ethical and political dimensions of the European Union's foreign policy role in the world today.

Each chapter concludes with a guide to further reading. Where possible direction is given to readily available books and articles. Readers are also pointed to relevant European Union documentation and websites.

A Note on Terminology

The European Union only came into being with the ratification of the Maastricht Treaty in 1993. Legally, the post-1993 European Union is a conglomerate whole comprising the three European Communities – the European Economic Community, the European Coal and Steel Community and the European Atomic Energy Community – as well as the structures of the Common Foreign and Security Policy and Justice and Home Affairs cooperation mechanisms. The term European Union is therefore used to describe and refer to this conglomerate entity. The term is also used to refer to actions of parts of the conglomerate. If actions are carried out, for instance, under the legal auspices of the Communities, the term European Union will also be used if these actions clearly represent the policies of the conglomerate whole. There is also some anachronistic use of the term in the sense that although the European Union was only legally created in 1993, its history is of the growth and expansion of the Communities so as to make the Union possible. In this sense the term European Union is sometimes used in this book to refer to a discernible historical entity.

There are similar difficulties with the term European Community. It is mainly used here as a singular word that, however, denotes the three Communities that since 1993 comprise part of the Union. It is also sometimes used to describe the conglomerate whole that prior to the Maastricht Treaty comprised both the Communities and the mechanisms of European Political Cooperation.

In this book the emphasis is on the foreign policy of the European Union, not the foreign policy of the European Union and the member states. The European Union acts in close cooperation with member states but it also operates as an independent, although not autonomous (of the member states) actor in foreign policy. European Union foreign policy therefore is not the same as the foreign policy of the European Union and the member states. That would be the subject of a separate book.

Finally, on the question of the denomination of currency, the European Union now gives its accounts in Euros. Until the creation of the Euro, accounts were denominated in European Currency Units

(ECU). In this book, figures are given in both Euro and ECU – depending on the time period to which they refer.

Guide to Further Reading for Chapter 1

This chapter has engaged with some of the more common understandings or theories of European Union foreign policy activity by dealing with the main points made by critics. For detail and discussion on the 'capability–expectations gap', first formulated by Christopher Hill, see the collection edited by John Peterson and Helene Sjursen (eds), *A Common Foreign Policy for Europe? Competing Visions of the CFSP* (London: Routledge, 1998). The procedural/institutional literature can be found in a number of edited volumes – a recent treatment is in Reinhardt Rummel (ed.), *Toward Political Union: Planning a Common Foreign and Security Policy in the European Community* (Nomos: Baden-Baden, 1992). See also Fraser Cameron, *The Foreign and Security Policy of the European Union* (Sheffield: Sheffield Academic Press, 1999). Useful evaluations of the practice of European Union foreign policy that utilise the institutional split as a framework for analysis include Phillipe de Schoutheete, *La Coopération Politique Européenne* (Brussels: Labor, 1980) and Simon Nuttall, *European Political Cooperation* (Oxford: Clarendon, 1992). The attribution of 'presence' in international affairs to the European Union can be found in David Allen and Michael Smith, 'Western Europe's presence in the contemporary international arena', in *Review of International Studies*, Vol. 69 No. 1, 1990. For an extended treatment of European Union as a foreign policy actor in the context of some detailed empirical work see Charlotte Bretherton and John Vogler, *The European Union as a Global Actor* (London: Routledge, 1999). A wide-ranging discussion of security dilemmas facing the European Union (and Europe as a whole) that avoids the institutionalist trap is James Sperling and Emil Kirchner, *Recasting the European Order: Security Architectures and Economic Cooperation* (Manchester: Manchester University Press, 1997).

There are few book-length empirical studies of European Union foreign policy activities with the partial exception of studies of the Union's relations with East and Central Europe. See Martin Holland, *The European Community and South Africa: European Political Cooperation Under Strain* (London: Pinter, 1988), Roy H. Ginsberg, *Foreign Policy Actions of the European Community: The Politics of Scale* (Boulder:

Lynne Rienner, 1989), Hazel Smith, *European Union Foreign Policy and Central America* (London: Macmillan, 1995) and John Peterson, *Europe and America: The Prospects for Partnership* (London: Routledge, 1996). On European Union policy towards East and Central Europe see John Pinder, *The European Community and Eastern Europe* (London: Pinter/RIIA, 1991), Heather Grabbe and Kirsty Hughes, *Enlarging the EU Eastwards* (London: Pinter/RIIA, 1998), Alan Mayhew, *Recreating Europe: The European Union's Policy towards Central and Eastern Europe* (Cambridge: Cambridge University Press, 1998), Karen Smith, *The Making of EU Foreign Policy: The Case of Eastern Europe* (London: Macmillan, 1999).

A comprehensive collection of relevant documentation can be found in Christopher Hill and Karen E. Smith (eds), *European Foreign Policy: Key Documents* (London and New York: Routledge in association with the Secretariat of the European Parliament, 2000). A mixed but lively collection is in Jan Zielonka (ed.), *Paradoxes of European Foreign Policy* (The Hague/London/Boston: Kluwer Law International, 1998). A start towards the issue-area approach as a way of understanding the foreign policy of the European Union is made in Carolyn Rhodes (ed.), *The European Union in the World Community* (Boulder: Lynne Rienner, 1998). By far the best introduction to the foreign policy of the European Union and one that takes a geographically demarcated approach is Christopher Piening, *Global Europe: The European Union in World Affairs* (Boulder: Lynne Rienner, 1997).

2 Laying the Groundwork: 1945–68

A common foreign policy for all or part of Europe might have seemed an impossible dream way back in 1945. Yet a contemporary European Union foreign policy, which aims and often succeeds in the organisation of a common, though not yet comprehensive, foreign policy for 15 European states has emerged – partly as a result of efforts to solve post-Second World War political and economic problems. Its development was initially shaped by two international tensions; the first was the all-encompassing Cold War which lasted from around 1947 to 1989 and the second was the continuing effort by the West Europeans to develop a global identity which would be separate from its closest ally, the United States. European Union foreign policy as we see it today, however, only became possible when the Community became able to 'speak with one voice'. That voice was first articulated throughout the common external tariff (CET) – which was established in the late 1960s and very visibly allowed the Community to play a coherent and cohesive role in the international political economy.

EUROPEAN IDEAS FOR EUROPEAN UNITY

Before any idea of a European foreign policy could be conceived the idea of a common 'Europe' would have to come first. The idea of a European federation is as old as the idea of the state itself (about 500 years) – for after every major war between states in Europe proposals emerged whose intent was to bind those states together so that war between them would become impossible. Federated states would, by definition, share a common foreign policy, thus there would be no reason for war between them. Variations on this theme can be seen in the seventeenth-century 'Grand Design' for a European 'Republic' of Henry IV of France, Immanuel Kant's plan for 'Perpetual Peace' in Europe published in 1795, and the early nineteenth-century ideas of Saint-Simon and Augustin Thierry who advocated the establishment of a conflict-solving European Parliament.

In the twentieth century, the First World War provided the impetus for a number of plans for European unity ranging from the comprehensive plan for Pan European Union promoted by the Hungarian Count Richard N. Coudenhove-Kalergi to that actively pursued by leading French statesman Aristide Briand in his 1929 proposal for a European Federal Union. European integration gained support from across the political spectrum from left to right. Leon Trotsky supported a proletarian United States of Europe (although the idea was ridiculed by Lenin) and the Nazi leadership saw no inconsistencies with the idea of a united Europe led by Germany.

Despite this range of opinion in favour of some form of European integration there was no agreement as to the shape such integration might take. Some argued that economic integration should be primary; others that some form of political integration was necessary. The classical federalist ideas, that is, where federated states retain domestic authority but relinquish foreign policy and defence powers to a newly created centre, were not universally pursued. Briand, for instance, argued for 'European union' as distinct from 'European unity' – emphasising that member states of a European federation should retain their national sovereignty.

During the Second World War, US Secretary of State, Cordell Hull, a major architect and advocate of postwar planning, saw international peace and prosperity as being best promoted by *global* organisations. He rejected a system of regional blocs which he considered as being akin to the balance-of-power system of world politics – a system discredited in some circles for allegedly having contributed to the outbreak of two world wars. The US lack of interest in the promotion of regional economic and political organisation was somewhat at odds with that of the European resistance movements who had been discussing the possibilities of European unity throughout the war. US antagonism to regional blocs was also not shared by influential Europeans such as Winston Churchill, the British wartime Prime Minister – and Jean Monnet, a French businessman, who had worked for US governments during the First and Second World Wars, coordinating the supply of material to US allies. Monnet, for instance, had become convinced that the way to prevent another major European war was in the continent's integration.

POSTWAR PRIORITIES

In 1945, after the Second World War, victors and vanquished in Europe had suffered massive loss of life and wartime destruction of economic infrastructure. Of the allied powers which had defeated the Nazi-led Axis alliance, the Soviet Union had suffered the most dreadful human losses, amounting – at probably a conservative estimate – to some 20 million people. The figures for loss of life elsewhere, if not as awful as in the USSR, were still high. The estimated figures for Chinese casualties are around 10 million people dead and for Japan some 2 million. Britain lost just under half a million people as did France. Germany and Italy, the defeated European powers, lost between 4½ and 5 million people and just over 400,000 people respectively. Six million Jews were systematically murdered in an act of planned genocide by the Nazi leadership in Germany. The largest numbers of Holocaust victims came from Poland (1,750,000), Hungary (650,000) and Romania (320,000) but the rest came from all over Europe – from Norway to as far south as Greece.

Economies were also devastated. Economic losses affected winners and losers. Inflation rose throughout Europe and in Germany; in the immediate aftermath of the war, chocolate and cigarettes replaced the worthless currency as a medium of exchange. In sum, the scope and scale of wartime destruction informed the attitude of postwar planners who wanted to find ways to prevent such a brutal war ever happening again.

Britain suffered major economic losses – roughly one-quarter of national wealth went in the war effort. Having led the allied war effort before the US entered the war in 1941, it had borrowed extensively from the United States in order to maintain wartime expenditures. At the end of the war the British government needed to find funds to rebuild its own economy, pay wartime debts (mainly to the US) and was also faced with the bill for postwar occupation forces throughout the globe. British governments had spent most of the war years negotiating economic agreements with the US; the British considering that they were winning the war for the West and, therefore, the Americans should help to pay for victory. By contrast, the US considered itself munificent in respect of an ungrateful Britain that would not accept that it was no longer a world power and which was trying to maintain that status at the expense of the US taxpayer.

In 1945 both Conservative and Labour governments, despite what they hoped might be a temporary economic malaise, still considered Britain a world power, on a par with the United States. The British Empire had not yet disintegrated and sterling was still a widely used international currency. Britain – along with the US – had taken the lead in forging the political and economic institutions of the new international order and, as the initial leader of the anti-Nazi wartime alliance, it retained a certain political status, at least in Europe.

France, which had been engaged in three bloody wars against Germany in a hundred years (the 1871 Franco–Prussian war, the 1914–18 'Great War' and the Second World War), was primarily concerned with maintaining the security of the state against any possible resurgent German militarism. France was determined that Germany should never be allowed to rearm to the extent that it could again prove a threat to its neighbours. Postwar French policy was to oppose any reindustrialisation of Germany and to try to shift the industrial centre of gravity in Europe from Germany to France.

Of the major protagonists in the war only the United States remained relatively unscathed. Some 300,000 US citizens had lost their lives – a significant enough number for grieving friends and relations – but in terms of the impact on the economic development of the US the impact was minimal. This contrasted with the experience of the Europeans who had lost a significant source of manpower that could have been used for economic reconstruction. The United States benefited economically and politically from the war. The dollar replaced sterling as the world's central currency and the US – with the Soviet Union devastated and China in the grips of civil war – the world's only superpower. The United States was, for the first time, willing to take the role of world leader – turning away from its previous policy of international isolationism to create and take the lead in postwar global economic and political institutions. These were the two international financial institutions negotiated at Bretton Woods in the United States – the International Monetary Fund (IMF) and the World Bank – and the United Nations.

The main concerns of the United States were strategic and political. Although the US had emerged from the war as the strongest economic power, the postwar Truman administration did not trust its former ally, the Stalin-led USSR and feared Soviet expansionism worldwide, including within Europe. US fears were heightened because of the popularity of indigenous Communist movements within West and East Europe; those Communist parties had a real popular appeal because their leaderships and members had, in many cases, formed the nucleus of the wartime resistance movements that had stayed in occupied Europe to fight the Nazis from within, rather than from exile abroad.

In the first two years after the war the global economic institutions created at Bretton Woods and the mainly US-funded UN Relief and Rehabilitation Administration (UNRRA) proved incapable of providing the necessary assistance to restore Europe's agricultural and industrial production to pre-war levels. The very cold winter of 1946/47 accentuated the problems of food shortages, inflation and general lack of resources in Europe. In March 1947 France and Britain responded to the continuing perceived threat of German rearmament by signing the Treaty of Dunkirk – intended to express mutual solidarity against a Germany which was still seen as providing the main security threat in postwar Europe. Meanwhile, the United States demonstrated that it was prepared to take on a worldwide anti-Communist mission when President Truman, in the wake of Britain's withdrawal from Turkey and Greece in 1947, issued his now-famous 'doctrine' – asserting the willingness of the US to 'assist free peoples to work out their own destinies in their own way'.

The priorities of the capitalist powers for postwar Europe therefore coalesced around a number of related objectives. The first was economic reconstruction, the second was what became known as the 'problem of Germany' and the third the development and maintenance of a united front against what was perceived as an expansionary Soviet Union. The United States' response, in a change of policy from the promotion of international institutions, was to support the building of a strong regional association of states in Europe. The objective was the promotion of a united Europe, or at least a united capitalist Europe. The US plan would encourage a controlled reindustrialisation of Germany within the context of a European-wide organisation of liberal and democratic capitalist economies that would be supported in their regional reconstruction efforts by US aid. In this way, German reindustrialisation would take place under international supervision and, given British lack of interest in participating in regional institutions, in actuality, under French supervision. French security fears would be thus assuaged, European economic reconstruction would be facilitated by economies of scale and the Soviet threat would be met by a strong, renewed Europe which could make use of German industry in a Western capitalist bulwark against communism. In the process, the population of Europe would perhaps find that liberal capitalism could respond to their needs – so making the domestic appeal of European communism less alluring.

The United States was assisted in its policy objectives by the currents in European thought which had pushed for European integration both before and during the war. It was also able to provide substantial leverage in that when Secretary of State George C. Marshall announced the United States' intention to further assist in the reconstruction of Europe in his June 1947 speech at Harvard, he made it clear that US aid would only be forthcoming in response to a coordinated European plan for economic recovery. Marshall did not go so far as to endorse European economic and/or political integration but he did insist on some form of collective European response prior to any disbursement of funds in what would become known as the European Recovery Programme (ERP), or 'Marshall Aid'.

THE EARLY EUROPEAN REGIONAL ORGANISATIONS: 1947–51

In the immediate postwar Europe it had seemed that pan-European unity was a political possibility. In 1946 the various 'federalist' groups in Europe had combined to form the European Union of Federalists which organised the 1948 Congress of Europe at The Hague. Here Churchill repeated wartime calls for a 'United States of Europe' – not necessarily with Britain inside such an organisation. The conference resulted in the establishment in 1949 of the initially ten-member Council of Europe, whose founder members were Britain, France, Belgium, Luxembourg, the Netherlands, Ireland, Italy, Norway, Sweden and Denmark. The Council of Europe disappointed many of the federalists, however, as the British insisted on an inter-governmental institution that, although having a fairly broad political remit, had, at least initially, no effective or independent decision-making powers. This was definitely not an organisation which would evolve a common foreign policy for Europe.

Shaping Postwar Europe: Geographical Division and the Attempt to Separate 'Politics' from 'Economics'

In 1947 Europe was still undivided and, except for Germany which was occupied and administered by the United States, Britain, France and the Soviet Union (the victors in the Second World War), a continent of sovereign nation-states. Between 1947 and 1951, dramatic geopolitical change took place in the European continent. Europe became divided – a bifurcation of the continent that would last some 40 years. Institutional structures began to be organised on either a *West* or *East* European basis. Both West and East European institutional structures attempted to separate economic from political and foreign policy questions. This was the period, therefore, which marked the start of a *political* division of the continent that was expressed in *geographical* terms – East/West – and a *functional* separation of policy management for both pan-West and pan-East European blocs. In this context there seemed little likelihood of a common European foreign policy – either in pan-European terms – or even within the confines of the Western or Eastern blocs.

The division of the European continent began in the economic arena. The conditionality of Marshall Aid – ensuring that European recipients of US aid worked collectively – was accepted by the two major West European powers, Britain and France. In 1947, these two states, along with 14 others and representatives of occupied Germany, formed the Committee on European Economic Coopera-tion (CEEC), institutionalised the following year as the Organisation for European Economic Cooperation (OEEC). The effect of the Soviet Union's refusal to participate and its prevention of Polish and Czech participation was to consolidate this first major postwar European economic organisation as an essentially West European organisation.

The OEEC was not, however, an organisation of European, even West European integration. France remained unwilling to allow the formal incorporation of the tri-zonal Western Germany (those areas controlled by the US, Britain and France) into the OEEC although it did allow tri-zonal representation into some of the organisation's deliberations. The United States continued to try to persuade the West Europeans to adopt a more integrated approach to the recon-struction of Europe than many were willing to countenance: the aim of the US being to allow for an internationally supervised German reindustrialisation as part of a united, economically strong Western block against the Soviet Union.

The Brussels Treaty Organisation (BTO) – the first of the postwar West European security institutions – was created in 1948 by the Treaty of Dunkirk powers, Britain and France, along with Belgium, the Netherlands and Luxembourg (the Benelux countries) as an alliance against Germany. But by the end of that year its main fear was that of the perceived threat from the USSR. The Communist coup in Czechoslovakia and the Soviet blockade of West Berlin helped to consolidate both the division of the continent and the urgency, from the perspective of all Western governments, of providing a cohesive front in the West. In 1949 the Federal Republic of Germany was created from the joining together of the US, British and French. and, in that same year, the United States formed the North Atla. Treaty Organisation (NATO), along with the Brussels Treaty powe and Italy, Portugal, Denmark, Norway, Iceland and Canada. By the end of 1949, therefore, Europe's security problems were resolved to the extent that the United States formalised its commitment to defend the West within NATO. The corollary of the creation of the transatlantic alliance was the unspoken agreement that any coordinated West European security policy would be supervised from Washington. In France, wartime memories remained strong, however, and the formation of NATO was as much a prophylactic measure against Germany as the Soviet Union.

As West European security policy was placed within a transatlantic framework, so West European economic policy became enshrined within a parallel organisational context. Economic integration proceeded to the extent that in 1950 the West Europeans were able to successfully establish and organise the European Payments Union (EPU). The EPU was made up of OEEC members and, through the facilitation of currency movements, was able to assist in the development of intra-European trade. Two postwar problems were settled, therefore, in that economic reconstruction was progressing steadily and the threat from Soviet expansionism was contained through the creation of NATO.

The 'problem' of Germany, essentially that of Franco–German relations, remained. France had tried to maintain a defensive economic alliance against Germany through proposals for the creation of a French/Italian/Benelux tariff agreement (known as Fritalux) but by 1950 the Dutch were arguing that Germany should be permitted to join any such arrangement. French plans to form some form of Franco–British-based European Union were also stymied as the British were determined to pursue both a closer Anglo–US partnership – as distinct from any continental Union – and a continued global role in relation to the Commonwealth.

The French responded with a change of policy which built on the various discussions held during the postwar years, including those which had proposed a European customs union that might include West Germany. The French also drew from the experience of the International Ruhr Authority, whose members were the US, Britain, France and the Benelux states. The Ruhr Authority had been established in 1948 to administer the Saar region – which had been removed from German control after the war – and its establishment had given the member states control over the production and output of coal, coke and steel in this region. In May 1950 French foreign minister Robert Schuman, at the instigation of Jean Monnet, proposed a plan for a European coal and steel authority which would establish supranational control over all of German (and French) coal and steel production with the intention of creating a common market in these commodities.

The founder members of the European Coal and Steel Community (ECSC) were France, the Federal Republic, Italy and the Benelux states. Britain, although invited to participate, declined – concerned about both the supranational aspects of the plan and the move towards continental integration which it saw as inimical to its own policy of greater transatlantic ties. Germany supported the plan as it gave the Federal Republic a previously denied input into the management of German resources and also some hope of the return of the Saar (actually achieved in 1959) to the German state. The attraction for France was that it institutionalised French input into German reindustrialisation at a time when the US, having suffered the 'loss' of China to Communist forces in 1949 and the successful advance of Communist North Korean troops in the early stages of the Korean war the following year, was less inclined than ever to support French efforts to continue to prevent the reindustrialisation of Germany and its reintegration into Western Europe. For their part, the Benelux states were anxious to see the German 'problem' resolved in order to provide political and economic stability within Europe.

The European Coal and Steel Community (ECSC) Treaty was signed in Paris on 18 April 1951. The ECSC started work in 1952 with Jean Monnet as president of the Higher Authority – the central supranational organ of the ECSC. The first of what would become the European Communities and later the European Union, was a functionally economic institution that was designed to achieve political objectives. Robert Schuman's May 1950 statement was unequivocal in this respect. He argued that:

The contribution which an organised and active Europe can make to civilisation is indispensable for the maintenance of peaceful relations ... Because Europe was not united, we have had war. A United Europe will not be achieved all at once, nor in a single framework: it will be formed by concrete measures which first of all create a solidarity in fact ... The community of [coal and steel] production ... will clearly show that any war between

France and Germany becomes not only unthinkable but in actual fact impossible.

Although in the early 1950s, the West Europeans were still very far away from the concept of any common or coordinated foreign policy, the establishment of the ECSC, with its integration of the Federal Republic into the core of a Western European economic organisation, laid the groundwork for further discussions around the contentious issues of defence and security. The two related questions at the heart of the matter were how to best incorporate West Germany into a collective defence organisation against the Soviet Union and whether or not (West) European security organisation should be institutionalised separately from NATO. The question of political union and the related issue of a common foreign policy for (West) Europe were now on the agenda.

DEFENCE AND SECURITY: THE EUROPEAN DEBATE

In August 1949, Winston Churchill, the then opposition leader in Britain, publicly recommended the creation of an integrated European army which would 'act in full cooperation with the United States and Canada'. The idea was further developed by French policymakers in 1950, who were anxious to maintain a measure of control over German rearmament. The French premier René Pléven, supported by Jean Monnet, proposed to use similar methods to those that had been adopted in respect to German reindustrialisation with the putative ECSC. In October 1950 Pléven proposed the setting-up of a European army that would be fully integrated under supranational control. It included radical proposals that would be far from the idea of coordination of national divisions but would include troops from all the participating states which would be integrated at the lowest possible levels – a truly integrated army. In answer to the criticism that such an army would need to be placed under democratic control, the draft European Defence Community (EDC) Treaty included a clause (Article 38) that would allow for the establishment of a European Political Community (EPC) which would exert such oversight. The Treaty was signed in May 1952 by the same six states that had agreed to form the ECSC. Britain, Denmark and Norway attended the preparatory meetings as observers only, with Britain offering support but not participation in the new European army (by May 1952 Churchill was now British prime minister). The United States which was by now even more convinced that a democratic Germany must be allowed to participate in an anti-Soviet alliance – which should be composed of an integrated West European bloc alongside the US and Canada – strongly encouraged this new venture.

The elaboration of proposals for a European Political Community took place immediately after the EDC Treaty had been signed. The ECSC Assembly, which had been charged with this task, produced a plan which would give a measure of supranationality to the EPC. Included in the proposals was the establishment of a common foreign policy which would coordinate the foreign policies of member states. The central supranational authority would be able to carry out foreign policy activities but only with the agreement of the member states of the EPC. The common foreign policy would, essentially, be subject to national control.

In August 1954, after four of the six states had ratified the EDC Treaty and Italy was about to do so, the French National Assembly refused its agreement. Rightwing Gaullists and leftwing Communists were suspicious of the supranational elements of the Treaty and the French nation as a whole was reluctant to surrender even partial control over French military resources in return for an agreement which would allow German rearmament. There was also concern that, without the participation of Britain, Germany would dominate the proposed European army as French capabilities had to meet military commitments worldwide and Germany could concentrate its military redevelopment in Europe.

In October 1954, in response to the collapse of the EDC Treaty which had left Germany strategically anchorless in Europe, Britain, with US backing, proposed the creation of the Western European Union (WEU). The WEU was established in 1955 and comprised the Brussels Treaty powers, the Federal Republic and Italy. In addition, the Federal Republic of Germany (FRG) was recognised by the Western powers as a sovereign state and was invited to join NATO which it did in 1955.

By 1955, therefore, the three great postwar problems had been settled, for better or worse, to the satisfaction of the major Western powers. West Europe had rapidly recovered its economic health; such rapid recovery sprang from a number of elements including, among other things, the import of Marshall Aid funds and the accelerated industrialisation brought about by the Korean War. The German problem was resolved to the extent that the country was divided but the West was securely incorporated into the Western liberal capitalist democratic framework. And, last but not least, the transatlantic anti-Soviet alliance, supported by a Western Europe integrated through its membership in NATO, was firmly established.

Also by 1955 the foundations of a peculiarly distinct European 'construction' were in place. West and East were divided politically and geographically. A sharp functional separation of policy was also developing. Military, defence and security policy was to be coordinated through NATO in a transatlantic system of cooperation. Economic policy in the key areas of coal and steel was to be organised by six West European states, at European level. After the EDC debacle, however, the responsibility for a 'European' foreign policy remained at the level of the nation-state.

CONSOLIDATING DIVISIONS: 1955–60

The 1950s saw a discernible trend towards multinational cooperation between states and a willingness by states to surrender aspects of their sovereignty in some policymaking areas. At the same time, however, the period 1955–59 saw the institutionalisation of strategic and ideological divisions in Europe. Western European states also divided up the policymaking areas around which they would agree to cooperate. In this they were influenced by the *functional* approach to integration, which was based on the idea that pragmatic, incremental steps towards integration around 'non-controversial' and 'technical' questions such as economics or welfare issues would provide the surest route to eventual political integration. *Federalist* ideas relating to constitutional union around a strong central executive were no longer on the agenda.

The ideological and strategic division of Europe was consolidated in 1955 as the Communist powers responded to the incorporation of West Germany into NATO, by signing the Warsaw Treaty. East Germany was brought into the security alliance which became known as the Warsaw Pact, alongside the Soviet Union, Albania, Bulgaria, Czechoslovakia, Hungary, Poland and Romania. The Communist states had already established the Council of Mutual Economic Assistance (CMEA or COMECON) in 1949 in order to organise economic cooperation between the member states.

Meanwhile in Western Europe in May 1955, the Benelux states proposed that ECSC member states and any 'interested parties' should meet to discuss further European economic integration. Jean Monnet again used his influence to gain French support and in June

1955 the ECSC foreign ministers met at Messina in Sicily to discuss the Benelux proposal. Paul-Henri Spaak, the Belgian foreign minister, was deputed to produce a report on how economies could be progressively merged, a common market created, social policies harmonised and common institutions established. The Messina conference also instructed its representatives to consider how the ECSC member states could collectively work on 'the peaceful development of atomic energy'. All the Messina proposals were framed by the intention 'to work for the establishment of a united Europe'.

Britain had signed an association agreement with the ECSC in 1954 and as an important European power was the particular 'interested party' to which the Benelux call was addressed. Britain was, therefore, invited to participate in the Messina process and sent a civil servant as its representative. In late 1955 with the consolidation of proposals for a customs union, however, Britain withdrew, as it was unwilling to enter into any union which would involve discrimination against its Commonwealth trading partners. The two Rome Treaties that were signed on 25 March 1957 that established the European Economic Community (EEC) and the European Atomic Energy Community (Euratom) only created, therefore, a 'Europe' of 'the Six'. The EEC, commonly referred to as 'the common market', and Euratom began functioning in January 1958.

Britain seemed to have assumed that the European Communities, like the previously mooted EDC, would not come to fruition. As the Messina talks progressed through 1956, Britain became concerned, however, that it was going to be left out of a French-led European economic bloc and sought to mitigate any future harmful effects in respect of British trade. To this end it proposed the establishment of a free trade area of all the OEEC states. If the plan had come into effect this would have meant that all OEEC members, including the future EEC member states, would have been committed to abolishing tariff barriers between themselves but would not have been compelled to develop a common external tariff towards third countries. The essence of the proposed common market (of the Six), however, was the eradication of internal barriers to trade and the establishment of a common external tariff. If the British proposal had succeeded the plans for a common market of the Six would have been weakened to the extent that an EEC as planned could not have been successful. The British proposal, sometimes known as the Maudling plan after the British minister responsible, was rejected by the Six and, in response, the British pursued their free trade plans with six OEEC states which were not members of the EEC. In 1959, Britain, Denmark, Norway, Sweden, Austria, Switzerland and Portugal agreed to form the European Free Trade Association (EFTA) and in January 1960 EFTA was established by the Stockholm Convention.

EFTA was particularly attractive to the Scandinavian states which had since 1945 attempted to cooperate between themselves despite being divided in their geopolitical interests; Sweden, Austria and Finland being neutral states while Denmark and Norway were allied to the West. As a result there was little probability that the Nordic states would be able to form or join an avowedly integrationary institution which gave powers on any issue to centralised institutions. These problems were evident in 1948 when Sweden's proposal to create a Defence Union of Denmark, Norway and Sweden was unsuccessful. However, in the same year Denmark, Iceland, Norway and Sweden succeeded in establishing a Joint Nordic Committee for Economic Cooperation. This institution, like its 1951 successor, the Nordic Council, was established on intergovernmental lines.

One important codicil to the breakdown of the Maudling plans for free trade between the OEEC countries was the transformation of the OEEC into the Organisation for Economic Cooperation and Development (OECD) in 1960. The United States argued for greater economic coordination between the Western allies and the OEEC member states were joined by the United States and Canada to form the OECD – to the relief of the French who had feared that Britain would lead an anti-EEC movement from within the OEEC. Such moves would be harder to pursue within the expanded OECD given the United States' enthusiastic support for the EEC.

EFTA was in no sense an integrationary institution. It was strictly intergovernmental in its institutions and its main external function was envisaged as providing some forum for negotiation with the EEC. This organisation, like the intergovernmental OECD, Council of Europe and the Nordic Council, was never likely to provide the basis for institutionalised European collective organisation in the field of foreign policy. The institutions which might have provided a base for the incremental development of a foreign policy capacity (in the way the functionalists predicted) were those involved with collective security and the defence of Western Europe. By 1960, however, the only significant collective security and defence institution for Western Europe was the transatlantic NATO – whose leadership was non-European. NATO was led by the United States and was therefore most unlikely to provide the base for a European foreign policy which by definition would be different from US foreign policy. It would be the European Communities, within the framework of the EEC Treaty of Rome commitment to an 'ever closer union', that eventually provided the basis for a common West European foreign policy.

LAYING THE FOUNDATIONS FOR FOREIGN POLICY COLLABORATION: 1961–69

Throughout the 1960s, the Six continued to attempt, unsuccessfully, to find ways to coordinate foreign policy outside of the institutions of the Communities. At the same time, the evolution of the internal capacities and visibility of the European Communities, particularly the EEC, necessarily gave the EEC international capabilities and status so that it evolved as a consequential actor in world affairs – without the EEC's member states having made any conscious decisions to this effect. The French-led EEC began to separate out its European interests from more general 'Western' interests; this separation of interest was clearly seen when the EEC became embroiled in political and economic conflict with its ally and erstwhile sponsor, the United States. The French President, Charles de Gaulle, resolutely refused to permit the EEC institutions to acquire any foreign policy competencies. The continued de facto evolution of the Community's external responsibilities, however, along with a change of leadership in the core EEC states of France and Germany combined at the end of the 1960s to facilitate the acceptance by EEC member states that the Communities would require some form of organised collective foreign policy – partly to prevent the Commission taking the lead in what member states saw as their sovereign prerogative, the area of foreign policy.

The First Attempts at Foreign Policy Cooperation

From June 1958, when General Charles de Gaulle became head of state, the French pursued a European policy, the aim of which was to establish a political authority that would institutionalise political and foreign policy cooperation between West European states in an inter-governmental form separate from the Brussels-based institutions of the European Communities. Whatever intergovernmental system of cooperation that emerged was also intended to provide a supervisory function over the Community institutions. This proposed intergovernmental system would develop European policies, distinct from those of the United States, on both domestic and international issues.

Between 1959 and 1963 discussions between the Six with respect to European foreign policy cooperation took place at two levels. The first was in terms of the attempt to discuss substantive foreign policy issues collectively. The second level was the eventually unsuccessful attempt to establish an institutionalised system of West European foreign policy cooperation. The meetings to discuss foreign policy cooperation began in Rome in January 1960 and were suspended in January 1963 after de Gaulle unilaterally vetoed Britain's application for membership of the European Communities. During that period the foreign ministers had discussed issues ranging from relations with the Soviet Union, to the Congo crisis and Cuban missile crisis of October 1962. These meetings could not develop as much more than the exchange of views until the more fundamental issue, of whether the Six wished to cooperate and on what basis, was resolved.

In 1959 de Gaulle had initially proposed that the foreign ministers of the Six should meet regularly to discuss foreign policy issues and that a secretariat for such political cooperation be established in Paris. De Gaulle's EEC partners rejected the idea of the secretariat but agreed that the foreign ministers should meet periodically. In 1960 the French President vigorously pursued his idea of an intergovernmental Europe – proposing regular summits of the heads of state and government of the Six and restating his preference for the establishment of a Paris-based secretariat for this organisation. Christian Fouchet, a French diplomat, was deputed to formalise these proposals and, in 1961, produced a report whose objective was the creation of a common foreign and defence policy for Europe.

The Fouchet Plan would have been acceptable to all the Six if de Gaulle had accepted amendments that responded to the concerns of the smaller EEC member states. The Dutch were particularly anxious that the putative West European bloc be firmly attached to NATO in order to retain the US commitment to defend Europe in case of future war. They were also concerned that France and Germany might establish a *directoire* which would dominate the new institution. This would have had the immediate effect of institutionalising French leadership of Europe given that Germany, the defeated Second World War power, would not have been permitted (and also had no desire) to attempt to exert any political leadership in the new organisation. As safeguards, the Dutch and Belgian states would have settled for one of two options; one was the acceptance into this new intergovernmental institution of Britain which could have acted as a counter-weight to France and West Germany. The other was the consolidation of the power of the institutions of the European Communities. In late 1961 Britain made it clear that it did not want to participate. The cause of the eventual inability to agree, however, was de Gaulle's refusal to accept a public commitment to NATO and his rejection of amendments that would have spelt out NATO support for the Community within the second Fouchet Plan of 1962.

French diplomacy did, however, result in one significant step on the road to West European political cooperation. De Gaulle had worked closely with the West German Chancellor, Konrad Adenauer, throughout the negotiations on the future of West European cooperation. The relationship laid the basis for the formalisation of Franco–German *rapprochement* and in January 1963 both states signed the Treaty of Franco–German Cooperation, sometimes known as the *Elysée* Treaty.

The mid-1960s marked the nadir of attempts at foreign policy cooperation within the context of the Communities. De Gaulle maintained his opposition to any increased powers for Community institutions to the extent that he refused to permit France to participate in the Community decision-making structures for six months in 1965/66. The famous (or notorious) 'Luxembourg Compromise' of 1966 allowed an accommodation which, although ambiguous, seemed to give member states equal decision-making capacities with the European Commission, the most important of the Community institutions, on all issues. Thus when the member states completed the merger of the institutions of all three Communities in 1967, the newly created European Commission adopted a consensual approach to dealing with Community decision-making. One consequence of the Commission's cautious approach to the member states was that it was unlikely to be the initiator of ideas that would strengthen the 'union' of the Six. It could not therefore act as an initiator for any proposals for a common European foreign policy.

In 1967 de Gaulle made an attempt to revive the idea of intergovernmental political and foreign policy cooperation at the Rome Summit of the Six. France wanted the foreign ministers to meet regularly again in order to discuss, among other things, the Middle East crisis and the division of Germany. The Dutch were still adamant, however, that initiatives on political cooperation should not proceed without the involvement of Britain. The Six failed to reach a compromise that would have allowed further foreign policy cooperation to take place; instead they merely noted that political and foreign policy cooperation would take place when 'experience and circumstances' were propitious.

The Community's External Relations Capabilities

The European Communities derived rights, responsibilities and powers with respect to non-member states and international organisations and hence *international* capabilities from two sources. The first was from the competencies allocated to the Community institutions by the Treaties of Paris and Rome. The second was from the evolutionary practice of both Community institutions *and* member states. The competencies allocated through the Treaties were enshrined in international law. The responsibilities derived from the practice of the Communities were also protected by international law – by way of the body of case-law established through the activities of the European Court of Justice (ECJ) – which was initially established as part of the ECSC and whose competencies were extended in 1957 to include all three Communities.

The member states had allocated limited external relations powers to the ECSC and Euratom. The EEC, by contrast, was allowed significant competencies and also developed external responsibilities as a consequence of its domestic (intra-EEC) powers devolved on the EEC institutions by the 1957 Treaty. The founding treaties established that all three Communities possessed an international personality, that is they could be recognised as independent actors in international law.

The ECSC's central institution, the Higher Authority, had few external relations competencies except for the important right to receive diplomatic credentials from non-member states' ambassadorial appointments to the ECSC: the first such ambassador being from the United States. The Higher Authority was empowered to establish diplomatic relations with non-member states: a permanent delegation being established in London in 1955. Its more minor responsibilities were to exchange information with the Council of Europe, the OEEC and the UN. In general, the Euratom Commission was permitted more latitude than the ECSC's Higher Authority in terms of relations with outside bodies. Euratom was given authorisation to make agreements with third (non-member) states, international organisations and nationals of non-member states. It could also enter into association agreements with third states, unions of states and international organisations. The Euratom Commission, similarly to the Higher Authority, was responsible for the exchange of information with the Council of Europe, the OEEC and the UN. It was also given the responsibility of ensuring appropriate contacts with the General Agreement on Tariffs and Trade (GATT). The Commission and the Euratom Council (directly representing the member states) were both to have input into decisions regarding international agreements.

The EEC's external competencies were similar to those of Euratom in terms of its ability to enter into international agreements and in terms of the prescribed interaction between the Council of the EEC and the Commission in decision-making. It could send and receive diplomatic representatives, although after 1959, an exchange of letters between the Council and the Commission, confirmed that this prerogative would not solely belong to the Commission: the Council and the Commission would share the responsibility. The Commission of the EEC was given the responsibility of maintaining 'all appropriate relations' with the UN and the GATT. The EEC should form cooperative relations with the Council of Europe and the OEEC.

The significance of the EEC as an external actor, however, lay much more in the policy areas over which it had direct responsibility, rather than its institutional powers. The most important of these were trade, including trade in agricultural goods, and development policy. These external competencies were clearly set out in Article 3b of the Rome Treaty – whereby one of the functions of the EEC was to establish a 'common customs tariff and ... a common commercial policy towards third countries'. Article 3k of the Treaty went on to declare that another activity of the Community would be 'the association of the overseas countries and territories in order to increase trade and to promote jointly economic and social development'. Trade and development powers therefore, along with the ability to enter into international agreements, gave the newly-formed EEC a very wide scope in global affairs indeed.

Trade

The Rome Treaty stated that the common market should be established by the end of a twelve-year transitional period: this would mean the abolition of intra-EEC barriers to trade and the establishment of a common external tariff (CET). After the transitional period the Commission, on behalf of the Community, would assume the responsibility, over and above the member states, of the initiation and negotiation of commercial policy. The Commission could not *conclude* trade agreements – this was the responsibility of the Council of Ministers – and it was constrained in the sense that it was obliged to report to a committee of representatives of the Council of Ministers which, once established, was initially known as the Article 113 Committee after the relevant Treaty provision. These Treaty provisions, however, laid the foundations for the emergence of the Community as an important international actor.

One of the first examples of Community visibility in international trade was in the context of the 1961/62 GATT talks – sometimes known as the 'Dillon Round' of multilateral trade negotiations. Here the Commission was very much still an ancillary actor. The member states had only just started the process of harmonisation of commercial policy and the Commission was therefore in the position of helping to represent the diverse *national* interests of the member states, as opposed to a Community interest. In the next GATT negotiations that lasted from 1963 to 1967 and were known as the Kennedy Round, the Community became a much more active and effective participant. This was despite the fact that at the beginning of this period the Community had not yet established common policies in the areas on which it would be expected to negotiate and it was also, at the same time, having to deal with serious internal conflict. In terms of the former it had not, by 1963, finalised its own agricultural or commercial policies, both subjects on which it was expected to take a position vis-à-vis the other GATT member states. In terms of the latter, internal quarrels were manifest with respect to the issue of British membership and the French 'empty chair' Luxembourg crisis of 1965/66.

In terms of the Community's development as an international actor with a common foreign policy the Kennedy Round was important for three reasons. First, it compelled EEC member states to produce common policies on which they could then negotiate within GATT. It would not be too much of an exaggeration to argue that the common agricultural policy (CAP), for instance, evolved as a product of negotiations between the member states in relation to their negotiating position with the United States in GATT. By way of this process, the EEC became a more cohesive domestic and external actor. The Kennedy Round negotiations also helped the Commission, acting on behalf of the Community, to become a highly visible actor in international affairs. This encouraged outside states and international organisations to treat the Community as a significant, *unitary,* international actor. One example of this was the 1966 formation of a Nordic trade delegation within GATT, comprising Denmark, Finland, Norway and Sweden, which was designed to defend their interests in respect of their trading relationship with the EEC. Lastly the Kennedy Round helped to define the emergent European Community as an international actor in its own right in contradistinction to its major ally, the United States. The EEC was starting to express a Western identity with separate and sometimes conflicting interests from those of the United States.

The common external tariff (CET) was established in July 1968, some 18 months ahead of schedule, and the customs union to which member states had derogated part of their economic sovereignty was therefore created. The establishment of the customs union, combined with nearly a decade's experience of coordinating member-state interests in international commercial affairs, added to the gradually expanding status and visibility of the Community as a credible international actor.

Development

The EEC Treaty, largely due to the insistence of French negotiators, laid down specific provisions with respect to future relationships with those 'non-European countries and territories which have special relations' with the member states. The term 'special relations' began as a way to describe the direct links between four of the founder member states – all except the Federal Republic of Germany and Luxembourg – and colonies and overseas territories. As the colonies became independent these treaty provisions were used to provide the framework for association agreements with both the former colonies of the original Six and those of new member states. Part Four of the Rome Treaty details the principles that should govern trade and investment between the two groups of states and accompanying Protocols to the Treaties called for an association with 'independent countries of the franc area' – essentially Morocco and Tunisia – and also specifically declared that there should be an 'economic association' agreement with Libya. An indirect form of development assistance also emerged from the Rome Treaty in that French overseas *départements* – which in 1958 still included Algeria for instance – were considered as an integral part of France and as such benefited from 'internal' development aid, including the important aspect of guaranteed markets for agricultural trade. EEC agricultural protectionism, in other words, gave economically developing areas located *within* the EEC advantages over those located outside the Community. This last aspect of EC aid applied of course as much to southern Italy and rural France as to overseas French *départements*.

Part Four of the Treaty left to an accompanying protocol the working out of a detailed convention between specified dependent territories in Africa, the Pacific and the Caribbean, and the EEC. Of those states eligible only Guinea refused to participate in agreements both before and after independence in 1968; President Sekou Touré viewed EEC involvement in Africa as neo-colonialism. The 1958 Implementing Convention contained trade and aid provisions; it opened up EEC markets to the dependent territories but demanded reciprocal access to markets. Aid was allocated by grants through the newly established European Development Fund (EDF) to which all member states contributed irrespective of whether or not the donor states had any 'special relations' with beneficiary states. This last provision was important in helping to establish the pattern for an important aspect of future EC foreign policy. This was that EC policies towards areas of the world where only some of the member states had historic, strategic or policy interests should be institutionalised and implemented by way of collectively financed multilateral programmes.

Rapid decolonisation took place in the late 1950s and early 1960s and the newly independent states negotiated to replace the 1958 Convention with a more appropriate agreement. In 1963 17 African states and Madagascar – known as the African and Malagasy Union – agreed the first of the Yaoundé treaties with the EEC. The treaty was signed in Yaoundé in Cameroon in July 1963 and came into force in 1964 for a five-year period. It was replaced in 1969 by the second Yaoundé Treaty that covered the period from 1971 to 1975. The first Yaoundé agreement, like the Implementing Convention, contained aid and trade provisions – most of the aid being allocated to the 18 independent states – although a small portion was reserved for remaining dependent states and French overseas *départements*. Trade preferences were still formally reciprocal, and were known as 'reverse preferences', but the 18 associated states were permitted to impose protective duties for revenue purposes or for protecting infant industries. The Yaoundé agreement also established what would become future EC foreign policy practice in terms of dealing with groups of states; this was the creation of a multilateral institutional framework which had the effect of both organising the EEC's relations with the group of countries concerned and with bringing those countries together as a functioning regional unit.

The Yaoundé agreement set up an Association Council which comprised representatives of the EEC Commission and Council and a delegate from each associated state. The Association Council was paralleled by an Association Committee – comprising officials from the component parts of the Council; a Parliamentary Conference which brought together parliamentarians from the EEC's Assembly (later known as the European Parliament) and parliamentarians from the associated states; and a Court of Arbitration which was composed of judges from EEC and associated states. There was no deliberate attempt to encourage regional integration between the 18 associated states. Indeed, the wider issues of the shape and scope of African integration were being fought out in other fora, most notably in the negotiations to create the Organisation of African Unity (OAU) which was established in 1963. The institutional structure, however, ensured that on certain vital issues such as commodity prices, exports and economic development, regional discussions would necessarily take place in order to formulate a negotiating strategy with the EEC.

The first Yaoundé Convention was innovative in terms of the economic instruments created to implement the development provisions of the treaty. The EDF was extended to offer loans, in addition to the grants it had offered through the 1958 agreement. The 1963 convention also permitted the European Investment Bank (EIB) to offer concessionary loans to associated African states.

The other group of states specifically referred to in the Rome Treaty were the Maghreb states – Libya, Morocco and Tunisia. Libya did not seek to claim the special status granted it in the Rome Treaty. Its major export was petroleum which was not subject to EEC duties and therefore it did not require any special trade arrangement with the EEC. Algeria's post-independence government sought relations with the Community but there was no movement from any of the EEC states to establish links with what was seen as a radical anti-imperialist state. Tunisia and Morocco continued to benefit from preferential trading arrangements with France throughout the 1960s and although community trade agreements were signed with both states in 1969 bilateral arrangements between member states and the Maghreb countries remained important.

Applications and association: the emerging global economic and political role

From the very beginning the EEC proved a magnet to states which either wished to join the Community or that wished to obtain economic and/or political benefits through close association with the EEC. In the 1960s a number of West European states either applied directly to join the EEC or gave serious consideration to doing so – although none was successful. Ireland, Denmark and Norway applied – as did Sweden which made a qualified request in terms of specifically seeking a membership which would safeguard its neutral status. Austria requested some form of association agreement in 1961.

Britain applied to join the Community in 1961 and again in 1967; both efforts were unilaterally rejected by France, mainly because of de Gaulle's fear that Britain would seek to represent an Anglo-American interest within the Community that would not be compatible with French-led 'European' policies. For de Gaulle, Britain seemed too acquiescent to US leadership in nuclear and strategic affairs – and not willing enough to embrace a 'European' identity which, on occasion, for instance in the GATT trade talks or in terms of global monetary negotiations, might hold a different per-spective from that of the United States. The Community was not, however, entirely institutionally cut off from Britain throughout the 1960s. The WEU provided a forum whereby an 'exchange of views on the European economic situation' could take place between Britain, the Six and a member of the European Commission. Despite French reluctance, talks continued to take place until 1969 when France, in response to a British proposal to discuss the Middle East, threatened to boycott them altogether if foreign policy discussions continued.

By contrast the Community found it easier to consolidate its growing international role south and east of its territory. In 1959 Greece applied and in 1961 achieved an association agreement which contained an in principle EEC commitment to eventual Greek membership of the Community. The association agreement liber-alised trade and provided for eventual economic union between Greece and the EEC. It also permitted Greece to benefit from EIB concessionary loans. An Association Council comprising Council and Commission members as well as representatives of the Greek government was established to oversee the agreement. When the Greek military took over government in a coup in 1967 the

Commission responded by refusing to recommend the continuation of aid to Greece. In a decision which can be seen as one of the first clear expressions of a Community foreign policy it refused to recommend further aid for political reasons – to express its disapproval of the anti-democratic forces that had taken power in Greece. The member states had initially been reluctant to take action against Greece – a fellow NATO member – but were firmly guided into such action by the Commission acting on behalf of what it saw as the best political interests of the Community.

The Community entered into a number of other association and trade agreements in the 1960s. Turkey applied for association in 1959 with the agreement being concluded and entering into force in 1964. This agreement, like the Greek arrangement, envisaged eventual Turkish membership. By the end of the 1960s Spain was also negotiating for association with the EEC. In 1960 the Israeli government had requested some form of association but the Community delayed negotiations and, in 1964, only agreed a restricted trade accord as it did not wish to give political signals to Arab countries that it was favouring relations with Israel. In order to emphasise Community 'even-handedness' in international affairs the EEC had rapidly agreed a 1962 request from Iran for a trade accord, completing the negotiations in record-breaking time by achieving an agreement the following year. When Israel renewed its bid for association in 1966 the Commission was again not shy in expressing a political as well as economic rationale for its own recommendations to the Council. The Commission argued that Europe had 'special responsibilities towards Israel'.

The Community further consolidated its emerging international role and visibility when it negotiated trade agreements with Lebanon, Nigeria and the East African countries of Kenya, Uganda and Tanzania. The last three collectively signed the Arusha agreement with the EEC in July 1968. The EEC continued to attract attention as a potential partner for the South as exemplified by India's 1968 application for a trade agreement and also by various 'non-agreements' in terms of unsuccessful attempts at partnership. The clearest example of the latter came with the sustained and, in the 1960s, fruitless, attempts by Latin American states to establish a trading regime with the Community. Nevertheless the Communities institutionalised links with Latin America to the extent that in 1965 the Higher Authority of the European Coal and Steel Community established a 'liaison office' in Santiago de Chile. This office became the Latin American Delegation of the Commission of the European Communities in 1967.

Conflict with the United States: The Shape of Things to Come

The United States had been a prime mover in the creation of the Communities and, in the early 1960s, continued to support the consolidation of the EEC as a trading bloc even though the gradual establishment of the common external tariff had the effect of discriminating against US exports. The 1960s, however, were marked by a series of conflicts between the United States and the EEC. President de Gaulle believed that France and, by extension, the French-led EEC had different and conflicting strategic, monetary and trade interests from those of the United States.

In 1962 President Kennedy announced a 'grand design' for Euro–American partnership which envisaged an economically strong and politically united West Europe as a linchpin in the Western anti-Soviet alliance. This vision of the EEC was of a political entity with more or less identical interests to the United States with Britain fully integrated into the Community. De Gaulle, however, pushed for and obtained an independent nuclear capacity for France, withdrew France from NATO's military command structure in 1966 and twice unilaterally vetoed Britain's application to join the Community. The French President challenged what he considered to be the exorbitant privileges accorded to the US because of the central role of the dollar in the international monetary system. De Gaulle also helped to develop and promote a common agricultural policy for the EEC which, along with its overall trade policies including the preferential arrangements with former colonies, helped to defend French domestic interests but laid the basis for continued friction with the United States.

The first important EEC/US conflict occurred in 1963/64 with the infamous 'chicken war'; so-called because this particular trade dispute centred around EEC duties on US frozen chicken exports which were increased as a by-product of the implementation of the first stage of the common agricultural policy. Poultry was one of the US exports which had been discriminated against since the EEC had started to implement the CET in 1960 but a temporary agreement had been reached during the 1961/62 GATT Dillon Round negotiations. In 1963 the US charged the EEC with not fulfilling these GATT obligations but the EEC refused to compromise, partly because it did not want to unravel the internal consensus which had been forged in respect of the CAP and partly because it was retaliating to 1962 US trade restrictions on EEC exports to the United States. The 1963/67 Kennedy Round of GATT negotiations resolved some of the trade quarrels between the EEC and the United States but established the pattern for future multilateral global trade negotiations whereby the major protagonists were the United States and the European Community. In the Kennedy Round little progress was made on the promotion of agricultural free trade and in the reduction of non-tariff barriers to trade but considerable tariff reductions – between 35 and 38 per cent – were finally agreed in the area of industrial trade.

Another point of conflict with the United States was with respect to the trade preferences granted to developing countries. The US had not opposed the first Yaoundé Treaty – considering this as a con-comitant of the Rome Treaty obligations. The United States and Britain were less favourably disposed to the Community's extension of trade agreements to the rest of the world as both states considered that such agreements might encourage developing countries worldwide to discriminate against them in favour of trading links with the EEC.

There were also points of discord between the United States and EEC member states, particularly France, on broader foreign policy issues. France for instance condemned the 1965 US invasion of the Dominican Republic. The West Europeans as a whole were not enthusiastic about the growing US military involvement in Vietnam. They were also anxious lest the bilateral United States–Soviet Union arms control talks might presage the creation of Soviet Union–United States condominium that might take decisions on European security without European input.

CONCLUSION: THE FOUNDATIONS LAID

The European Community emerged out of a post-Second World War political and economic environment that saw the institutionalisation of geographical and ideological splits in Europe and the functional separation of policy areas within different international organisations. This functional differentiation proved difficult to contain and, as the EEC proceeded to implement the provisions of the Rome Treaty, it began to develop a de facto foreign policy role for itself. This role was based on a French vision of a strong, inter-governmental Europe with its own trade, monetary and political interests that did not always coincide with those of the United States. Although French-led, this vision of a Western European entity which was strategically interdependent with the United States although politically and economically independent of it, was more-or-less shared by all the EEC member states. By the end of the 1960s therefore the EEC was developing, albeit in a somewhat inchoate manner, the foundations of a foreign policy that was 'European' in two senses. First, it collectively organised the previously separate external policies of EEC member states and, second, where these collective policies were developed they were, in important areas, distinct from and sometimes conflictual with United States' interests and policies.

EC foreign policy coalesced around the competencies allowed the Communities via the treaties and also through the pragmatic evolution of the organisation's increasing ability to 'speak with one voice' – most notably though the implementation of the CET. Trade, development, interregional cooperation and enlargement oversight were important issues that required a de facto foreign policy voice. The intermingling of security, defence and political agendas with all these issue-areas provided an impetus for the Union to attempt to institutionalise foreign policy activities. The tendencies of actual European Union foreign policy practice to step outside the formal parameters of its attempted institutionalisation provide the key to any understanding of European Union foreign policy.

Guide to Further Reading for Chapter 2

For broad historical context see F.H. Hinsley, *Power and the Pursuit of Peace* (Cambridge: Cambridge University Press, 1988) and J.A.S Grenville, *A World History of the 20th Century, Volume 1* (Glasgow: Fontana Press, 1986). The immediate postwar context of efforts to integrate Europe is comprehensively reviewed in Michael J. Hogan, *The Marshall Plan: America, Britain and the Reconstruction of Western Europe, 1947–1952* (Cambridge: Cambridge University Press, 1987).

There are numerous introductory textbooks that give useful accounts of the history of the EC. These include Leon Hurwitz, *The European Community and the Management of International Cooperation* (Westport, Connecticut: Greenwood, 1987); Brigid Laffan, *Integration and Cooperation in Europe* (London and New York: Routledge, 1992); William Nicoll and Trevor C. Salmon, *Understanding the European Communities* (London: Philip Allan, 1990); Neill Nugent, *The Government and Politics of the European Union*, fourth edition

(London: Macmillan, 1999). A reader which gives excerpts from pertinent documents is David Weigall and Peter Stirk (eds), *The Origins and Development of the European Community* (Leicester and London: Leicester University Press, 1992). There is little easily accessible information on the growing international role of the EC during the 1960s but interested students should consult the invaluable Gordon L. Weil, *A Foreign Policy for Europe* (Bruges: College of Europe, 1970) and Richard Bailey, *The European Community in the World* (London: Hutchinson, 1973). A discussion of the Fouchet proposals can be found in Simon Nuttall, *European Political Cooperation* (Oxford: Clarendon, 1992). Some discussion of the early US/EEC conflicts can be found in Roy H. Ginsberg, *Foreign Policy Actions of the European Community* (Boulder and London: Lynne Rienner/Adamantine, 1989).

3   Institutionalising European Union Foreign Policy

The history of the development of a European Union foreign policy is a history of a struggle by key decision-makers to try to compartmentalise European Union activities so that the Union does not deal with sensitive foreign policy issues – only with technical, non-controversial areas of policy. The idea was to try to institutionally separate technical or economic issues – what is sometimes called 'low politics' from political or 'high politics'. The Commission was supposed to take the lead in the former while the member states would maintain their sovereign prerogatives in respect to the latter. In practice, however, European Union foreign policy has always been implemented through the various different institutional and procedural channels of the European Union – using instruments provided by both Community and intergovernmental pillars of the European construction. The debates over the institutionalisation of European Union foreign policy reflect the tension inherent in the enterprise – how to achieve commonality of policy and action while at the same time maintaining the singularity of member-state national autonomy.

This chapter describes and analyses the institutionalisation of a common foreign policy from 1969 onwards. These developments took place within the context of institutional division and legal separation of competencies – into those governed by 'Community-based' procedures and those that have taken on a more intergovernmental form. The chapter also demonstrates how the distinct philosophy, set of objectives and mode of decision-making that underlay Union foreign policy came into being. Decision-making procedures and institutional responsibilities became stubbornly bifurcated between 'Community' procedures based initially on the treaties of Rome and Paris and European Political Cooperation, later Common Foreign and Security Policy procedures, based on intergovernmental arrangements institutionalised within separate 'pillars' or sections of the various treaties.

DEVELOPING THE FORMAL FRAMEWORK: 1969 ONWARDS

The successful 'relaunching' of foreign policy cooperation, after the failure of similar attempts in the 1960s (see Chapter 2), took place in 1969 at The Hague summit of Heads of State and Government (HSG). In trying to combine lofty ambitions for political union with the more modest objective of a commitment to harmonise foreign policies, the 1969 Summit ended up by agreeing a long-term orientation towards an increasingly collective approach to foreign policy. After the 1987 Single European Act (SEA), this commonality of foreign policy became institutionalised within a treaty-based framework which allowed for individual member-state idiosyncrasies at the same time as insisting on certain common normative commitments and, to a certain extent, a legal obligation to engage in common policies. With the ratification of the Maastricht Treaty on European Union (TEU) in 1993, those common commitments have evolved into the Common Foreign and Security Policy (CFSP). The Amsterdam Treaty, which came into force in 1999, codified and extended foreign policy instruments. It did nothing, however, to resolve the underlying tension of a foreign policy which was both common and extensive in practice in many issue-areas, yet in terms of institutional structure maintained a fiction that foreign policy 'proper' only took place through the mechanisms of the CFSP institutional structure.

Pragmatism and Flexibility

The first step in the institutionalisation of foreign policy coordination, in the 1970s, the effort to create a forum where information could be shared, points of view harmonised and where, if 'possible or desirable', joint foreign policy activities could be undertaken, was termed European Political Cooperation (EPC). (The term EPC was often used as a synonym for cooperation on foreign policy although political cooperation also covered areas such as justice and police cooperation.) The development of EPC was characterised institutionally by pragmatic, incremental and flexible adjustments jointly and consensually agreed by member-state representatives. Sporadic attempts at radical change designed to achieve a qualitatively different foreign policy were not successful. Any hint of a more formalised EU foreign policy which might have imposed statutory obligations on member states or which in any way could be seen or portrayed as abrogating the sovereignty of member states, particularly on the sensitive areas of security and defence, was rebuffed. Some of the more radical proposals did, however, succeed in establishing new ideas that were, in some instances, progressively incorporated into later versions of the Union's foreign policy.

One feature of the institutionalisation of foreign policy cooperation was the gradual, if partial, incorporation of Community institutions into the legal and procedural framework governing EU foreign policy. The Council of Ministers has always been involved as the foreign ministers who play the governing role in foreign policy cooperation are the same foreign ministers who manage the affairs of the Union. There has also always been a pragmatic recognition of the role that the Commission necessarily plays in the articulation and implementation of a common foreign policy. The member states, however, only reluctantly allowed the European Parliament an input into the foreign policy process. One significant feature of the gradual institutionalisation of foreign policy coordination, therefore, was that this process continued with only the barest of democratic input until the mid-1980s when, in some member states, most noticeably Ireland, the foreign policy issue became a subject of public debate. The foreign ministers also made vigorous efforts to exclude the European Court of Justice (ECJ) from jurisdiction over foreign policy matters.

The CFSP created at Maastricht represents a recognition that the line between foreign policy as something carried out by member states acting collectively but in tandem with the Community, and so-called Community external responsibilities which are supposed to be 'non-foreign policy issues' is hard to sustain. It also recognises that an EU common foreign policy is neither exclusive in that it covers every aspect of foreign policy of interest to each member state nor is it 'single' in that it is the only foreign policy framework available to the member states. The policy is common, in other words, to the extent that the member states agree that it ought to be. The creation of the CFSP as a treaty-based institution indicates that the Union, in its dealings with the outside world over a large number of issues, increasingly espouses a common foreign policy shared, to a greater or lesser extent, by all member states. This is so for many issues, including those once commonly thought to be the exclusive preserve of the nation-state, for instance in the security area. This is so in terms of relations with allies as well as adversaries – including the relationship with the West Europeans' most important partner, the United States. The CFSP as an institutional framework has thus developed to provide an arena for common decision-making on issues of 'European' interest – allowing the member states to 'speak with one voice' – and, should they so choose, to engage in 'common actions'. In 2001, therefore, the CFSP increasingly acts as an umbrella forum for the whole gamut of EU foreign policies although it still does not encompass the entire range of Union capacity and competencies in its dealings abroad.

THE NON-BINDING INSTITUTIONALISATION OF FOREIGN POLICY COORDINATION: 1969–81

Formal foreign policy cooperation and coordination were initially institutionalised within the context of declarations issued by Summits of the Heads of State and Government of the Community and non-treaty, therefore non-binding, frameworks established by periodic reports agreed by foreign ministers.

The 1969 Hague Summit

At the end of the 1960s, even after the resignation of de Gaulle in April 1969, France continued to play a dominant role in the revital-isation of the Community and the resuscitation of attempts at foreign policy cooperation. De Gaulle's successor, Georges Pompidou, initiated the December 1969 Hague Summit which had on its agenda the three related items of enlargement, economic and monetary union, and political union. Although the idea of political union remained vague it was, broadly speaking, meant to encompass some method whereby both the applicant states and the Community institutions could be brought in to a more coordinated and cohesive decision-making structure within the Community framework. The six member states at The Hague decided that although membership should be offered to four applicant countries, that is Britain, Denmark, Ireland and Norway, it should be tied to a commitment to Community institutions and practices which would be strengthened and deepened in a concurrent process to the enlargement negotiations. Stressing the 'irreversibility' of the Community, the member states at The Hague argued that the next stage in Community evolution would mean 'paving the way for a United Europe capable of assuming its responsibilities in the world of tomorrow and of making a contribution commensurate with its traditions and missions'. Another impetus to the development of increased political cooperation by the member states was the ambition to control or at least to supervise the Commission which, with the common external tariff now in place, was now able to play a powerful economic role internationally.

The HSG discussed the possibilities of taking steps towards political union through the harmonisation of their foreign policies and instructed their foreign ministers to report back within one year on 'the best way of achieving progress in the matter of political uni-fication, within the context of enlargement'. New member states would be expected to accept, not just the founding treaties of Paris and Rome, but any newly created mechanisms for political union. This was an important point, as all subsequent enlargements of the Community/Union have continued to insist on such an acceptance as a point of principle. Applicants must agree to abide by the treaties which have anyway a legal, binding effect, the secondary legislation created by the EC/EU and the customs and practice developed by the EC/EU since its establishment (the *acquis*). The Hague Summit established a benchmark which included not just the customs and practice evolved in respect to the treaties, sometimes known as the *acquis communitaire*, but also those surrounding the more nebulous political cooperation aspects of the community – which have become known as the *acquis politique*.

The 1970 Luxembourg Report

A committee of national civil servants, headed by the Belgian Political Director, Viscount Etienne Davignon – after whom the report is sometimes named – drew up the report requested at The Hague. After being submitted to the member governments and debated by the European Parliament it was approved by the foreign ministers in October 1970. The report took into account the sensi-bilities of the member states on foreign policy cooperation that had prevented agreement being reached in the 1960s and attempted to breach the gap between grand ambition – to speak with one voice – and the low commitment levels of the individual member states to pool sovereignty on issues pertaining to security, defence and nationally perceived 'vital interests'. The preamble to the Luxembourg report retained the rhetorical sweep of The Hague dec-laration and in doing so put on paper the outline of what would become a clear EC philosophy underlying its future foreign policy. At the same time it introduced a set of cautious, limited objectives for this new exercise in European Political Cooperation (EPC) on foreign policy. The report also innovated a number of procedural forms, designed to help initiate this new practice of foreign policy coordination and cooperation. There was virtually no public input into the process of adoption of the report – save the reference to the Parliament whose members, although directly elected parliamentarians in their own states, were (in 1970) appointed and not elected to the European Assembly. This report marked the first successful attempt at foreign policy cooperation by the member states of the European Community. It was important because the 'Luxembourg approach' provided the model for future institutionalisation of the common foreign policy. The core of the approach is that of a rhetorical commitment to the vague objectives of Union along with a sometimes inchoate but persistent idea that the member states possess a distinctive 'European identity' in the field of international relations – accompanied at the same time by modest short-term aims and incremental steps in procedural innovation.

Philosophy

The Luxembourg report emphasised that the European Communities formed the 'nucleus' of 'European unity'. Projects designed to bring about the 'ever closer union' envisaged within the Rome Treaty would have the EC at the centre of such a union. Membership of the EC, however, was not open to all European states – only those that were 'democratic ... with freely elected parliaments'. At the time this provision excluded not only the states of Central and Eastern Europe but fascist Spain, dictatorship-led Portugal and the military-controlled state in Greece. Foreign policy cooperation was therefore to be linked with the broad objective of Community-building which was itself to be underpinned by a very specific philosophical and normative commitment – the consolidation and expansion of liberal representative democracy in Europe. The report recognised that the Community, because of its internal common policies, was developing an increasingly cohesive role in the world. The goal therefore was to parallel those Community developments with political cooperation so that 'Europe' could eventually 'speak with one voice' in order to be able to carry out its 'imperative world duties'.

Aims

The specific aims of foreign policy cooperation between the six member states were cautious in the extreme. The commitment was to share information and consult with each other on 'the major issues of international politics'. They would also aim to harmonise their views, concert their attitudes and 'take joint action when it appears feasible and desirable'. As the document was ratified by neither Community nor national legislation these objectives were not binding or enforceable. Even had these objectives been made the subject of a treaty their formulation was loose enough to enable an extremely flexible interpretation as to the obligations of the member states towards each other. Again, the Luxembourg report set the standard for future developments. Although foreign policy cooperation would eventually evolve into a common policy and be enshrined within a legal basis, commitments would deliberately be loose and subject to the broadest interpretation by member states which would, in the main, seek to maintain the widest possible remit for national autonomy.

Procedural innovation

The Luxembourg report established substantially new, yet cautious and pragmatic, mechanisms for implementing this novel aspect of Community-building. The foreign ministers attempted to bridge the gap between those states which had rejected foreign policy cooperation in the context of the Community institutions in the 1960s and those which had seen a Community involvement as necessary and appropriate. The solution found was to draw a distinction between the activities of foreign policy cooperation and those of the Community and at the same time to recognise and utilise the obvious organic links between EPC and the Community. This distinction, although precarious theoretically and blurred in practice right from its inception, provided a formula with which all member states could agree. After a couple of decades of suspicion, mistrust and false starts, therefore, the member states were at last able to commence the foreign policy cooperation that had previously eluded them.

The distinction between European Political Cooperation and the Community was operationalised in four ways. The first was the prescribing of alternative decision-making procedures in EPC to that of the Community. The second aspect of procedural innovation was the creation of new institutions that would, at the level of the Community, deal solely with foreign policy cooperation. Thirdly, the distinction between EPC and the Community was to be visible in that the foreign ministers meeting in EPC were to meet in the country of the member state holding the Presidency, as opposed to any of the cities housing the Community institutions (except of course when Belgium, France or Luxembourg held the Presidency).

The cumulative effect of these changes contributed to a fourth aspect of procedural change with the transformation of the role of existing Community institutions in terms of their contribution to EPC as compared to their position within the treaty-based institutions.

The foreign ministers of the Community were allocated the central decision-making role in this new institution. They were, however, not to meet as the Council of the Communities (as prescribed by the Community legislation for treaty-based competencies) but as a *conference* of foreign ministers – meeting every six months or when necessary if convened by the Presidency. The Presidency would be held by the same foreign minister which held the presidency of the European Communities and, as in the Council of the Communities, the Presidency would change every six months. The presidency was specifically given the authority to arrange consultation in cases of 'serious crisis or special urgency'. The Presidency was also allocated the responsibility of consulting and informing the applicant states of discussion in EPC. The Commission was to be consulted on Community-related business and the European Parliament's Political Committee was to be informed once every six months of activities within EPC. The European Parliament was also to be provided with an annual report by the Presidency of progress in foreign policy cooperation.

The Luxembourg report created new institutions to facilitate foreign policy cooperation. The most important was the Political Committee which comprised the Political Directors of the member-state foreign ministries and which was to report to the Presidency and was to meet at least four times a year. The Political Committee was given the authority to set up working-groups and 'panels of experts'. Finally each state was to appoint a 'correspondent' to help organise the practical aspects of coordination between each member state. This last provision effectively set up yet another Luxembourg innovation – the 'group of correspondents'.

Decision-making

Decision-making rules were not made explicit in the Luxembourg report but it was clear that the foreign ministers would make any necessary decisions. This of course was somewhat different to the Community procedures where the Commission and the Council both had important decision-making capabilities. In European Political Cooperation consensus would be the operating principle. This was also different to the Community where, in certain circumstances, it was theoretically possible to make decisions on the basis of a qualified majority procedure related to a system of weighted voting. This last difference was not, however, one of substance as Community decision-making also tended to seek consensus in order to avoid a repetition of the 1965/66 'empty-chair crisis' when France had created a veto for itself over and above the Community's treaty-based legal framework (see Chapter 2).

Both the foreign ministers' decision-making role and that of the Presidency within EPC were much more authoritative than their equivalent roles within the Community. The Presidency of EPC would have more authority than the Presidency of the Council of the Communities in that it alone was given the right to call meetings, to chair those meetings and to set the agenda (although member states were given the right to propose any matter for discussion). Conversely the Commission's role was much diminished in EPC. In the Community, the Commission was the 'motor of integration' and the only legal initiator of policy: at Luxembourg it was allocated the lesser function of occasional adviser. The Parliament's position in EPC remained substantially similar to its then role within the Community – as a purely advisory and uninfluential body. Another crucial institutional difference between EPC and the Community was the absence of any role for the European Court of Justice in foreign policy cooperation. In sum the effect of these procedural innovations was to institutionalise EPC as a Community-related but *intergovernmental* activity – moving away from Community decision-making procedures which, in some respects, had *supranational* features. It would be wrong, however, to assume from this process of differentiated decision-making that member states intended that EPC become an optional activity which might be undertaken separately from Community membership. The link between the two aspects of Community-building – EPC and the treaty-based functions – was made explicit in part four of the report which stated in Article 1 that 'Ministers stress the correlation between membership of the European Communities and participation in activities making for progress towards political unification.'

The 1972 Paris Summit

The member states met again in Paris in October 1972 to discuss among other things progress in foreign policy cooperation. In the run-up to the meeting the old disagreement as to whether a permanent secretariat for EPC was necessary was raised and again remained unresolved – leaving intact the status quo of the rotating presidency supported by national civil servants. The Summit itself concluded by offering a reiteration of the grand objectives relating to speaking with one voice but settled for only modest procedural improvements to the EPC machinery. These included an agreement that foreign ministers should meet quarterly instead of twice a year. They were also enjoined to maintain close contact with the Community institutions in respect of the political aspects of Community activities and 'Community policies under construction'. The foreign ministers were instructed to prepare another report on ways to improve European Political Cooperation. The institutions of the Community were invited to report back, before 1975, on how future political union, which remained the self-declaimed aim of the Paris Summit, could be achieved. The Paris summit stated its intention to complete 'before the end of the present decade' the amalgamation of the 'whole complex of the relations' between the member states within 'a European Union'.

The significance of the Summit was limited to four issues. One is that after previous years of lack of progress, the Summit recorded that foreign policy cooperation was actually occurring and likely to intensify. The second feature of the Paris Summit was the recognition that in this new enterprise of foreign policy cooperation the Commission was likely to be a necessary partner. The third notable aspect was that the discussion of political union was divorced from that of procedural improvements to EPC. The last area of note was that political union was not dropped as a medium-term goal despite its bureaucratic separation from discussions on foreign policy cooperation.

The 1973 Copenhagen Report

The foreign ministers, again guided by the draftsmanship of Etienne Davignon, completed and approved the report on ways to improve foreign policy cooperation in July 1973 in Copenhagen. A formal written procedure was used to secure assent from the Heads of State and Government and this was given by the end of August. The report made few innovations, staying within the framework established at Luxembourg in 1970, but did succeed in elaborating a more detailed procedural framework. The major difference from the Luxembourg report was the absence of an extensive overarching philosophical framework. The reason for this omission was that at the same time as the foreign ministers were preparing the

Copenhagen report they were also engaged in a more ambitious venture – to define the European identity internationally, particularly in relation to the United States, their major ally. The member states, which were in early 1973 engaged in a somewhat acrimonious debate with the US on the issue of Community/US relations, were anxious to stress both the 'original contribution' of 'Europe' to international affairs and its loyalty to 'its traditional friends and to the Alliances of its Member States'. This balance of interest – between an EC anxious to assert its independence and at the same time to preserve US security leadership – was further addressed in a document on the 'European identity' which was approved in Copenhagen in December 1973. It served to provide the philosophical accompaniment to the procedures for improved foreign policy cooperation worked out in the earlier July report.

The Copenhagen report is important because it signified that political cooperation was actually taking place – an annex was attached to the report identifying 'results' that had *already* been achieved in the practice of foreign policy cooperation. It also proclaimed that the practice of political cooperation had – even in the short time of its operation – succeeded in establishing a 'coordination reflex' among member states. The report is also significant because it reaffirms that the hybrid intergovernmental/supranational procedures established at Luxembourg had become standard practice. Efforts were made to improve working practices but no substantial changes to the principles underlying them were seriously mooted.

Aims

The aims of consultation, harmonisation and joint action where necessary or desirable were reaffirmed. The foreign ministers also committed themselves to seek 'common policies on practical problems'. The policies must concern 'European interests whether in Europe itself or elsewhere'. The emphasis on discussing 'practical problems' presaged what became the characteristically British view of foreign policy cooperation – that it should be a pragmatic venture – and not used as a tool in any grand design for a united Europe. A new element introduced was the idea that member states were *obligated* to consult with each other on foreign policy issues. The relevant clause was written so as to preclude any legal commitment but nevertheless some element of political or moral obligation was envisaged with the statement that 'each State undertakes as a general rule not to take up final positions without prior consultation with its partners'.

Procedural innovation

The Copenhagen report strengthened the Luxembourg features – consolidating the dominant position of the foreign ministers and the Presidency in political cooperation and reinforcing the member states' input into the procedure via a formalisation of the role of the Political Committee. The relationship with the Commission remained little changed from Luxembourg although the guidelines pertaining to that relationship served to express both its ambiguity and the ambivalence of the foreign ministers towards the Commission's role. Thus the changes in the relative weight of the major institutions of the Community in decision-making in EPC (as compared to their role in the Community's treaty-based procedures where the Commission had more powers), that had been initiated at Luxembourg, were retained and further institutionalised at Copenhagen.

The decision taken at the 1972 Paris Summit to increase regular ministerial meetings to four a year was confirmed. It was also decided that foreign ministers could meet in places other than the country of the Presidency 'when they happen to come together on other occasions'. This somewhat coy turn of phrase referred to the occasions when the foreign ministers met as the Council of the Communities. Thus the Copenhagen report recognised that the distinction contrived at Luxembourg between EPC and Community decision-making was, at the very inception of foreign policy cooperation between the member states, proving difficult to enforce in practice.

The foreign ministers had also become aware from their intervening experience that the Presidency's role was crucial. As well as the task of setting agendas and organising meetings that were foreseen by the Luxembourg report, the Copenhagen report iterated the Presidency's increasing responsibilities. The Presidency was responsible for collective implementation of decisions made in European Political Cooperation consultations, and meetings with ambassadors of the member states on EPC-related issues. Given that a permanent secretariat had been ruled out, it was decided that the Presidency could call upon the assistance of other member states if necessary.

The Community institutions were still kept at arms length from the process of political cooperation although the report stated that 'the Commission would be invited to make known its views in accordance with current practice'. This rather oblique statement masked the fact (recognised in the annex to the report) that since its inception in 1970 the Commission had been operating as an active participant in EPC – most visibly and successfully in its coordination of economic issues within the negotiations of the Conference on Security and Cooperation in Europe (CSCE). Formal coordination between the Commission and the foreign ministers was further supposed to be facilitated by the provision in the report instructing the foreign ministers to inform the Council of issues discussed in EPC that may have relevance to the Community, via the member states' permanent representatives (COREPER) in Brussels. Although the foreign ministers were instructed to transfer information, this instruction was in some senses slightly odd given that the foreign ministers would be effectively informing themselves (the Council) of decisions they had themselves made. The fact of 'double-hatting' provided some obvious if elementary coordination between the Community institutions and EPC and of course served to maintain the distinction – so important for some of the member states such as France and Britain – between Community and EPC activities.

In contrast to the Commission's persistent involvement with EPC, the Parliament's ability to influence foreign policy cooperation was only marginally improved. It was to be permitted four (instead of two) meetings of its Political Committee (the then Parliamentary committee for foreign affairs) with ministers a year. The Political Committee of EPC was also instructed to inform foreign ministers of any Parliamentary resolutions relevant to foreign policy deliberations. Most of the responsibility for coordinating European Political Cooperation fell on the Political Committee. Those responsibilities were enumerated in the Copenhagen report and the Political Committee was authorised to meet as frequently as necessary to discharge these responsibilities. As well as preparing for the ministerial meetings and supervising the working parties and panels of experts, the Political Committee was also entrusted with coordinating member states' consultations prior to meetings of the UN General Assembly, the Economic and Social Council and the Food and Agriculture Organisation that had formerly taken place within the WEU context. Also added to the Political Committee's oversight role was a responsibility to ensure effective coordination of embassies and ambassadors in third countries and international organisations. A further responsibility was supervision of the group of Correspondents – the national civil servants given the responsibility, at

Luxembourg, of practical coordination of the new EPC procedures between and within member states.

The Copenhagen report attempted to associate the member states' ambassadors and representatives in third countries and international institutions more closely with the work of foreign policy coordination. Each member state committed itself to appointing a member of staff in the other member states' capitals who would deal exclusively with EPC. Representatives in international organisations were specifically instructed that they must attempt to seek 'common positions'. Finally, the foreign ministers agreed a technical and important innovation that was the institutionalisation of a telex link between the member-state foreign ministries. Its French acronym was COREU – as it is still known.

Decision-making

There was no alteration made at Copenhagen to the central position of the foreign ministers in decision-making although there is much clearer understanding than in the Luxembourg report of the close and necessary relationship between the Community institutions, particularly the Commission, and European Political Cooperation. Nor was there any change to the principle of consensus among the member states. Voting procedures were not mentioned at Copenhagen and the unwritten rule remained that progress on questions of both procedure and substance in foreign policy cooperation could only proceed by unanimous agreement between the member states. The Commission could advise on certain specified issues, but it could not, theoretically, participate in decision-making.

The 1973 Document on the European Identity

The philosophy underpinning the Community's new determination to speak with one voice in international affairs was set out in a document 'on the European identity' adopted in December 1973. Its immediate genesis was the series of political and economic frictions that had bedevilled EC–US relations throughout the early 1970s. The Europeans and the US disagreed on Vietnam, international monetary relations and the relative merits of Israeli and Palestinian claims in the 1973 October war. The United States, previously accustomed to bilateral dealings with the West European states, also had to attempt to define its relationship to the enlarged (in 1973 to include Britain, Denmark and Ireland) and economically more powerful EC. In April 1973 Nixon's high-profile National Security Adviser, Henry

Kissinger, had argued that what was required was a new Atlantic Charter (a wartime document drawn up between President Roosevelt and British Prime Minister Winston Churchill) to organise economic, political and defence relationships between the two partners. This objective would probably have been acceptable to the member states except for the fact that the Kissinger proposal relegated the Europeans to the status of junior partner as he insisted that the US had global interests to protect while the Europeans possessed only regional interests.

The foreign ministers were thus propelled into a delineation of the European role in international relations at a very early stage in the process of foreign policy coordination among themselves. How would this role be distinct from that of the United States and at the same time supportive of a broad Western strategic consensus?

The member states attempted to resolve the dilemma by asserting that the Europeans possessed a common identity and a unique contribution to bring to the management of international affairs based upon common interests and related to a European civilisation composed of a variety of cultures but upholding common values, principles and concepts of life. This contribution was based on the 'fundamental elements of the European identity' which included principles of representative democracy, the rule of law, social justice, economic progress and respect for human rights. Two corollaries flowed from the articulation of the European identity. The first is that future member states would have to share the same 'ideals and objectives' as a prerequisite for membership. The second corollary is that the European contribution to contemporary international relations, based on this distinct identity, could only effectively be made if the member states could learn to 'speak with one voice'.

It was more difficult for the member states to spell out their contradictory relationship with the United States. The 1973 document acknowledged the protection given to Europe by the continued stationing of US troops and nuclear arms in Western Europe. It also mentioned the 'close links' between the US and EC member states, based on shared 'values and aspirations founded on a common heritage'. At the same time the foreign ministers attempted to chart an independent political course (of the United States) in the sphere of international relations. The EC intended 'to maintain a constructive dialogue with the United States' and to develop cooperation with them on a basis of equality and in a spirit of friendship. In other words the foreign ministers wanted a partnership of equals not of subalternship.

The document is significant for two reasons. First of all it articulates an identity for the 'European construction' which links membership to a very specific political philosophy. Only applicant states, which share the iterated features of European identity, would be permitted to join the Community and its associated political cooperation. The Luxembourg provisions regarding the democratic credentials of future member states were thus reinforced. Second, the report details the importance of the US relationship to the vicissitudes of developing European foreign policy cooperation. European Political Cooperation is based upon US security leadership within NATO and yet at the same time was an effort by the West Europeans to maintain an international political identity distinct from that of the United States. The Community's sometimes contradictory relationship with the United States shaped the debates over how foreign policy cooperation should develop for the next 20 years. It was not until the end of the Cold War and the Maastricht Treaty, which institutionalised a cooperative 'division of labour' between the two 'pillars' of the Western alliance, that the relationship was more or less clarified. The 1973 document on the European identity was, therefore, the first of a series of attempts to try to chart the relationship between an increasingly more representative, more economically powerful and potentially more politically significant Community and its ally, the United States.

The 1974 Gymnich Agreement

Disputes with the United States over its perceived right to be consulted on foreign policy were resolved in April 1974 with the adoption of the 'Gymnich procedure' – designed to offer a mechanism for 'friendly countries' to be made aware of deliberations in European Political Cooperation and to allow for their input. The necessity for some form of procedure to allow consultation with allies had become particularly obvious after both Nixon and Kissinger had complained that the European allies were adopting foreign policy positions in areas of mutual concern without consulting the United States. The foreign ministers, meeting informally at Gymnich in Germany, agreed a formula whereby the Presidency, if all the foreign ministers agreed, would consult their allied partners on issues to be discussed in EPC. The agreement was unwritten and somewhat vague but it proved acceptable to the

United States and remained the basis for Community/US political consultations until their formalisation in the early 1990s.

The 'Gymnich agreement' should not be confused with the 'Gymnich-type' meetings which are a way of referring to the once-a-presidency informal meetings where the foreign ministers (and their spouses should they so wish) meet with each other in the country holding the Presidency in order to discuss 'off-the-record' issues of the day.

The 1974 Paris Summit

The now nine Heads of State and Government met again in Paris at the invitation of President Giscard d'Estaing in December 1974. Their discussion focused on the French proposal to institutionalise the now regular summit meetings in a European Council. The European Council was to be an intergovernmental institution that would meet three times a year. It was to be composed of the HSG, assisted by the foreign ministers and the President of the Commission. Its intention was to assist in 'progress towards European unity' and to this end it would act as a coordinating body which could produce general policy orientations on all issues relating to the common interests of the European Council member states. These would include matters relating to the Community, foreign policy cooperation in EPC and any other matters requiring discussion. Thus foreign policy cooperation in EPC was to be linked to Community decision-making at the highest political level. The Paris communiqué stressed that the European Council would aim to achieve 'common positions' in international relations. The President-in-Office of the European Council (the HSG of the country holding the six-monthly rotating presidency) would 'be the spokesman for the nine and will set out their views in international diplomacy'.

The Summit did not entirely neglect supranational aspirations in its creation of essentially intergovernmental machinery for member-state consultation. One very minor change was made to increase Community involvement in foreign policy coordination through the decision to allow the Parliament to ask questions of the foreign ministers and to receive replies. A perhaps more major nod in the direction of supranational ambitions was the instruction to Belgian Prime Minister Leo Tindemans to prepare a report on European Union to be submitted in 1975.

The significance of the Summit was less the role given to the European Council in international diplomacy, as in practice the foreign ministers continued to take the lead in this area, and more the tacit recognition of the inextricable links between Community policies and foreign policy cooperation. The institutionalisation of the Commission's involvement within the European Council – just four years after the Luxembourg report had aimed to exclude the Commission from discussion of non-treaty matters – provides evidence of the steady blurring of Community/foreign policy competencies. The genuflection to Parliamentary involvement also emphasised the close relationship of treaty- and non-treaty-related activities of the Community and its member states. Another feature of consequence was that, given that all previous proposals to further establish union had at their core attempts to establish a common foreign policy, the proposed report on European Union would inevitably involve reopening the debates on the nature of foreign policy cooperation within the 'European construction'.

The 1975 Tindemans Report

The 1972 Paris Summit had requested reports on European Union from the institutions of the Community including the Commission, the Parliament, the European Court of Justice and the Economic and Social Committee. In 1974, Tindemans was given the task of assessing the progress towards European Union by utilising the completed reports from the institutions, consulting member-state governments and taking into account public opinion. The result was presented to the European Council in December 1975, published in January 1976, discussed by the European Council on a number of different occasions until at the November Hague meeting a suitably diplomatic formula was found which would allow Tindemans' proposals to be dropped. Nevertheless the report produced a number of different ideas on substantive and procedural aspects of foreign policy cooperation that retained their force with many being recycled at future evolutionary stages in the development of a common foreign policy for the EC/EU.

The report did not deal with foreign policy per se but its major focus was on the Union's external identity. While not attempting to define European Union, which Tindemans saw as a changing phenomenon, he did advocate the building of an institutionally more cohesive body, particularly in external relations. He argued that the distinction made between political and economic matters should be ended and that the Union should discuss foreign policy, security, defence, external economic relations and development as part of an overall Community policy. In concrete terms he proposed the end of the separation of the two sets of institutional procedures governing decision-making in Community external economic relations and in EPC. Probably the most controversial of the Tindemans recommendations, however, was the idea that in foreign policy, member states should be obliged, through legal mechanisms, to seek common policies (as is the case in the treaty-based Community areas of competence). Tindemans proposed that in foreign policy discussion 'the minority must rally to the views of the majority at the conclusion of a debate'. Allied to this notion of a new legal obligation – sanctified by a new treaty – was a further politically contentious idea. This was the suggestion that the European Court of Justice be given jurisdiction over all aspects of Union decision-making – including foreign policy.

No agreement could be reached on these proposals whose implementation, apart from anything else, would have demanded a qualitative change in the way that foreign policy coordination was developing. Instead of pragmatic, incremental cautious steps towards a common foreign policy, the establishment of the new Union with wide-ranging foreign policy competencies would have to have been accompanied by some form of major constitutional debate in the member states. None of them was willing to risk opening up debate on such sensitive issues as sovereignty and national security and therefore the Tindemans initiative failed in its immediate objectives. The European Council would only agree to call for further annual reports from the foreign ministers and the Commission on progress towards Union. In practice the reports were destined for obscurity but the Tindemans ideas remained the subject of continued debate.

The 1978 Improvements to Procedure

In 1978 during the Greek accession negotiations, it became necessary to collate the procedural reports agreed in respect of the management of foreign policy cooperation – so as to acquaint Greece with its future responsibilities in European Political Cooperation. Greece, as an applicant state, agreed to adhere to EPC procedures – although it was not expected to go along with every pronouncement that would have been made within EPC prior to accession. The procedural texts were amalgamated and organised by the Group of European Correspondents in the *coutumier*. Belgium, in practice, took on the responsibility of keeping these current. It was also

Belgium that initiated the practice of collecting the most important statements of each Presidency in what is known as the *recueil*.

The 1981 London Report

The next stage in the institutionalisation of the process of foreign policy cooperation came at the initiative of the British and in the wake of the 1979 Soviet invasion of Afghanistan when European Political Cooperation had manifestly been unable to provide a speedy and cohesive response to the crisis. The British argued for an increased political commitment to EPC, an improved procedure for dealing with international crises and a strengthening of diplomatic and administrative support for the Presidency. The report agreed by the foreign ministers in October 1981 adopted most of the changes identified by the British and also built on suggestions from the Federal Republic of Germany which, among other things, had wished to include security issues within the ambit of EPC. The coming to power in France of Mitterand in May 1981 and the appointment of a former European Commissioner, Claude Cheysson, to the post of French foreign minister helped to facilitate discussions about the position of the Community institutions in EPC. The report, however, was bereft of large visions of a future Union and instead concentrated on procedural issues. There was no radical change in ideas developed at Luxembourg and Copenhagen and merely some fine-tuning of the diplomatic apparatus.

Aims

The foreign ministers underlined the objective agreed at Luxembourg and Copenhagen to consult partners by stressing the fundamental nature of this commitment. Partners would be consulted before final national positions were adopted and before the launching of 'national initiatives on all important questions of foreign policy'. The report stated that joint action 'not merely a common attitude' should be increasingly possible. One slight change to the responsibilities admitted of EPC was the reference, in the preamble, to the highly sensitive topic of security. The foreign ministers reported that the flexibility of EPC procedures had permitted discussion of 'the political aspects of security'. This apparently innocuous reference demonstrated that old barriers to the discussion of the sensitive issue of national security were being breached.

Procedural innovation

The London report marked the consolidation of the intergovernmental features of EPC such as the predominant role allocated to the foreign ministers and the Presidency. At the same time the report formalised the growing involvement of the Community institutions and as such recognised that foreign policy cooperation had evolved as a complex and hybrid structure with both intergovernmental and supranational characteristics.

Foreign ministers were authorised to continue with the 'Gymnich-type' meetings established in 1974 and they were also given explicit permission to meet on the same occasion as the Council of the Communities. The core of the London report was an elaboration of the duties and responsibilities of the Presidency. The Presidency would continue to organise the meetings with the help of the Political Committee. It would also be the spokesperson to the media – after having consulted the foreign ministers. Third countries or groups of them that wished to establish relations with EPC were to do so via the Presidency. In order to cope with what is clearly seen as a high-profile and onerous set of duties the Presidency was permitted to make use of civil servants from the preceding and successor presidencies. These civil servants would be employed in their home embassy of the capital of the Presidency but would work under the direction of the Presidency. Mirroring this arrangement at the administrative level was the 'troika' facility established where the previous and successor foreign ministers were given a support role to the Presidency-in-office. The troika arrangement satisfied the need for political and administrative support for the Presidency and, at the same time, avoided the creation of a common secretariat to administer EPC – a still sensitive subject for some of the member states.

Included in the report was an unambiguous commitment to the Commission being 'fully associated with political cooperation, at all levels'. Furthermore, the report enumerated the previous decisions taken to maintain contact with the European Parliament (EP), noted where improvements in EPC/European Parliament consultation had taken place and suggested ways in which it could be further improved. The section on relations with the Parliament noted that the President gave a speech to the Parliament at the beginning and end of the six-month term of office and this 'usually' included political cooperation issues and it also pointed out that the Presidency regularly held informal meetings with the leaders of the political groups in Parliament. The foreign ministers gave a vague commitment to take the resolutions of the EP more into consideration in their deliberations and, more concretely, noted that after the meetings of the European Council, the President would address the parliament on all issues discussed including foreign policy matters.

Other procedural improvements related to the efforts to secure a clear method of cooperation between member states' embassies in third countries. The London report noted that Heads of Missions abroad did meet regularly with their counterparts and encouraged them to submit reports to the foreign ministers either on the request of the Political Committee or 'exceptionally' on their own initiative. In the last section of the report, the foreign ministers addressed the issue of how to work more effectively together in times of international crises. They agreed that a meeting of the Political Committee or the ministers could be convened within 48 hours at the request of three member states. Working groups were encouraged to carry out some strategic thinking on potential crises and to provide options for foreign ministers in such circumstances.

Decision-making

The intergovernmental aspects of decision-making were slightly altered by the recognition that the Commission must be fully associated with European Political Cooperation. Given that the Commission was constrained in its operation by very specific decision-making procedures, this implied some recognition by the foreign ministers that, in some circumstances, collective or supranational decision-making rules may apply. The ministers, however, remained governed by the principle of unanimity. The London report had been designed to facilitate existing decision-making roles – not to change them.

GIVING FOREIGN POLICY A TREATY BASE: 1981–93

Debates in the 1980s on Community foreign policy moved the European construction in the direction of a harmonisation of the treaty and non-treaty aspects of foreign policymaking and implementation. The Community's foreign policy became enshrined in two international treaties – the 1987 Single European Act and the 1993 Treaty on European Union – the latter recognising and constitutionalising the existence of a *common* though not *exclusive* foreign and security policy for the member states and the Union. Prior to enshrining European Political Cooperation and the Common

Foreign and Security Policy in international legislation (the SEA and the TEU respectively), the foreign ministers and the Heads of States and Government considered and rejected a number of different proposals from the Community institutions and the member states which had as their aim the further institutionalisation of some form of foreign policy cooperation. Agreement to formalise foreign policymaking within a juridical structure was only reached after a series of intergovernmental conferences held throughout the mid-1980s and early 1990s.

The 1981 Genscher-Colombo Initiative

In January 1981 the German foreign minister Hans-Dietrich Genscher launched what became a series of ideas to try to reinvigorate the Community and to move forward to European Union. At the centre of his proposals was the suggestion that the new Union should adopt security and defence responsibilities. Italian foreign minister Emilio Colombo also joined the fray in January 1981 – arguing, among other things, for a common European approach to security which could be managed through improvements to the process of foreign policy cooperation within EPC.

The Genscher-Colombo initiative was presented to the other member states in November 1981 in the form of a draft European Act and a draft declaration on economic integration. The proposal referred to Community and EPC-related issues but at its core was the idea for an amalgamated common foreign policy which would include security. Included in the vision of an amalgamated Union – bringing existing European-level economic and political responsibilities together with expanded competencies that would not only include security and defence but also cultural and legal questions – was the proposal to establish a single institutional framework to manage these responsibilities. The treaty framework would bring together the European Council, an increased number of Councils of Ministers (to deal with the new security, defence, cultural and legal areas) and the existing Community institutions.

The single institutional framework was not a proposal to implement a common decision-making approach that might harmonise political cooperation (foreign policy, security, defence, culture and law) and Community (economic) procedures. In many ways the proposal, if acted on, would have meant an institutionalised separation of Treaty of Rome and Paris procedures from the political cooperation procedures. This is because the new 'political' aspects of the Draft Treaty were to be administered by a new secretariat of European political cooperation while the Council secretariat would have continued with its own separate existence in relation to economic issues. The initiative was strongly intergovernmental in intent – as it envisaged a continuing dominance of the member states in decision-making – but nevertheless, because it also envisaged a single institutional framework, the outcome of the Treaty, if it had been implemented would have been a continued institutionalisation of a rather hybrid structure – an intergovernmental organisation with strong supranational features intrinsic to it. The European Council, however, deferred judgement and merely 'received' the Draft Act in November 1981. The foreign ministers and the Commission were asked to further elaborate the Genscher-Colombo proposals and report back to a further meeting of the HSG.

The 1983 Solemn Declaration on European Union

Despite intensive discussions within the Community institutions and with the member-state governments there was little concretely achieved as a result of the German and Italian initiative. The result was a Solemn Declaration which, apart from having no legal force, did not include any commitment to anything other than the most minor changes to the substance and procedures of foreign policy cooperation. Ireland, Greece and Denmark were particularly opposed to any inference that the Community was to be given any responsibility in the area of security policy. The compromise reached in the declaration was to slightly expand the formula agreed in the 1981 London report. Instead of being only permitted to discuss the 'political aspects of security' (as in the London report), foreign ministers would now be able to discuss the 'political and economic aspects of security'.

The Solemn Declaration made few procedural innovations. As regards foreign policy cooperation it reiterated the role and function of the European Council and the dual role of the foreign ministers who met either as the Council of the Communities or as the foreign ministers meeting in EPC. Parliament's right to be consulted was affirmed and moderately enhanced in that the foreign ministers would continue to respond to parliamentary questions but from 1983 would also reply to resolutions that the EP might agree on foreign policy issues.

The 1984 European Parliament Draft Treaty Establishing the European Union

In 1979 the European Parliament had been directly elected for the first time. It had established a committee for institutional questions in 1981 whose members included Altiero Spinelli, an Italian Communist and strong advocate of European federalism who had served as a Commissioner from 1970 to 1976. Spinelli produced a 'draft Treaty establishing the European Union' which was agreed in February 1984 by the European Parliament. Its intent was to propose constitutional change that would have the effect – in a similar way to both the Tindemans and the Genscher-Colombo proposals – of bringing together the treaty-based institutions and procedures, European political cooperation and the European Council within a legal framework that would be sanctified by a new treaty.

Spinelli proposed a *common* institutional framework – not a *single* structure for decision-making. This was to be operationalised through a system whereby there would be three types of Union competencies: exclusive (to the Union institutions), concurrent (between the Union institutions and the member states) and those which would be exercised under the direction of the member states alone. Within each of these spheres, the Union was to be permitted to carry out its duties either through *common action* or through *cooperation*. Cooperation was an activity implemented by member states. Common action implied Union responsibilities and possible decision-making by majority voting.

The European Council was to be entrusted the task of deciding when a foreign policy issue should be handled either by the member states or the Union but the draft treaty suggested that the Union would be well placed to deal with the political and economic aspects of security, particularly in the four areas of armaments, sales of arms, defence policy and disarmament. The proposal did not, however, suggest any transfer of sovereignty to the Union on foreign policy. The input from the Union was to take place under the aegis of the cooperation procedure and member states would retain the dominant role in decision-making. The only sphere of foreign policy that would be enshrined in the common action procedure would be the external authority already delegated to Community/Union institutions as for example in trade policy. A suggestion for moderate reform was included in the provision that development aid policy should become an area for common action after a period of ten years. Other suggested innovations included the right of the Commission to initiate foreign policies and, in certain circumstances, to coordinate the diplomatic activity of member states. It was also suggested that the European Parliament and the Council should both have the authority to approve international treaties. An important feature of the proposals in the sphere of foreign policy was that, where the European Council did admit of common action, the member states were permitted to annul the action at any time by reverting to the cooperation procedure or vetoing proposals. The draft treaty also suggested that foreign policy decisions could be differentially implemented – in other words a decision would not necessarily be mandatory for all member states.

The draft treaty was an attempt to provide an acceptable, evolutionary path to European Union which would not offend the member states' sensitivities on key areas including national security. The sum total of its recommendations would not have altered the intergovernmental nature of Community/Union foreign policy-making but would rather have given some institutional cohesion to the practice of the Community which, by the 1980s, was undoubtedly engaging in a whole number of different foreign policy initiatives – many of which were stretching the Community's institutional framework to its limits. The draft treaty was not approved but its importance is in respect of ideas that it generated – many of which found their way into either the 1987 Single European Act or the later treaty on European Union.

The 1985 Dooge Report

Of the member state leaders Mitterand had been the most enthusiastic in respect of the ideas contained in the European Parliament's draft European treaty and it was Mitterand who suggested that the draft treaty and the 1983 Solemn Declaration should be used by the member states as the basis for drawing up a new treaty for European Union. Mitterand was particularly keen to establish a permanent secretariat for political cooperation that would function under the direction of the European Council. Mitterand's ideas added to the *pot pourri* of proposals for reforms, as did a British paper that called for modest organisational changes to Community decision-making and which was produced for discussion at the 1984 Fontainebleau European Council which met to discuss, among other things, the various ideas about the future direction of the Community. The European Council agreed to appoint an ad hoc committee on institutional affairs, composed of the personal representatives of the HSG, and chaired by the Irish representative, Mr Dooge. The committee offered an interim report in December 1984, producing the final 'Dooge report' in March 1985.

The Dooge report was noticeable for its moderation although it did conclude that the member states should proceed towards some form of Union. The report's provisions in respect of foreign policy coordination were discussed in terms of the problems of creating an 'external identity' for 'Europe'. Security issues were to be admitted into the purview of Union discussions but decision-making would have to take account of already established alliances such as NATO and the WEU. There was no recommendation to merge Community decision-making and EPC decision-making although the Dooge report did recommend a closer alignment between the two structures. The report advocated the creation of a permanent secretariat for political cooperation under the direction of the Presidency – partly to help in maintaining cohesion between the Community and political cooperation matters. In conclusion the Dooge report suggested that an intergovernmental conference be held to discuss the creation of a treaty on European Union – to be based on the Stuttgart declaration, the Parliament's draft treaty, the committee for institutional affairs' own report and the *acquis communautaire*.

The 1987 Single European Act

By the mid-1980s therefore a plethora of proposals had emerged – all of whose aim was to try, in some way or another, 'to transform … the whole complex of the relations between the Member States of the European Communities into a European Union' (1973 Paris Summit communiqué). Most of these proposals contained some reference to the possibilities of expanding the functional remit of foreign policy cooperation (particularly in terms of security) and all – either in a more or less attenuated manner – contained references to procedural and institutional changes within EPC and between EPC and the Community in order to achieve greater cohesion between the two spheres. These proposals were discussed and argued over at the June 1985 Milan European Council and the 1985 intergovernmental conference – eventually resulting in the signing of the Single European Act in February 1986, its ratification in 1987 and its coming into force on 1 July of that same year.

The June 1985 Milan European Council

The Milan European Council debated the widely agreed Cockfield Single Market proposals (named after the British Commissioner responsible for the internal market) on liberalisation of the common market by 1992 – as well as institutional questions in relation to the Community. An important institutional debate was over whether to maintain the veto which had been more or less accepted as the prerogative of each member state since the Luxembourg compromise of 1966. The Single Market or '1992' proposals were linked to institutional questions in that suggestions were made that legislation intended to implement the '1992' proposals should be agreed by majority vote. The European Council also discussed the various proposals for improved foreign policy cooperation and the future roles of the Parliament and the Commission. No agreement being possible, the Italian Presidency proposed that an intergovernmental conference (IGC) should be called to resolve these problems – the results of which would be incorporated in amendments to the Treaty of Rome. The decision to hold the IGC was agreed by majority vote with Britain, Denmark and Greece dissenting. Given that the Community's decision-making practice had been to attempt to achieve consensus on important decisions the procedure – majority voting – has sometimes been seen as heralding the willingness of some of the member states to contemplate a 'two-speed Europe'. By this is meant that certain states would become more integrated more quickly with each other – thus forming a core and periphery in relation to European integration. However, the IGC was approved under the provision of the Treaty of Rome (Article 236) which only permits amendments to the treaty if *all* member states eventually ratify them and, therefore, no major change could take place without consensual support.

Subsequent to the Milan meeting the July Council of Ministers agreed that the IGC should take place later that year and that its conclusions would be presented to the December 1985 European Council. The participants would be foreign ministers, the Commission and also the foreign ministers of the two candidate countries, Spain and Portugal. The Committee of Permanent Representatives (COREPER) would prepare papers on the economic aspects of treaty revisions; the Political Committee of EPC would do the same for the political aspects.

The 1985 intergovernmental conference

The 1985 IGC met several times during September, October, November and December. Issues relating to the further liberalisation of the common market along with an agreement to support majority voting on internal market issues were fairly readily agreed. No such easy agreement could be attained on the question of foreign policy cooperation however. The Political Committee produced its draft in November. In that month the French proposed a treaty on 'European Union' that would bring together in one treaty both EPC and the Treaty of Rome-based competencies of the Community – while maintaining a procedural and institutional separation between the two spheres. By the time of the December European Council divergences between the member states continued to exist. These included the nature of the objectives to be pursued by European Political Cooperation, the question of what body should manage EPC, the question of scope in terms of whether security issues should be discussed, and the issue of how closely linked EPC should be to Community membership.

In December 1985 the European Council reached a compromise on the issue of political cooperation in that it was agreed that EPC should be institutionalised within a new treaty – thus for the first time providing a legal framework for European foreign policy cooperation – but it also agreed that EPC should be institutionalised under different provisions from those relating to Treaty of Rome competencies. The provisions relating to EPC were eventually included in the Single European Act which was *single* in that it brought together the hitherto separate Community and EPC activities of the ten member states. The EPC provisions, however, were placed in a section of the act – Title III – which was distinguishable from the rest of the Treaty in that its component members were termed 'High Contracting Parties', thus emphasising the undiluted sovereignty of the member states in foreign affairs. Title III was also excluded from the jurisdiction of the European Court of Justice. The content of the provisions relating to European Political Cooperation contained, for the most part, a codification of the agreements already reached in Luxembourg (1970), Copenhagen (1973) and London (1981).

The member states rejected the idea, initially mooted by Denmark, that other democratic states in Europe should be permitted to join EPC. Instead, in an annexed declaration to the Single European Act, the member states simply agreed to strengthen their relations with the democratic European states including those that were members of the Council of Europe.

Philosophy

The preamble of the Single European Act stated that the intention of the treaty was to contribute to the attempt to create European Union. Towards this end, the SEA brought together reforms to the Treaty of Rome and EPC (in foreign policy) in one treaty. The preamble stressed that the governing principle of the SEA was the signatories' commitment to democracy, human rights and the 'preservation of international peace and security'. Title III itself was mainly procedural with the High Contracting Parties committed to nothing more elaborate than 'to formulate and implement a European foreign policy'.

Aims

The main commitment by the member states to be incorporated in the treaty was to consult each other 'on any foreign policy matters of general interest'. The signatories would aim to maximise their collective influence internationally by coordinating and attempting to converge around agreed positions and they would also attempt to carry out joint action. Only the consultation commitment, however, was given much elaboration in that the SEA stated that consultations 'shall' take place before the member states reach final positions and member states abjured unilateral actions before taking 'full account' of the positions of its member-state partners and before having considered the possibility of adopting a 'European' position. The SEA also committed the member states to seeking 'common principles and objectives' and insisted that member states should 'endeavour to avoid' adopting national policies which could inhibit the Community's ability to act cohesively internationally. In other words, the short-term aims of the treaty were simply to codify the consensus agreed in the previously agreed reports. No vestige of legally enforceable obligation to cooperate was included in the treaty; instead a series of vague injunctions to cooperate were iterated in the SEA.

Some attention was given to the relationship between EPC and the external relations of the Community in that both were instructed to assure consistency between their policies. The provision within the 1983 Stuttgart declaration that 'political and economic aspects' of security could be discussed in EPC was formalised in the SEA. Any suggestion that the formalisation of the widening of the scope of EPC would lead to radical change in its aims and objectives – for instance for it to become a primary locus for West European discussions on security – was dispelled by the clause in the treaty which stated that the SEA would in no way 'impede closer cooperation in the field of security' within either the WEU or NATO for those member states which were also members of those organisations.

Procedural innovation

Few innovations were proposed – as the SEA did little more than juridically codify arrangements made in the intergovernmental reports previously agreed. Foreign ministers were to meet four times a year to discuss foreign policy and were also explicitly permitted to discuss political cooperation when they met as the Council of the Communities. In line with the practice developed in the 1981 London report, the SEA confirmed that an emergency meeting of either the Political Committee or the foreign ministers could be convened within 48 hours at the request of three member states. The Commission would be 'fully associated' with EPC and the Parliament would continue to be consulted and informed of developments. The roles of the Presidency, the Political Committee, the European Correspondents and the working parties were confirmed. The previously non-institutionalised European Council was formally recognised within the SEA as was its composition – of Heads of State or Government and the President of the Commission assisted by the foreign ministers and a European Commissioner. The European Council was to meet twice a year – in other words once less frequently than the schedule established by the 1974 Paris communiqué which had created the European Council.

There were two innovations to practice. The Commission was given a more responsible role in that both it and the Presidency of the foreign ministers were given joint responsibility for ensuring consistency between EPC and the Community's external policies. Second, the SEA agreed to establish a small secretariat for EPC which would be based in Brussels and whose function would be to provide administrative support to the Presidency.

Decision-making

There were no changes to EPC decision-making procedures that continued to operate on the basis of unanimity. The member states were exhorted to 'as far as possible, refrain from impeding the formation of a consensus' but this imprecation was not supported by any enforcement mechanisms.

The 1993 Treaty on European Union

In the late 1980s the emphasis within the Community was on the creation of the single market by 1992. In June 1989 the European Council decided to convene a new IGC on economic and monetary union in order both to facilitate and to reflect the dynamism of what were widely termed the '1992' proposals. After 1989, however, external events altered the context of Community discussions when the European and international political landscape changed dramatically: the Berlin Wall fell in November, German reunification began to take shape and Eastern Europe and the Soviet Union began to divest themselves of communism and move towards liberal capitalist systems. The decision of April 1990 to convene a parallel IGC on political union was partly as a response to these external stimuli and partly because of the apparent necessity to create political structures which could control and direct the putative economic and monetary union. Proposals to advance cohesion in foreign policy came from the institutions of the Community and influentially, in April 1990, from a Franco–German initiative designed to create a 'common foreign and security policy'.

The IGC on political union commenced its proceedings in Rome in December 1990. The intention was that both IGCs would complete their deliberations by 1992 so as to complement the achievement of the single market. International events such as the Gulf War of 1990/91 and the start of the Yugoslav crisis in 1991 ensured that discussions on how the EC could become an effective international actor excited external and domestic interest. The initial intention to merely complement the EC's increasingly dynamic economic structures with an appropriate political framework was submerged within a concern to develop an operational and effective joint foreign policy – particularly where the member states' European interests appeared to be jointly at stake.

Agreement was reached at Maastricht in December 1991 on a treaty on European Union that would incorporate both economic and political issues although it was not signed until February 1992. The Maastricht Treaty did not come into force until 1993 after referenda in Ireland (June 1992), France (September 1992) and

Denmark (June 1992 and May 1993) eventually approved ratification of the treaty.

The 1990/91 IGC on political union

The main item on the agenda of the IGC on political union was foreign policy and security although other issues were debated. Some had a clear relevance to foreign policy such as the proposal to increase cooperation on development aid. Others were more indirectly related. These included the bestowing of Union citizenship on all member-state citizens, the institutionalisation of cooperation in justice and home affairs, the insistence that commitments to democracy and human rights must underpin member states' – and therefore applicant states' – polities, and institutional reform. Also included was the eventually unsuccessful proposal to permit the European Union a federal vocation.

Prior to the IGC a number of different proposals from member states and Community institutions were circulated in respect of what a common foreign and security policy should consist of and how it should be managed. The Parliament wanted to bring together both EPC and Treaty of Rome-based external relations responsibilities. The Commission agreed and also suggested that the future European Union should be granted defence responsibilities through a linkage with the WEU. It also argued that the Commission should be able to initiate policy along with the foreign ministers and that, in some cases, foreign policy should be managed by majority vote and not by unanimity which had been past practice. The most important intervention in the debate was the joint Franco–German paper that recommended that the Union be given defence responsibilities – again through some form of relationship with the WEU. These two states were also willing to accept some form of majority voting in respect of the implementation of unanimously agreed foreign policy positions.

The IGC opened in December 1990 with a report from the personal representatives of the member states, on which there was a good deal of initial consensus in the realm of foreign policy recommendations. The almost purely theoretical distinction between the foreign ministers meeting as the Council of the Communities and meeting 'in EPC' was to be abolished. The Commissions's role would be upgraded. The EPC secretariat would be merged with the secretariat of the Council (in whose building it was already housed in Brussels). Another area of broad agreement was the Franco–German suggestion that majority voting could be used in the Council where general foreign policy positions had been agreed by consensus.

Discussion centred around the Luxembourg draft treaty whose broad thrust was to create three 'pillars' comprising Community, foreign and security, and justice and home affairs responsibilities. The Community pillar would underpin this 'Greek temple' approach – providing a single institutional structure for the Union. The most contentious issues revolved around three aspects of suggested foreign policy reform: defence, decision-making and the relationship of the Commission to foreign policymaking in the new Union. The agreed treaty reflected the compromise reached between the majority of member states that were anxious to proceed with a communitarian or more supranational policy and the minority, comprising Britain, Denmark, Ireland and Portugal, that on the whole preferred a more intergovernmental approach to foreign policy. A *common* foreign and security policy (CFSP) was agreed for the European Union. This policy, however, was again not an *exclusive* foreign policy for the member states and in this sense it was not a *single* foreign policy for the member states. The CFSP can only be seen as single in the sense in which the term was adopted in the SEA – that is as indicating that both foreign policy and Community policies continue to be integrated, along with justice and home affairs, into one single treaty and within one single institutional structure.

Philosophy

The commitment to 'the principles of liberty, democracy and respect for human rights' was incorporated in the preamble of the treaty. These commitments were given some force in the area of foreign policy. In Title V of the treaty which contained the 'provisions on a common foreign and security policy', one clause commits the Union 'to develop and consolidate democracy and the rule of law, and respect for human rights and fundamental freedoms'. The pursuit of individual liberties was of course part of a broader political project which saw the increased liberalisation of economic markets, as for instance in the '1992' project, as bringing both prosperity and peace. The political and economic philosophy was therefore that of liberal capitalism; not a completely unfettered capitalism, however, as policies were also incorporated in the TEU that were intended to assist the least developed areas of the Union and assist with 'strengthening of its economic and social cohesion'.

The preamble contained a commitment 'to implement a common foreign and security policy including the framing of a common defence policy, which might in time lead to a common defence'. This carefully worded statement could not disguise that the TEU did contain something of a qualitative change for European foreign policymaking. For the first time the member states admitted that the EC/EU was capable of carrying out a common foreign policy. This implied something more than intergovernmental cooperation – particularly given the additional claim that the EU would work not just towards common defence policies but towards a common defence. The implementation of a common defence for Europe would imply some element of sharing of command and control over national militaries and therefore a shift away from intergovernmental ideas of Europe towards the supranational idea. This shift was reinforced in Title V of the treaty which stated that the CFSP would cover 'all areas of foreign and security policy' and explicitly that the CFSP would 'strengthen the security of the Union and its Member States in all ways'.

The CFSP envisaged an influential and visible role for the European Union globally. In international affairs, the CFSP would promote peace, international security and international cooperation. It would support the UN Charter and the 1975 Helsinki Act which defined the remit of the Conference on Security and Cooperation in Europe (CSCE). It would also uphold the Paris Charter of 1990 which had signalled the end of the Cold War.

Aims

Unlike the Single European Act which had done little more than codify past practice, the TEU introduced new objectives for the CFSP. One change was more to the tone than the substance of the articles dealing with foreign policy. Member states 'shall' consult and 'shall' ensure' conformity in their national positions. They 'shall' avoid action that may damage the Union's effectiveness in international relations. The TEU therefore institutes a certain sense of obligation in the sense that member states commit themselves to finding and cooperating with common foreign policy positions. The commitment to cooperate is sharpened – and monitored in the sense that the Council is supposed to ensure compliance with the principles of the treaty. However, these principles remain difficult (if not impossible) to enforce.

In international organisations the TEU also stated that member states 'shall' uphold common positions. This latter injunction was potentially of some import given that the TEU stated that member states should take note of the CFSP even 'where not all the Member States participate'. Specific reference was made to the member states that were also permanent members of the UN Security Council. They committed themselves to 'ensure the defence of the positions and the interests of the Union'. This clause, notwithstanding the waiver stating it was 'without prejudice' to the responsibilities of the permanent members under the UN charter, did seem to imply that Britain and France were prepared to represent a 'European' as opposed to merely a national position in the Security Council.

Probably the most substantial of the new objectives was the introduction of a defence and security component to the CFSP which would be implemented by way of linkage with the WEU. The TEU specifically stated that this new European defence competency would not impinge on prior obligations to NATO or jeopardise any bilateral links between member states. However, the joint agreement within the treaty that the WEU was 'an integral part of the development of the Union' signified a more ambitious step in the creation of a common foreign policy than had been hitherto adopted.

Another objective pertaining to the CFSP but included within the remit of the Community pillar of the EU was the new commitment to the coordination of member states' and EU development aid. In addition, the provision of EU development assistance was closely tied to the philosophical underpinnings of the CFSP in that the Community's development aid was made specifically conditional on how it assisted with 'the general objective of developing and consolidating democracy and the rule of law, and to that of respecting human rights'.

Procedural innovation

Compared to the innovations in substantive objectives, procedural change was cautious and pragmatic. The Presidency's key role was confirmed – as was the support role of the troika. The European Council would define 'general guidelines' for foreign policy but the Council was given the responsibility of taking initiatives, making decisions and implementing them. The Commission remained 'fully associated' and for the first time authorised to initiate foreign policy proposals, along with the Council. The European Parliament retained its consultative status. The emergency procedure was further refined in that the Presidency, the Commission or any of the member states could request a special Council meeting to be held either within 48 hours or sooner if necessary.

The most important innovation was the merging of the Council of Ministers of the Community with the 'foreign ministers meeting in EPC' in the Council of the European Union. The always tenuous distinction between the two bodies was abolished. In addition the bureaucratic infrastructure was simplified so that the Committee of Permanent Representatives (COREPER) was allocated the responsibility of preparing all meetings of the Council including those to discuss foreign policy. The role of the Political Committee, which had hitherto been given the sole responsibility for administering foreign policy, was changed to that of a monitoring and oversight body. Finally, the secretariat for EPC established by the SEA was incorporated into the Council's general secretariat.

Decision-making

One change was brought in, however, with the introduction of ideas generated by the Franco–German proposals to the IGC and the earlier Spinelli proposals of 1984. The member states agreed that if the Council adopted a common position by unanimity, its implementation could be given the status of 'common action' and implemented by a qualified majority vote (QMV). The QMV was a system of weighted majority voting – already used to implement the internal market legislation – whereby each state was allocated a different number of votes according to its relative size. Britain, France, Germany and Italy had ten votes each; Spain had eight; Belgium, Greece, the Netherlands and Portugal had five each; Denmark and Ireland had two votes each – leaving Luxembourg with two votes. In the EU of twelve member states the qualified majority for the implementation of common action had to be at least 54 votes which had to be cast by at minimum, eight member states.

In the determination of common positions unanimity remained the rule within the Council. Majority voting on common positions within the Council was not ruled out – as was made clear in an annexed declaration to the TEU, where the member states committed themselves to refrain 'to the extent possible [from] preventing a unanimous decision where a qualified majority exists in favour'. On the whole, however, the balance between intergovernmentalism and supranationality remained tilted towards the former as the Council retained its right to redefine the scope of previously agreed common actions and thus prevent decisions being taken by the QMV procedure.

ENTERING THE TWENTY-FIRST CENTURY: COMMON FOREIGN AND SECURITY POLICY AS THE STATUS QUO

From the 1990s the European Union still maintained an active foreign policy towards the rest of the world but political and economic efforts were concentrated in Europe. It turned eastwards to deal with the transformation of East European states from communism to capitalism. It also continued to be a major player in the Yugoslavia conflicts (see Chapter 8). Foreign policy priorities focused on enlargement of the EU. The major institutional development was the signing and coming into force in 1999 of the Amsterdam Treaty – although the treaty itself was widely considered a 'tidying-up' and clarification exercise rather than heralding any radical departure from CFSP practice.

Towards the turn of the century, however, the major development came in the Franco–British talks designed to create a European Security and Defence Identity (ESDI). Unlike previous discussions, these talks were welcomed by the United States. The British and French were not arguing for an ESDI that would operate separately from their Atlantic partners or be divorced from the NATO context. ESDI was about how to ensure that the Europeans could act efficiently and effectively within the context of the Atlantic alliance. The circle that had so troubled European–US relations since the 1970s seemed to have been squared. The Europeans would develop a separate defence and security identity from the United States but would do this in the context of partnership with their allies and in the framework of NATO.

Policies continued to be developed and implemented through the mechanisms of both CFSP and treaty-based competencies. The procedures and practices of the Common Foreign and Security Policy, however, increasingly provided a framework wherein the broad outlines of strategies were agreed. The instruments for policy implementation were, however, as likely to be derived from Community instruments such as aid and trade concessions as much as the diplomatic *démarches* derived from the CFSP procedures. The CFSP procedures were also underpinned, at least in relation to the important foreign policy arena of enlargement, by the criteria agreed at the 1993 Copenhagen European Council. States would only be accepted as candidates for membership if they were committed to establishing market economies and democracy and were committed to upholding human rights and the rule of law.

The 1995 enlargement brought neutral Austria, Finland and Sweden into the Union in 1995 but it did not signify a change to Union foreign policy priorities or procedures. These states were able to work out a relationship with the Union so as not to compromise the basic elements of their foreign policy (see Chapter 8). Their long-established market economies and liberal democratic polities combined with their experience of working with the Union via their membership of the European Free Trade Association facilitated a seamless transition into membership and adoption of the *acquis* – including the foreign policy *acquis*.

The Amsterdam Treaty

The Amsterdam Treaty consolidated CFSP procedures. It re-emphasised the relationship with the Western European Union and stated that CFSP should include 'all questions relating to the security of the Union'. The treaty also explicitly stated that these security competencies included 'the progressive framing of a common defence policy'. It did not, however, signal any change of philosophy but instead institutionalised procedural innovation and amendments to decision-making procedures.

Procedural innovation

The major innovations of Amsterdam were in the creation of a Policy and Planning Unit for the CFSP, the creation of a secretary-general within the Council Secretariat to deal with CFSP, the transformation of the troika and the clarification of CFSP instruments.

The Policy Planning and Early Warning Unit (PPEWU) was designed to monitor and analyse developments in the CFSP and was to consist of personnel drawn from the general secretariat, the member states, the Commission and the Western European Union. The Secretary-General of the Council was given explicit responsibility for the CFSP and was given the title 'High Representative' for the common foreign and security policy. In more colloquial terms, the High Representative is sometimes known as Mr CFSP – the first appointee being Javier Solana, the former Spanish foreign minister. The troika – formerly composed of the current, preceding and successor Presidencies – was reconstituted. Its components became the Presidency, the High Representative, the Commission and, if appropriate, the successor Presidency.

The Amsterdam Treaty also systematised the instruments available to the CFSP. The objectives of the CSFP could be pursued through the definition of *principles* and *general guidelines*. The Union could adopt *common strategies, joint actions, common positions,* and *strengthen systematic cooperation between member states in the conduct of policy*. *Principles and guidelines* could include matters with defence implications. *Strategies* would be developed where member states had important interests in common. *Joint actions* would address specific operation matters. *Common positions* on the other hand defined the approach of the Union toward a particular geographical region or a thematic issue. The treaty also clarified the position of the Union's special envoys – insisting that the European Council may appoint special representatives on specific issues as it deems appropriate.

Decision-making

The Amsterdam Treaty did not signify a change from the underlying principle in Union foreign policymaking of attempting to achieve consensus and unanimity. Some procedural changes were made in that the use of qualified majority voting (QMV) was slightly extended in highly restricted circumstances and the right of states to engage in constructive abstention was introduced. This latter innovation meant that states that had abstained from voting could accept that the decision would not commit the abstaining state to implementation – but would also 'refrain from any action likely to conflict with or impede Union action based on that decision'. On procedural issues the Council was given the power to act through a majority of its members.

The European Security and Defence Identity

Since the Amsterdam Treaty was signed, the French and the British have come closer together with their ideas for the promotion of a European Security and Defence Identity. Meeting at Saint Malo in December 1998, British Prime Minister Tony Blair and French President Jacques Chirac agreed that the European Union should develop a 'capacity for autonomous action, backed by credible military forces'. The Saint Malo declaration, however, did not presage new developments in the institutionalisation of a European Union foreign policy. The European Council was envisaged as the key decision-maker on defence and military issues. Decision-making would remain intergovernmental – and the commitment to operating within the context of the Atlantic alliance was made explicit.

CONCLUSION

By 1993 a common foreign and security policy had been developed for the new European Union and institutionalised within international legislation. Its philosophical underpinnings comprised a commitment to liberal democratic political values and, economically, regulated market capitalism. The EU succeeded in both carving out a distinct 'European identity' separate from its transatlantic ally, the United States, and in maintaining a US involvement in joint protection of 'the West'. The management of the CFSP continued to share with its predecessor a mix of intergovernmental and supranational features, with the balance weighted towards intergovernmentalism but with an increasing move towards carefully controlled supranational elements in decision-making.

The Amsterdam Treaty consolidated institutional trends towards a 'pillar' structure within the European Union in which different ways of making and implementing policy were institutionalised depending on the issue under consideration. The pillar structure separated out Common Foreign and Security Policy procedures from procedures governing the Community aspects of the European Union. In terms of the European Union's overall relationships with the rest of the world, however, only some of its many activities were covered by the CFSP. Much of the European Union's foreign policy towards the rest of the world either fell under the Community structures or, increasingly, was implemented through more than one pillar of the European construction. This was obviously true of issue-areas such as trade, development, interregional cooperation and enlargement but was also true of how the European Union dealt with the most classic of foreign policy concerns – the area of security.

Guide to Further Reading for Chapter 3

The most useful historical survey, in English, of the evolution of EPC is Simon Nuttall, *European Political Cooperation* (Oxford: Clarendon, 1992). See also Philippe de Schoutheete, *La Coopération Politique Européenne* (Brussels: Labor, 1980). Good for detail on the period up until 1987 is Panayiotis Ifestos, *European Political Cooperation: Towards a Framework of Supranational Diplomacy?* (Aldershot: Avebury, 1987). The standard text on the early years of EPC is David

Allen, Reinhardt Rummel and Wolfgang Wessels (eds), *European Political Cooperation* (London: Butterworth, 1982). For member-state input see Christopher Hill (ed.), *National Foreign Policies and European Political Cooperation* (RIIA/Allen & Unwin, 1983). Alfred Pijpers, Elfriede Regelsberger and Wolfgang Wessels in collaboration with Geoffrey Edwards (eds), *European Political Cooperation in the 1980s: A Common Foreign Policy for Western Europe?* (Dordrecht: Martinus Nijhoff/TEPSA, 1988) contains, *inter alia*, a chronology of EPC from 1969 to 1987. Andrew Moravcsik's essay on 'Negotiating the Single European Act' in Robert O. Keohane and Stanley Hoffmann, *The New European Community: Decisionmaking and Institutional Change* (Boulder: Westview, 1991) is informative. A discussion of the foreign policy issues requiring resolution at the Maastricht conference is in Reinhardt Rummel (ed.), *Toward Political Union: Planning a Common Foreign and Security Policy in the European Community* (Nomos: Baden-Baden, 1992). This book also contains an appendix that gives extracts of some of the proposals circulating prior to Maastricht. Two studies which take into account the Maastricht reforms are Ole Norgaard, Thomas Pedersen and Nikolaj Peterson (eds), *The European Community in World Politics* (London: Pinter, 1993) and Martin Holland, *European Community Integration* (New York: St Martin's Press, 1993). The text of the SEA and the TEU can be found in Office for Official Publications of the European Communities (OOPEC), *Treaties Establishing the European Communities*, abridged edition (Luxembourg: OOPEC, 1987) and Council of the European Communities/Commission of the European Communities, *Treaty on European Union* (Luxembourg: OOPEC, 1992), respectively. For a discussion of the Amsterdam Treaty with useful factual appendices see Fraser Cameron, *The Foreign and Security Policy of the European Union* (Sheffield: Sheffield Academic Press, 1999).

4 How it Works in Practice

Since the 1970s the European Community/Union has developed an extensive array of foreign policies towards all parts of the world. Its policies have been addressed to allies as well as adversaries. Foreign policy has not been confined to the classical areas of security and defence but instead has covered a number of different issue-areas. A variety of different actors have implemented Union foreign policy through a variety of procedures and instruments. The legal and institutional bases of EU foreign policy have never been static. Instead they have constantly evolved as EU decision-makers have inventively and pragmatically developed the means necessary to implement changing policies to deal with changing circumstances. The making and implementation of European Union foreign policy has never followed the structural divide between Community and member-state competencies that some have tried to maintain (academics as well as policymakers). This chapter therefore looks at how European foreign policy works in practice. The chapter further develops the analytical framework introduced in Chapter 1 to provide an outline for the more empirical Chapters 5, 6, 7 and 8.

REPRISING THE GEO-ISSUE-AREA PERSPECTIVE

This book chooses a geographical perspective, combined with an issue-area analysis to review Union foreign policy. Geography refers to the regional focus of policy. An issue-area refers to a complex body of policies related to one core central theme. The key issue-areas identified are security and defence; trade; development cooperation; interregional cooperation and enlargement. The EU has clearly not been involved in each geographical area of the world in each issue-area to the same extent. At one end of the spectrum, for instance, trade is a major issue for the EU in its relations with many states (though not all), while enlargement is only a foreign policy issue-area applicable to Union relations with the rest of Europe. Again, because the Union is a dynamic entity, issue-areas change in importance as the EU changes. A new issue-area that will undoubtedly have great importance in the future for foreign policy, for example, is that of monetary relations. In addition, some issue-areas have changed in significance at different periods of the Union's history. Security and defence, for instance, have become important for the Union since the end of the Cold War and may become more so if the new Bush administration's tendencies to unilateralism force the Europeans to reconsider whether the United States of the twenty-first century can still be considered as reliable and predictable an ally as has been previously assumed.

The issue-area framework shapes the discussion of *what* the Union has done to whom (the geographical focus) in Chapters 5, 6, 7 and 8. Basic information on the scope and scale of Union foreign policy activities abroad is presented within the issue-area framework. The focus on *what* the Union has done is also a response to the very widespread (mis)understanding of the Union as having engaged in only a very small amount of foreign policy activity during its existence.

In Chapter 1, the review of each issue-area contained a schematic outline of the specific actors, instruments, legal bases for action and decision-making procedures utilised within discrete issue-areas. In this chapter, a fuller description and analysis of the various actors involved in the foreign policy process of the EU is provided. Here we identify *who* or *what* makes foreign policy in practice. In this chapter we also examine *how* foreign policy is made – and further review the different instruments of foreign policy, the legal bases of policy and decision-making procedures.

Actors and Instruments

The European Union does not have its own legal personality, that is its own separate identity in international law. Yet the Union does act in international relations as a more or less cohesive foreign policy actor. It is able to do so because the Union's constituent bodies possess legal identities and because these constituent bodies are coordinated through the various mechanisms set up by the framework created by the Union's constituent treaties. These coordination mechanisms were elaborated in the 1999 Amsterdam Treaty which consolidated the structures established by the 1993 Treaty on European Union that had established a 'three pillar structure'. The three pillars of the Union are the 'Community' pillar, the Common Foreign and Security Policy (CFSP) pillar and the Police and Judicial Cooperation in Criminal Matters (formerly Justice and Home Affairs) pillar. All three are coordinated and managed by the Council. As the name suggests, the 'Community' pillar left in existence an (amended) body of law that built on the 1951 Paris Treaty and the 1957 Rome Treaties and which effectively channelled the European Community into a new role – as part of the new Union. The CFSP and the JHA policy areas provided new and additional pillars for the new Union.

The effect of these changes can be confusing for analysing the Union's role in the world. Since Maastricht it is the European Union (EU) that should be understood as developing and implementing foreign policy. Yet the Union can only perform this role through actions of the Community and the member states. Foreign policy instruments available to the EU emanate from these two sources. Consequently, policies designed to achieve the EU's foreign policy objectives are developed and implemented by a number of different actors using a variety of different instruments. To further complicate matters, actors can also be instruments. For instance the European Investment Bank (EIB) is a key actor in relations with partner countries. It can also be used as an instrument of policy by the European Council should it decide to enhance the Union's activities in specific regions or countries by the use of EIB funding.

ACTORS

The actors involved in Union foreign policymaking and implementation may have different powers and responsibilities depending on which aspect of foreign policy is being considered. Outlined below are the major actors in the foreign policy process and their respective spheres of influence.

The European Council and the Council of Ministers

All aspects of foreign policy are, since the Maastricht Treaty, coordinated by the same body. This is the European Council, which is composed of the Heads of State and Government. The European Council meets only twice a year (except for occasional special sessions) and so in respect of day-to-day decision-making it is the Council of the European Union (informally known as the Council of Ministers) – acting directly on behalf of their own governments – which formulates and makes day-to-day policy. The General Affairs Council discusses and negotiates EU foreign policy. The General Affairs Council's members are, of course, the foreign ministers of the 15 member states. Since Maastricht the Council had responsibility for both the Community and CFSP responsibilities (and the JHA pillar) and was therefore in a position to coordinate member-state and Union activity. The TEU stipulates that it is the Council's responsibility to 'ensure the unity, consistency and effectiveness of action by the Union'.

The Presidency of the Council

A president who holds office for six months – January to June and July to December – heads up both the European Council and the Council of Ministers. Each of the member states takes its turn at the six-month Presidency. Thus the actual president is often referred to as the 'president-in-office'. The Presidency is assisted by the troika which initially was composed of current, preceding and successor Presidencies, sometime augmented to include the two preceding Presidencies and the two successor Presidencies. Since the Amsterdam Treaty, the troika has been composed of the president of the Council, the Commission and the Council's 'High Representative' for foreign policy (a civil servant). The function of the Presidency, in terms of foreign policy, is to organise and prepare meetings and to act as the official spokesperson for the European Union. Another function, which is more or less successfully carried out, is to act to achieve consensus between the 15 member states on foreign policy positions. The Council shares the right to take foreign policy initiatives with the Commission.

The Civil Servants – COREPER and the Political Committee

The Council of Ministers is assisted in its foreign policy function by various civil servants – the most important of which are the Political Committee and COREPER (the French acronym for the Committee of Permanent Representatives). The Political Committee is composed of the 'European Directors' in the home foreign ministries and is the senior advisory group to the Council of Ministers for foreign policy. COREPER is also composed of national civil servants but these are permanently based in Brussels. Since Maastricht they have taken over from the Political Committee the job of preparing the Council of Minister meetings on foreign policy issues. The Council is assisted administratively by a foreign policy secretariat that, also since Maastricht, is located in the Council's general secretariat in Brussels. The Amsterdam Treaty created the post of 'High Representative' for the Common Foreign and Security Policy. Based in the Council secretariat, the High Representative would advise and represent the Council (see Chapter 3 for detail).

The Commission

The Commission's role in foreign policymaking and implementation changes according to which particular aspect of foreign policy is under discussion. Broadly speaking, the Commission's role is co-equal to the Council in the areas of trade, aid and multilateral diplomacy. The Commission's most important external competence is in terms of the foreign policy aspects of trade, including the highly political issue of economic sanctions. In this the Commission has, at least theoretically, the lead role. At the other end of the decision-making spectrum the Commission has only a minimal input in security and defence policy. The Maastricht Treaty gave the Commission a significant increase in power in the foreign policy process when, for the first time, it was granted the legal power of initiative on foreign policy. Hitherto foreign policy initiatives had been a Council prerogative. This change to the Commission's competencies brought the Commission nearer to its role in the Community structure where on domestic issues it had held the right to initiate policy.

The Commission's administrative structure was overhauled by Romani Prodi, the President of the Commission in 1999, after a series of scandals had evinced significant member-state dissatisfaction with its operations – ending with the resignation of the entire 20-member Commission in 1999 and its replacement with a team dedicated to Commission reform. Up until 1999, the Commission had been organised into directorate generals (DGs) which had accumulated policy responsibilities in different areas. The most important of these in respect of foreign policy were DGI, the external relations directorate, and DGVIII, the directorate responsible for development cooperation. The Prodi proposals for reform of the Commission abolished the numbering system for the directorate generals and attempted to rationalise Commission functions and Commissioner responsibilities.

The Commissioner for external relations, Chris Patten, is now responsible for all aspects of external relations with some suggestion of a coordinating responsibility for other commissioners dealing with external relations. Although this has yet to be fully worked out in practice, this may mean that Chris Patten will attempt to coordinate what used to be termed DGVIII functions – with external relations functions. DGVIII was the directorate responsible for development issues including the important task of managing the large institutionalised network of cooperation with the African, Caribbean and Pacific (ACP) countries. The Commissioner responsible for Development and Humanitarian Aid, Poul Nielson, is responsible for both development cooperation in general and also the European Community Humanitarian Office (ECHO).

This is not to say that other parts of the Commission do not have some say in defining external policies. The Union's common agricultural policy (CAP), for instance, which used to be handled by DGVI, and is now covered by the Commissioner for Agriculture and Fisheries, has enormous political ramifications outside the EU's borders – both in terms of relations with economically developed countries like the United States and Australia and in terms of relations with poor countries reliant on agricultural exports to fund economic development.

Another important arm of EU foreign policy that is part of the Commission structure is the European Community Humanitarian Office (ECHO) which was established in 1993 to enable the Union to better coordinate its humanitarian aid. ECHO is responsible for short-term actions as well as for the development of a long-term strategy which includes 'prevention, preparedness, and if necessary relief and rehabilitation and their links with long term development'. ECHO is not an implementing organisation and its programmes are implemented by either the United Nations humanitarian organisations, the Red Cross and Red Crescent movement or the NGOs. ECHO has been innovative in that it has institutionalised the role of non-governmental organisations (NGOs) in the implementation of EU humanitarian actions. By 2000, over 150 member-state NGOs had signed its Framework Partnership Agreement (FPA). Thus ECHO has formalised the role of non-governmental organisations as actors within the EU's foreign policy process.

The Commission also has, as part of its structure, its own missions abroad – called delegations – which perform a variety of functions, depending on the size of the mission and the importance of the state or international organisation to the Union. By 2000 the Commission maintained 106 overseas delegations – covering 156 partner countries. Their functions range from information gathering, to ensuring that trade, cooperation and association agreements are being efficiently and properly carried out, to liaison with host governments on subjects which may have both political and economic ramifications. The role of the delegations in respect of the CFSP is to cooperate with the diplomatic representatives of member states overseas and, in international organisations, to help ensure that the CFSP is 'complied with and implemented'. The Commission's importance as a diplomatic actor can be demonstrated by the number of third states that maintain an independent (of the member states) diplomatic representation with the Community – some 166 as at 1999.

The Parliament

The 626-member (since 1995) European Parliament (EP), like the Commission, has different powers in respect of foreign policymaking depending on the issue under discussion. It is involved in Union foreign policy decision-making insofar as Parliament's assent must be sought before the Union may conclude any important international agreement. These include association, accession and cooperation agreements. Recent examples of agreements in which Parliament's approval had to be sought include the 'Europe' agreements with Central and East European states.

The Council and the Commission must consult Parliament on foreign policy and the president-in-office is required to deliver a report to the full Parliament session on Union foreign policy. Parliament also scrutinises Union foreign policy to the extent that its members may ask questions to the president-in-office at the monthly plenary sessions held in Strasbourg. The Strasbourg session sometimes serves to provide a high-profile forum for visiting heads of state (not heads of government) to expound their views on relations with the Union and Europe as a whole. US President Ronald Reagan, the UK's Queen Elizabeth II, Pope John Paul II and Czech President Vaclev Havel are among those who have taken advantage of this facility.

The Foreign Affairs, Security and Defence Committee of the EP has 130 members which makes it the largest of the Parliament's 17 standing committees. It draws up reports on diverse foreign policy issues and meets four times a year with the president-in-office of the Council of Ministers for an exchange of views. The Parliament has an international reach in that its members participate in joint parliamentary committees with parliamentary representatives from applicant countries, for instance Turkey and Malta. Parliamentarians also engage in permanent dialogue with their counterparts overseas via four parliamentary cooperation committees and 16 interparliamentary delegations (committees). The largest of these delegations, with 24 members each, are those to Russia and the United States.

The Parliament has provided official observers to elections abroad, participated in Union delegations to UN and CSCE conferences and participates in the annual North Atlantic Assembly of NATO.

The European Investment Bank (EIB)

The EIB was set up by the Rome Treaty and confirmed in its status by the Treaty on European Union as an institutionally autonomous yet integral part of the Union. The European Investment Bank is a non-profit-making lending institution whose initial purpose was to fund large-scale projects in the member states but which has developed an investment role in those states which are associated with the EC/EU through treaty-based relationships – for instance the African, Caribbean and Pacific countries associated through the Cotonou conventions. The EIB's Board of Governors is the overall policymaking body and is composed of one minister from each member state. The Board of Directors is the next tier down in the management structure and has 25 members who tend to be senior civil servants from national economics ministries or have experience in financial policy. Of the 25, 24 are nominations from the member states (three directors each from Germany, France, Italy and Britain; two from Spain and one each from the rest) and one from the European Commission. The body responsible for more day-to-day management is the Management Committee which is composed of the president of the EIB and the seven vice-presidents.

The Member States

The member states have been anxious to retain foreign policy as an intergovernmental part of the Union. The member states therefore have an important input into those areas of foreign policy which have retained formal intergovernmental characteristics as well as those which, legally, have become the prerogative of the institutions of the Union, for instance external trade policy. In the former case member-state input takes place via the Council of Ministers. In the latter case the Article 133 (ex 113) Committee (originally named after the relevant Treaty of Rome article) which is composed of national governmental representatives acts as a conduit for member-state input on external trade decisions. The member states are particularly important when it comes to implementation of the Common Foreign and Security Policy. As we shall see, the Union has some instruments at its direct disposal (for instance economic sanctions and aid) but it is the member states that can add teeth to EU foreign policy. For instance in case of war or violent conflict it is only the member states that can authorise their armed forces to participate in military action.

The Western European Union (WEU)

Although the European Union does not have a defence or military capacity it has, since the Maastricht and Amsterdam Treaties, developed an institutionalised link with a defence institution, the Western European Union. At Maastricht, the WEU was given the authority in Article J 4.2 'to elaborate and implement decisions and actions of the Union which have defence implications'. At Amsterdam, the Union agreed that the Common Foreign and Security Policy could provide for the progressive framing of a defence policy. The Amsterdam Treaty also decided that the WEU could be absorbed into the Union in the future, if the European Council were to agree on this course of action. Some efforts have already been made to coordinate EU and WEU liaison in that the WEU's headquarters were transferred from London to Brussels in the early 1990s but the operational relationship remains to be developed. This is partly due to the fact that membership of both organisations is not the same. EU members Ireland, Denmark, Sweden, Finland and Austria do not belong to the WEU although they have observer status.

At Maastricht it was agreed that Union security and defence policy should not be incompatible with NATO policies. In practice this has meant that, apart from providing the potential vehicle for an EU defence policy, the WEU has had as an important function a coordination role for the EU vis-à-vis NATO. It is this latter role which has shown visible results – helping to form the institutional base for a potential EU defence identity. Liaison with NATO is helped by the fact that NATO headquarters are also in Brussels. The WEU has taken over former NATO responsibilities including the Independent European Programme Group (IEPG) and the Eurogroup. The IEPG had responsibility for the coordination of the procurement of armaments; within the WEU it will be transmuted into a European armaments agency while the Eurogroup used to be the more general coordinating body, within NATO, for its European members.

The WEU welcomed its potential role as the 'defence component of the European Union' in a declaration relating to the Treaty of Amsterdam issued in 1997. It foresaw the development of the Western European Union as an essential element in the creation of a European Security and Defence Identity (ESDI) within the context of the Atlantic alliance. It also envisaged an increasing operational role for the WEU in the carrying out of the so-called Petersberg tasks. The Petersberg functions – that is humanitarian and rescue missions, peace-keeping and combat missions in crisis management situations – had been incorporated as EU functions in the Treaty of Amsterdam. These aspirations have not, however, been met – even though in 1999 the Union agreed a report that attempted to chart how the EU could use military capabilities to carry out the Petersberg tasks. Although WEU was mentioned in the 1999 Presidency report on strengthening the common European policy on security and defence, the chief military partner was not envisaged as the WEU, but the North Atlantic Treaty Organisation.

The North Atlantic Treaty Organisation (NATO)

NATO does not have any structural links to the Union yet in practice it is closely, both rhetorically and institutionally, linked to the evolution and implementation of EU foreign policies – particularly in the security sphere. Rhetorically, links to NATO are spelt out in both the Single European Act and the Treaty on European Union. Institutionally the EU is linked to NATO in an indirect although concrete manner through the WEU/NATO concept of the Combined Joint Task Force (CJTF). This was the plan, agreed by NATO in January 1994, to permit the WEU to utilise NATO back-up in areas which NATO has, since its inception, treated as 'out of area' operations. The CJTF operations may well form the basis for further evolution of the European defence identity given that they permit the flexibility for non-NATO and possibly non-WEU forces to participate. Such developments would also facilitate the evolution of a defence role for the EU, to which all the WEU member states belong and yet which also includes the four neutrals (Austria, Finland, Ireland and Sweden). This is because the EU could act as the institutional focus for all its 15 members in order to coordinate any participation in CJTF forces, particularly in any European theatre.

In 1999 the Union restated its intention to rely on NATO for operational support where it could feasibly do so but at the same time it recognised that some of the structural relations between the two organisations remained unresolved. A key problem is that membership of the two is not coterminous and that in some instances there is not necessarily a harmony of interests between them. One potential area of discord is Cyprus. The European Union contains Greece but not Turkey while NATO contains both states. It is unlikely, for example, that any 'peace-keeping' arrangement designed by the European Union without Turkish agreement would also be acceptable to NATO.

INSTRUMENTS

There is a huge variety of instruments available for EU foreign policymaking. These include political diplomacy; the economic instruments of economic sanctions, trade preferences and the provision of aid; the negotiation and conclusion of international agreements; and, indirectly, the utilisation of military force. The Union has explicit powers in respect of the first three; these have evolved from a combination of treaty-allocated competencies and pragmatic evolution. The EU does not have direct access to military instruments, where it either has to rely on the support of member states, other states like the United States or international organisations.

Diplomacy

The diplomatic instruments directly available to the EU stem from its competencies in respect of the Common Foreign and Security Policy. These instruments can be classified as passive and active. Passive diplomacy might include the issuing of a press statement or the sending of a *démarche* (statement of opinion) to a third country. In a sense the term 'passive' is a misnomer because even a statement of opinion, if made by 15 powerful and relatively cohesive states, particularly if combined with the threat (or promise) of the use of economic instruments, can provide a very powerful intervention in world affairs. This type of 'passive' diplomacy, however, can be contrasted with more active forms of intervention such as the participation by foreign ministers and Commissioners in political conferences, fact-finding missions, and negotiation with third parties and, occasionally, attempts at mediation in conflict and crises. The Presidency of the Council normally leads any diplomatic interventions although s/he is sometimes assisted by the troika. The Presidency as lead diplomat on behalf of the EU is most visible each year at the UN General Assembly in New York. Here the president-in-office provides a summary of EU foreign policy positions and concerns in an address to the Assembly. In diplomatic problems that require close coordination of both the economic and political, and the Community and the member states – such as the EU's activities in post-Cold War Central and Eastern Europe – the Council and the Commission Presidencies work together in what is sometimes known as the bicephalous Presidency.

Economic Instruments

The EU uses both negative and positive economic instruments in foreign policy implementation. Negative instruments are more commonly referred to as economic sanctions and include restraints on trade, aid and investment with the targeted country. Positive sanctions include the granting of trade preferences, particularly non-reciprocal trade preferences and the provision of aid – in the form of concessional loans or grants.

Since Maastricht, economic sanctions have been explicitly recognised as instruments of the Common Foreign and Security Policy (Article 301 – ex Article 228a) although the decision-making procedures follow the Community method in that the Council acts by a qualified majority after receiving a proposal from the Commission. The Union, however, only has direct powers in respect of the treaty-based trade, aid and (limited) investment competencies and instruments available to it. Thus the EU can impose effective trade sanctions as the member states have abrogated a great deal of sovereignty to the Union in this area. By contrast it can do little more than recommend to member states that they should impose restrictions on national aid budgets or investment flows from national banks.

The Union's external economic instruments are not always used to complement or implement foreign policy decisions. Nevertheless any economic instruments designed to have an effect externally – such as protective tariffs or quotas – may have an indirect impact on the Union's foreign policy activities. For instance EU policy on agriculture which, among other things, subsidises EU exports in order to keep export prices low, is designed to assist the Union's farmers – not to harm farmers overseas. The fact that it does so, by undercutting more efficient but unsubsidised production abroad, has, however, foreign policy ramifications in terms of relations between the EU and the governments of those states whose farmers are being affected by the EU's common agricultural policy. In this sense it is hard to find any external economic instrument that does not have some relationship – either directly or indirectly – to the Union's foreign policy activity and capability.

An important economic instrument available to the EU is the tariff. The cutting of tariffs – and indeed their abolition in some instances – is part and parcel of the armoury of foreign policy instrumentation. There are two ways in which tariff cutting can be implemented. The first is on a straightforward reciprocal basis and this approach is the norm in the EU's relations with economically developed countries. The second is on a non-reciprocal basis and is often seen as more appropriate for relations with the less economically developed countries (LDCs). In addition the EU has developed a Generalised System of Preferences (GSP) that allows preferential access to EU markets for certain products from LDCs – particularly though not only industrial goods.

There are a bewildering number of different instruments that the EU can use to implement aid policies. These include provisions for emergency aid, food aid, humanitarian assistance, development finance, financial aid and technical assistance. The EU has also developed various measures to provide support for those poorest states which rely on export earnings from a small number of commodities including the STABEX (stability in export earnings) and SYSMIN (support for mining sectors) schemes. Not all instruments are available to all developing countries. Those states associated through Cotonou, for instance, have a privileged access to the European Development Fund (EDF). This is a separate fund from the Union's aid budget, financed by contributions from the member states, that is set aside for the ACP states. (In 1996–2000 EDF funding amounted to around 13 billion Euros.) In contrast, humanitarian aid can be offered to any state in need of it: in 1998 just under 1 billion Euros of such assistance went to over 60 countries in Africa, the Caribbean, Europe, Asia and Latin America.

International Agreements

Much of EU foreign policy is institutionalised in the form of agreements between the various parties. This means that economic and political instruments are often (though not always) codified in the form of an international agreement. International agreements are important for three reasons. The first is the substantive material with which they are concerned (for instance tariff concessions, aid and political dialogue). The second is that in the process of negotiation the EU can attempt to resolve side-issues or to encourage the putative partner-state or organisation to share the EU's own foreign policy objectives. In the negotiations with South, East and Central

Europe for instance, these objectives included support for human rights, respect for minorities and moves towards market-based democracy. Thirdly, a concluded international agreement is a visible sign of EU recognition and, in the context of post-Cold War international relations, a sign of international legitimacy.

The EU has concluded hundreds of international agreements with third countries and international organisations. Thus the EU enters into both bilateral and multilateral agreements. International agreements range from those with the narrowest of concerns to those that relate to the most general of issue-areas. An example of a narrow type of agreement might be the setting of an individual tariff on a particular commodity with one specific state. The broadest type of agreements could cover the whole gamut of foreign policy areas including trade, aid, culture and political dialogue in relationship to large numbers of states organised in multilateral and regional organisations. Agreements with such associations involve the institutionalisation of relations between groups of countries that are geographically contiguous or functionally and/or historically linked to the Union. The cooperation agreement with the states of the Central American Common Market (CACM) is an example of the former. The Lomé (now Cotonou) Treaty signed with 71 African, Caribbean and Pacific (ACP) states is an example of the latter.

The essential foundations of the Union's competence to conclude international agreements are the trade and aid provisions of the various treaties – particularly the former. Out of these provisions have grown a whole number of diverse agreements – each type designed to fit the individual requirements of any particular situation. In this way the treaty provisions have allowed a necessary flexibility to meet vastly differing circumstances pre- and post-Cold War. These international agreements include straightforward trade treaties (some preferential and some not) and aid, cooperation and association agreements. The 'Europe' agreements signed with Central and East European states are forms of association. Cooperation and association agreements are likely to include some form of accompanying political dialogue. Some international agreements are signed only by the Community and some by the Community and by the member states – the latter being the so-called 'mixed agreements'.

Although not designed for this purpose, in practice, an important type of agreement for the Union's foreign policy purposes has proved to be that of accession. Any state wishing to join the EC/EU must, among other things, agree to observe what have become commonly known as the Union's *acquis politique*, that is the political under-standings that have been reached between the member states on important issues. The candidate state must also, since Maastricht, possess a domestic political system 'founded on the principles of democracy' and respect human rights 'as guaranteed by the European Convention for the Protection of Human Rights and Fundamental Freedoms'. These TEU provisions give powerful weight to the Union's foreign policy towards applicant states. In the case of Turkey and the Central and East European states, for instance, the EU has insisted that accession would be conditional on, among other things, these applicant states adopting and maintaining political systems where minority rights are protected. In this sense, accession agreements provide powerful instruments to help implement foreign policy.

The final set of international agreements to which the EU is party and which assist the pursuit of its foreign policy objectives are those that include the EU as a dominant partner within a wider grouping. These include the ERASMUS (European Action Scheme for the Mobility of University Students), EUREKA (European Research Coordination Agency) and PHARE (Poland and Hungary: Aid for the Restructuring of Economies) programmes – the last of which has been extended to cover a wider area of Eastern and Central Europe. The membership of these programmes includes EU and non-EU states although the EU plays a preponderant part in the development and management of policy.

Military Force

The EC had, prior to the Maastricht Treaty, been conceived of as a 'civilian power' – an international actor that would implement its foreign policies by non-military means. Post-1993, the new Union was not allocated military or policing functions. Neither the Maastricht nor the Amsterdam Treaties went so far as to institutionalise and operationalise the Union's increasing attempts to coordinate member states' activity in respect of military functions although the Maastricht Treaty had given the WEU the responsibility of carrying out the 'necessary practical arrangements' in respect of defence-related issues in Article 14 (ex Article J.4.2). By contrast, the coordination of judicial cooperation and policing in the fight against international crime was institutionalised in Title VI of the Treaty on European Union in the section on Justice and Home Affairs. The Amsterdam Treaty and subsequent European Councils recognised deficiencies in this area and in 1999 there were recommendations that defence ministers should meet under the umbrella of the General Affairs Council and that a permanent Military and Security Committee with an associated Union military committee should be established. In practice, however, the Union has not proved a useful umbrella body for the coordination of member-state military forces. The Union has manifestly failed to provide an institutional instrument capable of managing military instruments – being eclipsed by the United Nations and NATO as providers, respectively, of peace-keeping and peace-making forces.

LEGAL BASES

The legal bases for developing and implementing foreign policy in the different issue-areas has evolved with the evolution of the Union as a whole through the treaties and secondary legislation. The European Union, as we have seen, is sometimes characterised as a structure that rests on three 'pillars'. The first is the quasi-supranational structure based on the Treaties of Paris (1951) and Rome (1957). In 1993 the second and third were the intergovernmental structures of the CFSP and Justice and Home Affairs. All three pillars were coordinated within the 1993 Treaty on European Union (the Maastricht Treaty) and consolidated by the 1999 Treaty of Amsterdam. The Union develops and implements its foreign policies through the Community and CFSP frameworks. Foreign policy direction and coordination is meant to be provided by the CFSP machinery although the fragmentation of the EU structure still allows for policy to remain lacking in consistency and cohesion.

Implementation of foreign policy is by a variety of means; some of these means are coordinated via the procedures that apply to the CFSP – the second pillar. The CFSP is legally underpinned by Title V of the Treaty on European Union and its procedures are intergovernmental in nature. CFSP policies are under the control of the Council of Ministers. Some foreign policy instruments fall within the legal competencies of the Commission – the first pillar of the Union. Commission-led procedures follow the 'Community method' (discussed further below). In practice there are a great many 'grey areas' and discussions and decision-making on broad areas of foreign policy take place in the same fora – the difference arises in terms of which aspect of the policy is implemented through which legal framework. For instance, the diplomatic and security aspects of foreign policy in respect of the former Yugoslavia may be discussed by the Council and the same meeting may, during the same debate, discuss humanitarian aid to former Yugoslavia; implementation of different aspects of the overall policy will then take place through whichever is the appropriate legal and procedural channel.

One important legal difference between the intergovernmental Titles V (CFSP) and the rest of the Treaty is that the intergovernmental pillars are exempt from scrutiny by the European Court of Justice. There are thus no sanctions available – short of peer pressure – to enforce member-state compliance with CFSP policies and procedures. Conversely there are sanctions available to the Union in respect of states that do not comply with the 'Community' parts of the TEU. Both the Commission and the ECJ attempt to enforce the treaty as, for instance, when in 1994 the Commission brought a case against Greece before the European Court of Justice in respect of its blockade of the former Yugoslav republic of Macedonia. Although the Commission was eventually unsuccessful in its objectives, the action illustrates the competencies of the Community as part of the Union but outside the CFSP structures – in highly political foreign policy issues.

DECISION-MAKING

The Union has also paid a good deal of attention to how decisions are made – incorporating strictures on decision-making procedures into the treaties.

EU decision-making in general relies on negotiation and consensus to a much greater extent than decision-making within a national state where a majority party may seek to impose its policies on an oppositional minority party rather than to achieve consensus. The difference between EU and member-state decision-making is much less significant in the case of foreign policy, however. This is because foreign policy is much more likely to be a consensual activity between the major political parties in the member states with most governments willing to go to some lengths to involve opposition parties in major foreign policy initiatives. The EU therefore, much like a nation-state, seeks to minimise internal conflicts in order to present a united front to the outside world.

The Union's foreign policy decision-making procedures differ depending upon the policy-area under consideration. They can be characterised as either intergovernmental or supranational. In the former case it is member states that dominate decision-making and in the latter case it is EU institutions (Council, Commission and

Parliament) that have certain powers over and above the member states.

Intergovernmental Features

Two parts of the foreign policy process are explicitly intergovernmental in their decision-making procedures. The most visible is the CFSP. The less commented on though, particularly in the case of developing countries, the hardly less important intergovernmental part of the Union's foreign policy capacity, is the European Investment Bank.

The CFSP is almost entirely intergovernmental in two important ways. The first is that the member states via their representatives in the Council of Ministers dominate the decision-making process. The second is that for all-important decisions, the member states must be unanimous. Having said this, the Treaty on European Union recognises – explicitly and implicitly – some qualification of the unanimity rule. A significant qualification, for instance, is found in the procedure in respect of the sphere of 'joint actions'. Whenever the Council decides by unanimity that a particular policy may be the subject of a joint action, that action may be implemented by way of a qualified majority within the Council. It is this procedure that was widely seen as introducing an element of supranational decision-making to the CFSP. Yet this is not quite such a move towards supranationality as it might first appear given that the Council may review the mandate for the joint action at any time.

Some qualification of the unanimity principle can be found in the provisions of Title V that relate to member states' responsibility not to impede common policies or actions. A state may abstain (under provisions of the Amsterdam Treaty) and is not obliged to implement the decision on which it has abstained – although it 'shall accept that the decision commits the Union'. The tenor of CFSP decision-making, however, is to promote unanimity and consensus, particularly on strategic decisions. If abstentions, for instance, amount to more than one-third of the weighted votes, the policy cannot be approved. States also agree that should they have difficulties implementing a joint action they should not adopt individual solutions that 'run counter to the objectives of the joint action or impair its effectiveness'. These open commitments to refrain from acting in a manner contrary to Union policy are reinforced by the commitment that member states 'shall' coordinate national positions with EU foreign policy positions and that EU member states 'shall' uphold common positions in international organisations 'even where not all the Member States participate'.

Like the CFSP, the EIB's decision-making processes are dominated by the member states – with the Commission allocated a very minor consultative role and the Parliament no input at all. Voting follows more or less the same rules applicable to Council meetings and, depending on the issue being voted on, decisions are taken by either unanimity, qualified or majority vote. The major difference between the EIB's voting arrangements and that of the Councils is that a majority in the EIB must represent at least 45 per cent of the subscribed capital (which is derived from the member states proportionately to their wealth).

Supranational Features

Decision-making in respect of Union trade, aid and development policies and, importantly, international agreements, is made under the legal provisions of the Treaties of Rome and Paris as amended by the 1993 Treaty of Maastricht and the 1999 Treaty of Amsterdam. Decisions taken in these areas are defined by procedures first developed within the earlier treaties that involve the Commission, the Parliament and the Council in co-decision-making (as opposed to the Council having the final say). Decisions made through these procedures are sometimes referred to as involving the 'Community method'. By this is meant the negotiation and trade-off of interests and objectives, regulated by the treaties, between the various Community institutions until consensus can be achieved. Decisions taken within the context of the treaties can be understood as supranational in that they are made within a framework of law which overrides member-state law. Within that context, however, some aspects of treaty-based decision-making on foreign policy-related issues are more supranational than others – in that the member states possess a varying degree of influence over decision outcomes – depending on the treaty clauses from whence each particular policy competency stems. Changes to decision-making procedures in the 1993 TEU, for instance, both increased and decreased elements of supranationality in decision-making. The Parliament achieved increased powers. At the same time, however, the Council's pre-eminent position in the Community decision-making process was further institutionalised.

PRAGMATISM AND FLEXIBILITY – THE HALLMARK OF
EUROPEAN UNION FOREIGN POLICY

The making and implementing of Union foreign policy is dynamic
and organic – responding to changing circumstances with policies
that are flexibly implemented through pragmatic means. Political
obstacles may have sometimes stymied the development of a
coherent and effective foreign policy – but where the Union and the
member states have had agreed values and interests to defend, legal,
procedural and decision-making constraints have been of secondary
importance. This pragmatic perspective is amply illustrated in a
review of what the Union has actually done in foreign policy terms
– in relation to the North, South and the New Europe.

Guide to Further Reading for Chapter 4

An extremely useful book on institutional, legal and decision-
making aspects of the EU post-Maastricht is Clive H. Church and
David Phinnemore, *European Union and European Community: A
Handbook and Commentary on the Post-Maastricht Treaties* (London:
Harvester Wheatsheaf, 1994). More up-to-date discussion can be
found in Helen Wallace and William Wallace (eds), *Policy-Making in
the European Union*, fourth edition (Oxford: Oxford University Press,
2000). This book as well as the indispensable Neill Nugent, *The
Government and Politics of the European Union*, fourth edition
(London: Macmillan, 1999) provides the core texts in this area.
Useful general texts include Juliet Lodge (ed.), *The European
Community and the Challenge of the Future*, second edition (London:
Pinter, 1993); Ole Norgaard, Thomas Pedersen and Nikolaj Petersen
(eds), *The European Community in World Politics* (London: Pinter,
1993) and the more recent Fraser Cameron, *The Foreign and Security
Policy of the European Union* (Sheffield: Sheffield Academic Press,
1999). Work on the Parliament that contains some references to
Parliament's international role is Richard Corbett, Francis Jacobs and
Michael Shackleton, *The European Parliament*, third edition (London:
Cartermill, 1995). During the 1990s, the annual *Strategic Survey*
(London: International Institute of Strategic Studies) discussed
European security architecture including relations between NATO,
the WEU and the EU's security role. Another useful source is the
Adelphi papers series (London: International Institute of Strategic

Studies). The most useful source on interregional cooperation remains Geoffrey Edwards and Elfriede Regelsberger (eds), *Europe's Global Links: The European Community and Inter-Regional Cooperation* (London: Pinter, 1990). For detail on development policy the best source, apart from the general textbooks referred to above, are the publications of the European Community (Luxembourg: Office for Official Publications of the European Communities) and the *Bulletin* of the European Union (published monthly). Evaluations and discussions of topical development issues, as well as other external aspects of Union policy, can be found on the Commission's internet sites at http://www.europa.eu.int/comm/dgs_en.htm.

5 The European Union and the North

The European Union operates as a global actor and has extensive security and economic links with other industrialised, economically developed states. This chapter evaluates the Union's relations with the non-European OECD states (excepting the two recent members – Mexico and the Republic of Korea which are discussed in Chapter 7), that is the United States, Japan, Canada, Australia and New Zealand. Relations with the remaining states of the North, the extra-EU European states, are discussed in Chapter 8. Following the structure set out in Chapters 1 and 4, the policy towards each major actor is discussed in terms of relevant issue-areas. These are security and defence, trade, development cooperation and interregional cooperation. Given that this chapter discusses relations with extra-European actors, enlargement as an issue-area is not applicable. Within each issue-area, an evaluation is given of the relevant actors, instruments, legal bases and decision-making procedures.

EUROPEAN UNION RELATIONS WITH THE UNITED STATES

The United States has been, and continues to be, by far the most important of the Union's partners in the industrialised world. In 2000 the United States and the Union remained each other's most important trading partner. The two economic entities together account for 37 per cent of global trade in goods and 45 per cent in services. In political terms, the Maastricht and Amsterdam Treaties confirmed the priority given to the US-led NATO alliance as providing the linchpin for European security. The adoption of the 'New Transatlantic Agenda' with its accompanying programme of action by the EU and the United States in December 1995 confirmed the closeness of the relationship. Yet Union relations with the United States had not always been harmonious. Their development was marked by conflict just as much as cooperation.

Relations with the United States constitute the strategic matrix out of which the Community developed. In the 1950s, the United States imagined the creation of a West European association of states that would join the global battle against communism. The origins of the Community were as a prospective trade and political partner for the United States (see Chapter 2). Both EC leaders and US governments shared a vision of a free-market, non-Communist world in which the major threat was communism, particularly in the shape of the Soviet Union. The Union of the early twenty-first century is as structured and constrained by geopolitical factors as was the Community of the 1950s. The Union's commitments to and conflicts with the United States, its chief ally within the Atlantic alliance, continue to shape the strategic and economic policies internationally.

Security and Defence

EU member-state relations with the United States in respect of security and defence are conducted through and within a number of fora as well as bilaterally. These fora include the European Union and other Western multilateral institutions such as NATO. NATO remains the paramount security institution in Europe. Of the 15 European Union states (excepting Ireland, Austria, Finland and Sweden) eleven are full NATO members and consequently work closely with the United States on security issues within this institution. All EU member states, however, including the neutrals, are concerned about the transformed security context of post-Cold War Europe with dangers arising from, among other things, violent nationalist conflict, unstable borders and lack of supervisory control over Eastern European nuclear armaments. The Union can assume a potentially pivotal strategic role as coordinator of a European security policy which can bring to bear the interests of NATO and non-NATO EU members. Such policy can then be implemented by a number of actors – the Union itself, the member states and the various European security institutions such as NATO, WEU and the OSCE.

Security and defence issues, although only recently officially part of the remit of the Union, have always been a key area for both transatlantic cooperation and conflict. As the Community evolved into the Union, two distinct periods can be identified in the security relationship with the United States. The first was the conflictual years of the 1970s and 1980s. The second is the era of cooperative relations forged and consolidated subsequent to the fall of the Berlin Wall in November 1989.

1969–89: contradiction and conflict

Although de Gaulle has generally been given the credit (or the blame) for creating and aggravating conflict in EC/US relations, it was post-de Gaulle EC/US relations of the 1970s that were most fraught. Confrontations with the United States in monetary, trade and political issues occurred in the early 1970s and these had long-lasting effects on the transatlantic relationship – helping to create an atmosphere of mistrust and mutual recrimination. The 1970s was the early period of EU assertion of its own identity in international affairs and was characterised by United States suspicion and sometimes anger at an emerging economic rival which, at the same time, seemed to want to exert the privilege of political partnership in its expectation that the United States would continue to provide a security guarantee for Western Europe.

During the 'Second Cold War' of the late 1970s and the 1980s strategic goals remained shared but differences arose in terms of how to deal with global and regional international conflicts. The West Europeans were more ready to trade with East Europe and the Soviet Union and less keen on using economic sanctions to try to coerce Communist countries into altering their domestic regimes. The reluctance of EC leaders to support the United States in regional conflicts, for instance in Vietnam in the 1960s, developed into a more open disagreement with US policies in the Middle East in the 1970s and outright opposition to the Reagan administration's activities in the tense Central American conflicts of the 1980s. Nevertheless the then Community faced enormous contradictions and tensions at the heart of its foreign policy. West European leaders considered that it was vital for the continuing security of West Europe that the United States remain engaged in Europe through active participation in NATO and the stationing of troops and armaments in Western Europe. At the same time they argued that they wished the then EC to coordinate a more independent 'European' foreign policy in the international conflicts of the Cold War. For the United States it appeared that the EC was trying to face both ways at the same time.

In 1969 the 'Europe' of the six member states had agreed enlargement (a previous goal of US foreign policy) and negotiations began on accession with Britain, Denmark, Ireland and Norway. During the negotiations, in August 1971, President Nixon unilaterally abandoned the Bretton Woods monetary system which had guaranteed fixed exchange rates between the major West European currencies and the US dollar. It was the unilateral nature of Nixon's action rather than the action itself which spurred the Europeans on to further integration – forcing them to consider both how they could coordinate a West European monetary system without the US and also accelerating serious thinking about political and economic integration that had begun at the 1969 Hague Summit which had agreed enlargement and where the European construction had been relaunched. Even the British, with their pro-Atlanticist governments, were forced to consider that the United States might not remain a permanently trustworthy ally and that their interests might best be served by having close relations with the EC as well as with the United States. Kissinger's clumsy attempts to launch a new partnership with the West Europeans through his 'Year of Europe' scheme in 1973 brought further antagonism as the President's National Security Adviser made it clear that he foresaw the United States as a global player and the West Europeans in a supportive but junior *regional* role.

Matters were made worse in October 1973 when the Yom Kippur war between Israel and the Arab states broke out and Arab states declared an oil boycott on those EC states which were perceived to be pro-Israel, with the Netherlands (along with the United States) singled out for a total oil embargo while Britain and France, at the other end of the scale, were excluded from Arab actions. Other Community states were supposed to have been the target of gradual cuts in supply. The EC responded politically in November by issuing a statement on the Middle East that supported both the legitimate rights of Israel and the Palestinians and called for the resolution of the conflict to take place at the United Nations – not at any specially organised conference. This position was different from that of the United States which saw itself as the key player in the region, which did not offer diplomatic support to the Palestinians and which had wanted to organise a Geneva-based conference with itself, the Soviet Union and the regional players to try to resolve the conflict. Although Britain and France had largely been displaced from their historic Great Power role in the Middle East after their unsuccessful invasion of Egypt in 1956 (the Suez crisis), these two states still resented the United States' attempts to exclude them from diplomatic influence in the region.

Throughout 1973 foreign ministers of the now enlarged Community attempted to bring together some form of response to United States' calls for a renewed partnership at the same time as they sought to assert their status as an equal, not a junior partner, to the United States. The result was the Document on the European Identity (see Chapter 3) which at the same time as declaring its commitment to US leadership within NATO, attempted to chart an independent political and *global* role for the Community. Disagreements continued, however, as the United States called for the EC/9 to join with it in a new organisation designed to coordinate the activities of oil and energy consumers. Although the International Energy Agency was set up in 1974 with some Community participation, France refused to join, further underlining the rifts in EC–US relations. In March 1974 the conflict was made even more visible when President Nixon made a public statement attacking the Community and its member states for their perceived opposition to United States' policies. These open disagreements were only resolved after a German initiative which proposed that the United States government should be consulted by the EC foreign ministers before arriving at any final decisions on foreign policy. This was the famous 'Gymnich agreement' of 1974 which was never institutionalised but which nevertheless permitted some measure of coordination between the two partners.

During the 1970s, the best example of Community and United States harmony in respect of the pursuit of common objectives in foreign policy was the Conference on Security and Cooperation in Europe (CSCE). This conference was initially designed to settle pan-European border issues unresolved since the end of the Second World War and to try to formalise security relations between East and West Europe in the context of the then period of détente. It was initiated in Helsinki in 1973 and continues as a forum for East–West cooperation (since 1994 institutionalised as the Organisation for Security and Cooperation in Europe). In the establishment of the CSCE and in its consolidation in the 1975 Helsinki conference and the 1980 Belgrade follow-up conference, EC foreign ministers acting in EPC and Commission officials acting under the legal framework provided by the EC treaties worked, on the whole successfully, to achieve security, political (including human rights) and economic objectives that were common to both the EC and its major partner in the Atlantic alliance, the United States. One of the reasons for the lack of friction between the two allies, however, was that the United States considered the CSCE relatively unimportant and was content to allow the EC to pursue its diplomatic objectives on what were seen by the United States as 'European' issues.

The Community's interventions in the Middle East, however, continued to provide a source of irritation for the United States. The European Community's Euro–Arab dialogue which began in 1973, under the aegis of the Community's treaty-based competencies, provided a forum exclusive of the United States and Israel. The EC attempted to focus discussions on economic issues but, as the Arab involvement with the EC was predicated on obtaining some form of hearing for the Palestinian cause as much as on improving trade links, and as most of the EC member states were anyway more inclined than the United States to consider both Arab and Israeli claims, the process of involvement, as it appeared to the United States, seemed to take the West Europeans further away from the United States and more towards an independent foreign policy. In the late 1970s the EC (organised in EPC) called for the Palestinians to be given a homeland and in 1980 issued the now famous Venice declaration. The June 1980 statement recognised both Israel's right to a secure existence and, for the first time, a Palestinian right to self-determination. Although in practice the Venice declaration did little more than herald a series of unsuccessful visits to the region by the Luxembourg foreign minister and president of the Council of Ministers, Gaston Thorn, it caused open conflict with the Carter administration which opposed and attempted to prevent this European initiative in the Middle East.

Despite the Carter administration's generally supportive attitude to the Community, there were two other important international crises in which the EC and the United States came into conflict at the tail end of his administration. The first occurred in November 1979 when Iranian revolutionary guards took US embassy personnel hostage in Teheran. The second was the invasion of Afghanistan by the Soviet Union in December 1979. In the first the EC member states offered diplomatic support to the United States but only reluctantly and with some months' delay imposed economic sanctions on Iran. Delay also occurred in the EC response to the immediate imposition of US economic sanctions on the USSR after the Afghanistan invasion. The EC foreign ministers failed to meet in the wake of the Christmas 1979 invasion and it was left to the Commission to pass regulations which prevented EC member states from supplying grain to the Soviet Union in place of suspended US grain exports. The EC also did not follow the lead of the United States in its call for an international boycott of the 1980 Moscow Olympics.

The Reagan years (1980–88) saw increased tensions in the wider Western Europe–United States security relationship; tensions which were also played out in the Community's relationship with its transatlantic partner. The West European states were concerned about what was widely perceived as a somewhat cavalier attitude by Reagan in respect of European security, displayed in an inept handling of management issues in the alliance relationship and a tendency towards unilateral decision-making on issues which directly affected European security. The Carter administration had taken an unpopular decision to produce an enhanced radiation bomb, the so-called 'neutron bomb' (which, crudely speaking, killed people not property), for use in the defence of Western Europe, and the Reagan administration confirmed it would continue to produce such a bomb soon after the presidential inauguration of 1981. Reagan's admission that it would not be inconceivable that a nuclear war could be fought out over European territory alarmed both European publics and West European elites who worried about the possibilities of the United States uncoupling itself from the defence of Europe. The installation of intermediate range nuclear weapons (including the cruise missiles later used in the 1990/91 Gulf War), designed only to be used in Europe, ratcheted up public concern – with millions of Europeans taking part in demonstrations against their deployment in the early 1980s. West European leaders were conscious that the public relations battle had been lost to the extent that large sections of Western publics did not know or did not accept the argument that the Soviet Union was equally responsible for the seemingly increased threats to European security because of its modernisation and development of nuclear weapons (the SS-20 missiles) which were only likely to be used on the European continent.

Reagan's decision to promote research and development on the Strategic Defence Initiative (SDI) was also not widely popular. The fear of West European elites was of strategic uncoupling; of publics was the apparent threat of 'star wars' between the then two superpowers, the United States and the Soviet Union, with a less well-defended Europe left to almost literally pick up the pieces in case of war. Overriding and bringing together all these concerns was that West European governments feared a public anti-Americanism which would force those governments to either withdraw from NATO or to take a much more distinctive 'European' line within it. These were important worries both for the social democrats of newly democratising Spain whose foreign policy hinged on a commitment to joining both NATO and the European Community and, equally, for the more conservative governments of Britain and West Germany who feared that a tide of anti-Reaganism might help to bring more leftwing governments to office in their countries. Fears of United States' unilateralism appeared to be corroborated even towards the end of the Reagan administration when, at the 1987 Reykjavik summit, President Reagan came very near to promising President Gorbachev complete elimination of all United States' missiles stationed in Europe – without any consultation with European leaders!

The tensions evident within the broader context of United States/European alliance were played out in the Community's relations with the United States; most specifically in the Community's reaction to the various regional crises in which the United States attempted to play a leadership role in the 1980s. The Reagan administration preferred to conduct its relations with the Europeans on a bilateral basis (as did, on occasion, the West European states) but the Community was directly involved in the most serious disagreements on security issues which were displayed in respect of the Poland crisis of 1981 and the Central America conflict of the 1980s. Differences between the two partners were also manifested in the different approaches to Maurice Bishop's leftwing government in Grenada (1979–83) and to the Libyan regime of Colonel Muammar Ghaddafi.

Throughout 1981 the major West European powers disagreed with the new US administration on how to handle the Polish government's increasingly tough approach to its dissident and trade union movements, culminating in General Jaruzelski's declaration of martial law on 13 December 1981. The United States pushed for the imposition of sanctions on the Soviet Union because of its support and direction of Polish hardliners. The EC displayed somewhat contradictory policies towards Poland in early 1981 with the DG responsible for agriculture banning beef exports on health grounds and the European Parliament in November deciding that 10 million ECU of beef should be donated to Poland. Nevertheless the overall thrust of EC programmes could be clearly differentiated from those of the US. The US supported sanctions; the EC opposed them. The EC offered inducements including economic aid to Poland. The United States opposed the provision of inducements. Subsequent to the declaration of martial law the EC maintained its cautious approach to sanctions, implementing only limited restraints on EC/USSR trade and continuing with its food aid to the Polish people.

Neither was there agreement on a common approach to the Central American crisis of the 1980s. The Nicaraguan revolution of

1979 which brought the leftwing Sandinista government to power was viewed by the United States in Cold War terms as a revolution directly sponsored by the Soviet Union in the US 'backyard' and as a result a direct threat to its national interests. The United States financed, trained and organised military forces based in Honduras which waged a war of attrition against the Nicaraguan government and at the same time attempted to delegitimise and isolate the Sandinistas internationally. By contrast the West Europeans, strongly led by the European Commission and the European Parliament, argued that the revolutions of Central America, including the leftwing guerrilla challenges to the state in El Salvador and Guatemala, were a result of poverty and structural inequality, not Soviet involvement. The Community opposed US intervention in Central America, actively campaigned to promote peace in the region and included Nicaragua in its regional aid packages. The Community's foreign policy encompassed financial support for the Sandinista literacy campaign in 1980/81, through to implementation of an institutionalised dialogue (the San José process) with the five Central American states (including revolutionary Nicaragua) in 1984 and continued active diplomacy in support of the Latin American states pursuing peace (the Contadora group) throughout the 1980s. The Reagan administration put enormous diplomatic effort into an unsuccessful campaign to persuade the Europeans to back its policies and resented European lack of support on what it considered was a major test of alliance solidarity.

In October 1983 when the United States government invaded tiny Grenada (population 100,000), a member of the Commonwealth, without informing Britain, or indeed any of its Western allies, each individual member state protested. The Community had, prior to the invasion, agreed substantial aid to Grenada as a way to encourage it to moderate its moves to the political left. On the other hand, although the West German foreign minister Hans-Dietrich Genscher did call an emergency EPC meeting, the member states did not make much use of the mechanisms of the Community subsequent to the invasion. This was mainly because the then Greek President-in-Office refused to allow discussion of Grenada because of a Greek grievance relating to Cyprus. The last major crisis involving Community relations with the Reagan administration occurred when the United States bombed Tripoli, as a response to alleged sponsorship of international terrorism, in April 1986. Only Britain offered support for the mission, providing refuelling facilities and allowing US airbases in Britain to be used. Nevertheless the British government also participated in a collective Community response to the United States which did not support comprehensive economic sanctions on Libya and advised the United States to show restraint in its handling of the crisis. George Shultz, the United States Secretary of State, later recalled that the Dutch President-in-Office, Hans van den Broek, whom he referred to as the 'head of the European Community', had telephoned to warn of the potential damage to transatlantic relations because of the US handling of the Libya issue.

The last years of the Reagan presidency were weakened by the Irangate crisis in which senior US officials were found guilty of breaking national and international law in the supply of arms to the Nicaraguan contras (those fighting against the Sandinista government) and of trying to exchange arms for the release of Western hostages held in the Middle East. Earth-shaking political events nearer to home were forcing Community foreign policy eastwards. When the Berlin Wall finally fell in November 1989, both the European Community and its transatlantic partner were faced with such a new and unforeseen political landscape that both partners were pushed into a much more collaborative relationship than that which had been evidenced in the 1970s and 1980s. There were two main worries. Would a united Germany stay with the West? And what would it mean for European and Western stability if the Soviet Union disintegrated into fractious smaller states, some with control over nuclear weapons and, just as threatening to Western states, control over access to oil. The potential problems relating to uncontrolled immigration, unstable borders, civil war, nuclear terrorism and drug smuggling formed the new agenda for Community/United States relations.

1989 onwards – cooperation and division of labour

The post-Cold War era introduced a period where the two partners, despite the occasional disagreement, worked in a more cooperative manner in security issues than ever before. This was partly because the Europeans recognised that they did not have the operational capacity to take the lead in security issues. It was also partly because the increasing resort to multilateral organisation – such as NATO or the United Nations – for peace-keeping, peace-making and peace-building tasks necessarily involved an acceptance of a significant role for the United States. It was also partly because there was no basic disagreement on strategic objectives – the most important being support for the transition to liberal capitalism for the former Soviet Union and the East and Central European states (see Chapter 8).

The Bush administration had been propelled into a reconsideration of its relationship with the Community, partly because of the momentous changes occurring in Eastern Europe but also because of fears of the economic implications of the '1992' or single market project for the United States. The United States assured itself that 'Fortress Europe' was not on the horizon for US business (see below) but at the same time the Bush administration began to develop an appreciation of the advantages open to it should it develop stronger relations with the Community as a collective entity, side by side with its bilateral relations with individual member states. President Bush and his Secretary of State acknowledged the pivotal role of the Community in the reshaping of Europe and redirected United States policy to incorporate the Community in a joint management of political and economic transformation in Europe (see Chapter 8).

The first important security challenge outside Europe in the post-Cold War period was the 1990/91 Gulf War and in this the Community displayed little collective will, leaving the war to be led by the United States within the framework of a United Nations action. The Gulf War was a watershed in Community/United States relations. Despite the apparent assertion of an independent foreign policy identity during the 1970s and 1980s (at least on some issues) the Gulf War seemed to reinforce United States' leadership of a security alliance, not of two cohesive partners, but of the United States and twelve disparate actors. This leadership was consolidated when Europeans, including the ex-colonial (and UN Security Council members) powers of France and Britain were sidelined in the consequent Arab–Israeli peace negotiations. On the other hand the Bush administration made concrete its objective of dealing with a collective Europe on security and other issues by agreeing a set of formalised institutional relationships between the Community and the United States in the November 1990 Transatlantic Declaration.

The Clinton administration overtly geared its domestic political agenda towards economic rejuvenation, selling himself as the domestic policy president – in contrast to George Bush's image as the 'foreign policy' candidate. Europeans feared possible renewed United States isolationism as Clinton looked to reinforce trading ties with Asia and the North American Free Trade Area (NAFTA). However, Clinton's economic agenda pushed the new administration into an activist stance worldwide in the promotion of free trade and open markets. Clinton recognised a need for political stability in order to secure the conditions to maximise international trade and, like Bush before him, recognised the importance of the European Community (the Union after 1993) as a partner in the promotion of economic and political objectives. Clinton supported the moves to further European integration, with a united Germany at the centre of the integration project, and initially encouraged a division of labour in security responsibilities. The European Community was to take the lead in Eastern Europe and, with the breakout of war in Yugoslavia, in the Balkans. It was only with the failure of EC/EU foreign policy to contain the war that Clinton exerted leadership, pushing NATO into military action against Bosnian Serbs and forcing a political settlement on the warring parties at Dayton, Ohio in November 1995 (see Chapter 8). It was also the United States which assumed leadership in the military offensive against Belgrade over Kosovo in 1999 (see Chapter 8).

Three related issues shaped Union relationships with the United States in this period of cooperation. The first was the Union's prioritisation of the management of change in Eastern Europe as its number one foreign policy objective. Here the United States accepted, approved and supported (more or less) EU initiatives. The second issue was how to transform Cold War institutions into effective and efficient instruments of peace and security in post-Cold War Europe. Here progress took place more as a result of ad hoc initiatives (as in the management of the conflicts in former Yugoslavia) than as a result of strategic planning (in contrast, for instance, with the meticulous US planning which had helped to create the security architecture of post-Second World War Europe). The transformation of institutions such as the OSCE and NATO into managers of postwar change – led by both the United States and the increasingly assertive European Union – is an example of this development.

The third milestone in EU/US relations was the agreement signed by the United States and the European Union in December 1995 on 'A New Transatlantic Agenda'. Both sides committed themselves to a series of political and economic objectives – to be developed and implemented jointly. The agreement was careful to acknowledge that the new Agenda was designed as complementary to policies developed and implemented within the context of NATO and not to diminish the importance of existing bilateral links between the United States and individual EU member states. Yet the Agenda did appear to represent a decision by the United States to concentrate more on relations with the collective organisation of the EU and at the same time to acknowledge the EU's pivotal role as the centre of the new politico-security architecture emerging in post-Cold War Europe. The 'New Agenda' was supported by a four-point action plan that included both political and economic objectives as well as agreements for closer cooperation between the two partners. Priorities for joint action in the area of security were itemised as including implementing the peace in Bosnia-Herzegovina, supporting the Middle East peace process, supporting democratic institutions and the development of market economies in Central and Eastern Europe, improving joint preventive and crisis diplomacy, defending human rights, reforming the United Nations, promoting nuclear non-proliferation, international disarmament and controls on arms transfers. These priorities looked set to shape the European Union and the United States joint security agenda for the twenty-first century. The 'New Agenda' explicitly acknowledged the intimate links between security concerns and economic trans- formation and liberalisation and therefore adopted a broad post-Cold War conceptualisation of security.

Actors, instruments, legal base and decision-making procedures

The EC member states had decided that the CSCE and the Middle East should be the priority areas for the intergovernmental mechanisms for foreign policy coordination in European Political Cooperation that had been created in 1970 (see Chapter 3). In practice, even as early as the 1970s, both these areas of foreign policy activity were conducted within the framework of EPC *and* the Community treaties. The use of both intergovernmental and treaty- based instruments to implement foreign policy continued in the 1981/82 Polish crisis. In July 1981 a meeting of foreign ministers within the context of both the Community and EPC was held to discuss Poland. This meeting displayed little regard for institutional formalities that decreed separation of treaty-based responsibilities from those ascribed to EPC. In addition the Community (treaty- based) sanctions were specifically imposed on the Soviet Union for foreign policy purposes. The Community also utilised both the instruments of intergovernmental cooperation and the treaties in the pursuit of its Central American policies, its response to the leftwing government of Grenada and the United States invasion and its approach to Libya. The Central America policy provides the clearest example of a Commission- and Parliament-led policy – of opposition to United States policies as part of a West European effort which to a greater or lesser extent succeeded in launching and maintaining a distinctive Community policy. The policy was articulated by Council, Commission and Parliament and was implemented through diplomatic and intergovernmental means or treaty-based economic instruments as was deemed appropriate. The United States considered the Community's policy as a common foreign policy, whether based on intergovernmental or treaty competencies. For instance George Shultz, in his discussion of Community reactions to the 1986 bombing of Libya, made no differentiation between Mr van den Broek's role as President of EPC and that of President of the 'Community'. Neither, one supposes, did Mr van den Broek consider it necessary to make the distinction.

Formalised instruments for political cooperation between the two partners were established in 1990 with the Transatlantic Declaration. These were consolidated and expanded by the Clinton administration in December 1995 with the agreement on 'A New Transatlantic Agenda'. All three of the major institutions of the Union participated in policymaking and implementation of policies towards the United States in the security issue-area. The legal bases for policies were a mix of treaty and intergovernmental procedures. Decision-making was pragmatic and the various instruments of the Community and intergovernmental cooperation were used.

Trade

The EU is the most important trading partner for the United States and vice versa, and in 1998 the overall value of two-way trade flow in merchandise trade came to a staggering $300 billion. The EU is also the largest source of foreign direct investment (FDI) in the United States at around 50 per cent of all FDI, while conversely the US is the source of around 42 per cent of all FDI in the Union – these percentages indicating very high levels of interdependent economic interpenetration.

Trade is an important but institutionally uncontroversial issue-area for the Union, in the sense that since the inception of the Community, the management of external trade has been accepted as an unambiguous competence of the Community institutions. Trade conflicts have, however, been a significant feature of EU–US relations and have both entered the realm of 'high politics' as issues in themselves, for instance, in the protracted GATT Uruguay Round negotiations (1986–93) and have interlinked with security issues, particularly in the area of economic sanctions. In the area of trade there is, similarly to the security issue-area, much more cooperation between the two allies than during the Cold War period. This is partly because Union trade policies have contradictory effects on US business. While, for example, the move towards a common market may sometimes have the effect of discrimination against foreign, including US imports, yet at the same time the implementation of single market rules can benefit US business established within EU territory. If the common market does help to achieve growth, as its advocates argue, then those growth effects are equally important for US firms established within EU territory as much as for EU business itself. At the same time, there is continued conflict – manifesting itself most strongly in the attempts by the United States to force European firms to stop investment and trade with Cuba through the Helms-Burton act, the EU refusal to import US hormone-fed cattle and the ongoing attacks by the US on the EU's use of trade preferences to support the uncompetitive Caribbean banana trade.

Because of the strong thematic element within trade-related issues, it makes more sense to discuss the development of the trade issue-area in terms of sub-issue-areas, rather than in terms of a chronological division between 1989 and beyond as in the security and defence relationship. The most important of these sub-issue-areas are the GATT, agriculture, economic sanctions, protectionism and monetary relations. Clearly, these are only analytically separate categories. In practice the issues and negotiations arising from problems associated with these sub-issue-areas intersected with each other and with the broader political and security aspects of EU–US relations.

General Agreement on Tariffs and Trade (GATT) and the World Trade Organisation (WTO)

The European Community represented the member states in the multilateral negotiating 'Rounds' of the GATT in the Kennedy Round which lasted from 1964 to 1967 and which achieved substantial reductions in tariff barriers to trade. The Community of six member states and the United States were the chief players in the Kennedy Round (see Chapter 2), as were the Community of nine and the US in the subsequent Tokyo Round (1973–79) and the Community of twelve and the US in the most recent Uruguay Round (1986–93). The Tokyo Round did not achieve substantial reductions in either tariff barriers or non-tariff barriers to trade although some technical agreements were concluded on issues related to common standards and customs valuations. The Uruguay Round, by contrast, involved 117 participant states, and ended with a much more comprehensive international trade regime that further opened markets for manufactured goods and, for the first time, extended world trade rules to include intellectual property rights and services. The Uruguay Round was also the first of the multilateral trading Rounds to successfully conclude an agreement which included agricultural trade but this was achieved only at the end of a protracted and acrimonious set of negotiations between the EC and the United States. The Uruguay Round also created the World Trade Organisation – designed to bring a more solid institutional base for monitoring trade rules and settling trade disputes. The Union and the United States have been keen to launch another round of multilateral trade negotiations but have been delayed from doing so after the 1999 meeting of world leaders at Seattle ended in chaos because of protesters demonstrating against the international financial institutions.

Agriculture

EU/United States conflict over agriculture resulted from the related issues of changing patterns of world agricultural trade and differing domestic agricultural support systems. When the EC was initially established it was an importer of agricultural produce and the United States was a major exporter. However, from its inception, the EC advanced the support of the agricultural sector as the major priority within the budget so that the bulk of the EC's budget (at least 60 per cent until the early 1990s with planned reductions thereafter) has been spent on financially supporting agricultural production. The Union has moved from a position of being a net importer to self-sufficiency, through to being a major exporter of agricultural produce and therefore a competitor to the United States. For the United States, this competition has been exacerbated by two developments. The first is the process of enlargement and the second is the system of EC farm support. With enlargement, the new member states are brought into a protectionist agricultural market which both encourages intra-Union trade at the expense of US exports and brings more products (for instance, citrus fruits after enlargement to Spain and Portugal) into the price support scheme that, the US argues, unfairly discriminates against US produce on international markets. This system has been heavily criticised, not just by the

United States, but by other agricultural exporters including Argentina, Australia, Canada and New Zealand for subsidising EC exports (and domestic production) so that produce is sold cheaply on overseas markets to the extent that some overseas producers can be forced out of business. The United States also subsidises domestic agricultural production but it has argued that EC export subsidies distort competition and it was deadlock over this issue that caused the two-year delay to completion of the GATT talks – from an original deadline of March 1991 to an actual agreement in December 1993. The EC finally agreed to cut subsidies – partly because of international – including US – pressure, but also because of domestic pressures to cut the heavy costs of agricultural subsidies. This long-running agricultural dispute was the source of strongly worded public discord between the two allies, particularly in respect of the GATT negotiations. In January 1992, for instance, President Bush accused the EC of setting up an 'Iron Curtain of protection during the GATT talks'.

The WTO dispute mechanism has been invoked by the United States on the issue of the Union ban on the import of cattle which have been fed growth promoting hormones. As at 2000 the EU was maintaining its ban – convinced by its interpretation of WTO rulings that it had a right to do so. In contrast the WTO directly ruled in 1997 and again in 1999 that EU trade arrangements in respect of bananas were illegal and authorised the United States to impose limited trade sanctions on the Union. As at mid-2000, the Union had still not found a legal method which would enable it to continue to favour banana imports from its partners in the African, Caribbean and Pacific (ACP) states and, at the same time, maintain a WTO-approved trading regime with other global banana producers – many of which are contacted to United States-based firms.

Economic sanctions

The restriction of trade has been an instrument which the Union has been reluctant to use to achieve its aims in international politics. This is in contrast to the position of the United States which has available to it a number of pieces of legislation which enable it to impose economic sanctions for political reasons and which has frequently resorted to their use for this purpose. One of the reasons for Union caution in respect of economic sanctions was its relatively greater dependence on international trade as a source of prosperity than for the United States. This meant that the EC was only prepared to support restrictions on access to markets as a very last resort. EC elites also supported 'constructive engagement' with revolutionary movements in order to promote moderation, and tended to develop strategies which included the provision of economic aid and the promise of access to EC markets as an inducement, rather than exclusionary strategies that relied on military and economic sanctions (see section above on security and defence). These different approaches caused intermittent conflict between the two partners when the EU imposed weaker restrictions than those implemented by the United States (on the Soviet Union in the Polish crisis in the early 1980s for instance), refused to go along with United States sanctions (north Korea) and sometimes actively campaigned against United States' imposition of economic sanctions (Nicaragua in the 1980s). Tensions were at their greatest when the United States attempted to force EU business to comply with United States legislation. The most notorious of these incidents were in 1981/82 when the Reagan administration attempted to stop European firms working with the Soviet Union on the completion of a pipeline which would supply natural gas to West Europe from Siberia. A more recent example was the Clinton administration's support for the Helms-Burton Act which seeks to impose penalties on non-US firms that do business with Cuba and which was vigorously opposed by the EU. By 1997 a united EU was pursuing complaints over restraint of trade on this issue through the judicial machinery of the World Trade Organisation (WTO). The EU eventually agreed to suspend its action within the WTO, after a compromise had been worked out with the Clinton administration that effectively ruled out the Act being applied to European companies and citizens. The Union was unhappy, however, that the Helms-Burton Act remained part of United States legislation, arguing that it provided for foreign (United States) extra-territorial controls over European companies which were illegal as they breached European Union member-state sovereignty.

Protectionism

The United States has consistently accused the EU of a protectionism directed against US trade through 'dumping', that is subsidising exports so that they are sold cheaper than market prices for the same but home-produced commodity, and other forms of discriminatory trading practices. Conversely the EC has alleged that United States legislation and trading practices discriminate against EC goods. These practices, according to the EU, range from 'Buy America' campaigns to the 'Super 301' clause of the 1988 US Omnibus Trade and Competitiveness Act that allowed the US government to impose sanctions on trade partners that discriminated against US exports 'unfairly'. Conflicts emerged in specific sectors, including the steel, aircraft, textiles, banking, telecommunications and audiovisual industries. Of themselves these trade disputes affect only specific sectors of business and the labour force. During the Cold War, however, the spillover effect of sectoral disputes, particularly those that involve well-financed lobbying (as in the aircraft industry), intersected with broader political issues to affect the texture of EU/US relations. The steel 'war' of 1982, for instance, in which the United States accused the EC of dumping and consequently imposed high duties on EC steel exports to the US, was only one issue in a host of often bad-tempered economic and political conflicts between the EC and the Reagan administration in the 1980s. By contrast, disputes have continued in the post-Cold War period but have not affected overall relations in the same way. The WTO ruling of 2000 which declared the United States foreign sales corporation tax scheme an illegal export subsidy and which was brought by the Union, did not have ramifications outside the issue-area of trade.

Monetary relations

Strictly speaking, monetary relations have not been an issue in the EU/US relationship. This does not mean that conflict and cooperation have not taken place between the two partners but that monetary matters that involved the West Europeans and the United States have been discussed in other fora. In the immediate postwar era the Bretton Woods system provided the framework for West European and United States monetary cooperation. After President Nixon unilaterally withdrew the United States from the system in August 1971, monetary cooperation increasingly took place in the various summits of Heads of State and Government (HSG) of the industrialised world. By 1993 the G7 – comprising the United States, Canada, Japan, Britain, France, Italy and Germany, with the European Commission represented as an observer – functioned as the coordinating committee for the world's currencies. Conflicts between the major partners then were played out in fora outside EU–US relations. This situation will of course change as Economic and Monetary Union (EMU) is consolidated. There is every likelihood that there will be some friction about the relative roles of the dollar and the Euro – involving significant political consequences including, for instance, the question of leadership of the major international financial institutions. (Analytically, we would then need to consider monetary relations as an issue-area of itself – rather than a subordinate category to trade.)

Actors, instruments, legal bases and decision-making procedures

The lead actor for trade-related issues is the Commission but to state this only tells part of the story. All three important Community institutions (including the Council and the Parliament) possess some legal competencies in the decision-making process. Through the Council, the member states played as much a part in the decision-making in respect of the trade disputes with the United States as the Commission. The Parliament has been able to voice opinions within the debates on GATT and other trade issues but has played a less important role than the other two institutions. The instruments utilised have been diplomatic negotiations and the provisions of the treaties which enable the Union to negotiate and implement trade and cooperation agreements with third countries and international organisations. The legal basis for the Union's various negotiations on trade-related activities with the United States can be found in Article 133 (ex 113). Decision-making procedures for Article 133 are set out in Article 300 (ex Article 228) and include a set of complex instructions on when and how the Council, Commission and Parliament should consult with each other before a decision can be reached.

Development Cooperation

Disagreements have arisen in respect of the differing policies of the transatlantic partners towards development cooperation although these have never led to serious conflict. One of the reasons for this is that, after the Mexican debt crisis of 1982, development strategies of the major Western powers were largely coordinated via the international financial institutions the IMF and the World Bank. The Union and the United States sometimes disagreed on which countries should receive aid (for instance in the 1980s the EC included and the US excluded revolutionary Nicaragua from regional aid packages) but on the whole agreed on the strategic direction of aid policies. Structural adjustment domestically (as defined by the IMF) in the direction of free markets combined with the promotion of export-led development strategies were encouraged by both the EC and the United States.

Disputes were tactical rather than strategic. One such was in respect of the EC's reciprocal preferential trading agreements with former colonies, the Yaoundé agreements of the 1960s (see Chapter 2) which the US argued discriminated against US trade. The next generation of EC agreements with its former colonies of the African, Caribbean and Pacific (ACP) states, the Lomé conventions (see Chapter 6), assuaged US complaints to the extent that preferential access was maintained for ACP exports to EC markets but on a non-reciprocal basis. In other words, EC exports to ACP countries were not given preferential treatment over and against US exports by way of Lomé. The major exception to this was in relation to the banana dispute, discussed above. There was also United States disquiet after the EC extended its Generalised System of Preferences (GSP) to developing countries outside the ACP framework in 1971, so as to permit some exports from these countries to enter EC markets either duty-free or at low levels of duty.

Development policies in the 1990s, however, displayed signs of cooperation not conflict. EU and US aid to Eastern Europe was coordinated via the European Commission-led G24 initiative (see Chapter 8). Both partners also cooperated in terms of aid to the developing states of the Mediterranean and Middle East in the wake of the Madrid peace process between Israel and its Arab neighbours. Similarly, the United States and the Union were partners in the relief and reconstruction efforts in South-East Europe in the late 1990s and early twenty-first century.

Actors, instruments, legal base and decision-making procedures

Discussions with the United States on development cooperation took place within the various contexts where the two partners met as there was no specific and separate forum in which development cooperation was discussed. The actors involved varied in respect of the issue under discussion. In general, however, the Commission assumed an increasing profile in this area. The most important areas of joint activity were in respect of the coordination of aid to Eastern Europe at the end of the Cold War. Here, the Commission assumed the lead role. The legal bases, instruments and decision-making procedures also varied in respect of the issue under consideration.

Interregional Cooperation

The term 'interregional' is conventionally used to describe the Union's relations between itself and other geographically contiguous groups of states. In the case of the EU and the US, however, it is not misleading to refer to 'interregional' cooperation given the size of the entities concerned. It was not until 1990, however, after pressure from President Bush and Secretary of State James Baker for improved consultation between the two partners that interregional coopera-tion was organised on an institutionalised basis. The 1990 'Transatlantic Declaration' formally committed both parties to consult each other on a regular basis at the level of Heads of State, foreign ministers and that of Commission and Presidential cabinet. The 1990 agreement bound the US presidency to meet once every six months with the president-in-office of the Community. It also committed the US Secretary of State to twice yearly meetings with EC foreign ministers at the same time as setting up a series of regularised consultation meetings between Commission officials and United States government representatives. A parliamentary delegation meets regularly with its counterpart representation from the US Congress. Cooperative relations continued to deepen throughout the 1990s and into the new century, particularly in terms of policy towards Eastern Europe. These new cooperative relations were made visible in the December 1995 adoption of a 'New Transatlantic Agenda' designed to further mutual political, economic and security goals.

The New Transatlantic Agenda has spawned various offshoots including the moves towards creation of the 'New Transatlantic Mar-ketplace'. The idea here is for both partners to work towards the elimination of barriers to trade in goods, services and investment. Side by side with the creation of channels at the official level has been the developing organisation of transatlantic business through the Transatlantic Business Dialogue – which has acted to make rec-ommendations to both the EU and the US on how to develop further relations. The result of some of these discussions was the Transat-lantic Economic Partnership launched in 1998 which is designed to provide a joint forum through which multilateral liberalisation of trade can be promoted.

Actors, instruments, legal bases and decision-making procedures

The Council, Commission and the Parliament play a role in inter-regional cooperation. The annual EU summits with the United States bring together the presidents of the Council and the Commission along with the president of the United States. The Commission is the lead actor in the various levels of trade dialogue while the Parliamentary delegation to the United States meets regularly with its Congressional counterparts to discuss political and economic issues. Instruments include diplomacy as well as the trade-based competencies derived from the Community. The legal foundations of trade-related decisions lie in Article 133 (ex Article 113). Decision-making on the broad strategic issues which flow from the institutional links between the two partners remains intergovernmental but decision-making procedures for specific issues follow from the legal bases underlying the particular substantive issue being discussed.

EUROPEAN UNION RELATIONS WITH JAPAN

EC/EU relations with Japan have been almost entirely confined to trade-related issues. In the area of *security and defence* there have been sporadic attempts at dialogue and coordination. In the 1970s the EC held 'high level consultations' with Japan to discuss EC enlargement. In the 1980s the EC troika of foreign ministers and their Political Directors (senior civil servants) met with their Japanese counterparts to share points of view on world politics. EC positions on important international crises such as the Iranian hostages issue of 1980 and the Central American crisis of the 1980s and which differed from those of the United States (see above) were closely followed by Japanese governments and used to provide some support for Japanese positions that were concerned about the bellicosity of the Reagan administrations of the 1980s.

It was only in 1990, however, that the EC began to consider seriously the possibility of substantial foreign policy coordination with Japan. This change of position of the EC was reflected in the 1991 EC/Japan Joint Declaration which, among other things, agreed to institute regular foreign policy cooperation at the level of, respectively, the President of the EC Council, President of the Commission, and the troika of the EC foreign ministers. They agreed to work together on strengthening the United Nations, supporting democracy, human rights and market economies, nuclear proliferation, support for developing countries, transnational 'challenges' such as the environment and international crime, support for Central and East Europe and stability in the Asia-Pacific region. The declaration, however, did not bring the political cooperation that had been envisaged with few joint political actions agreed – one being to initiate a register of Conventional Arms at the UN. Neither did the institutional arrangements work very effectively – with a 1995 Commission report still bemoaning the lack of effective political cooperation with Japan. One of the few concrete policies agreed by the EU in the broad area of security was the Commission's 1995 suggestion that should the UN Security Council be enlarged, the Japanese claim for a permanent seat should be supported.

In 2000 there were some attempts made to reinvigorate a political dialogue with Japan and plans were made to inaugurate a 'Decade of Japan–Europe cooperation' at the planned tenth European Union Japan summit in 2001. This new partnership was designed to promote political cooperation where possible as well as economic cooperation. In the interim, at the ninth bilateral summit held in July 2000, the two partners issued supportive joint statements on the Middle East peace process, the Korean peninsula, East Timor, the Balkans, the illicit trade in small arms and the biological weapons convention.

By far the most important of all the issue-areas in the EU–Japan relationship, however, is that of *trade* – providing a background of continuing low-level conflict to bilateral relations. The context for conflict is the three-way trade and investment relationship between the US, the EU and Japan, with these three economic competitors dominating world trade. Japan is the second largest national economy in the world and is third largest exporter to the Union (after the United States and Switzerland) and the second largest source of EU imports (after the United States). The main complaint of both the Union (and the United States) is of alleged Japanese protectionism which, it is argued, contributes to the fact that the EU has run a persistent trade deficit with Japan. The EU accused Japan of raising and maintaining structural non-tariff barriers to EU trade although, by the mid-1990s, the EU began to take a more sophisticated view about the deficit, looking at ways to encourage EU business to be more proactive in entering the Japanese market. In 1996, for instance, the EU–Japan Centre for Industrial Cooperation was set up in Brussels in order to provide training courses and support for EU managers working in the Japanese market. At the same time, the Union has been working with Japanese business and government to open Japanese markets and has suggested a number of deregulation proposals which, if implemented, it hopes will increase the EU's market position within Japan.

In the area of *development cooperation* there had been some discussion of coordinating activities but little of substance in practice. The area of *interregional cooperation* remained undeveloped until the creation of the Asia–Europe meetings (ASEM) in 1996 –

with the EU and Japan negotiating with each other either bilaterally or via international fora such as the G7, the OECD or the WTO. Although bilateral negotiations continue to provide the primary working framework for EU–Japanese relations, the ASEM summits, held in 1996 (Bangkok), 1998 (London) and 2000 (Seoul) have provided an incipient focus for multilateral cooperation.

Actors, instruments, legal bases and decision-making procedures

The major actor in the EU–Japan relationship remains the Commission although since the 1991 Joint declaration, structures have been established to provide for regular summits between the Presidents of the European Council and the Commission to meet with the Japanese Prime Minister. Provision was also made for biannual meetings of the EU troika of foreign ministers and the Japanese Minister of Foreign Affairs. Biannual meetings were also supposed to take place at the level of senior civil servants (Political Directors) of troika member states, the Commission and the Japanese foreign ministry. Another actor in the relationship is the European Parliament whose representatives have met with their equivalents in the Japanese Diet on a regular basis since 1978. Cooperation is conducted via a 20-member European interparliamentary delegation. The instruments, the legal basis for activity, the decision-making procedures and the instruments utilised were uncontroversial and arose from Article 133 (ex 113). The Joint Declaration of July 1991 between the EC member states and Japan structures the relationship.

EUROPEAN UNION RELATIONS WITH CANADA

Security and defence issues have not been significant in EU relations with Canada. There is provision to discuss security issues within the annual summits and regular meetings of ministers but these are secondary fora compared to other, multilateral frameworks, such as the United Nations, the G8 and NATO. There have not been major *trade* conflicts, albeit some irritations in the relationship. The two most significant of these were the dispute over seal pelts which led the EC to ban seal-derived products in 1983 and the fisheries issues – the latter of which was more or less resolved with the December 1992 fisheries agreement signed between the two partners. There are no formal agreements on *development cooperation*. In respect to *inter-regional cooperation*, there are currently no wider links incorporating the two partners although this may be an area of change in the future given that the EU is cognisant of the need to optimise its relations with the North Atlantic Free Trade Area (NAFTA) of which Canada – along with Mexico and the United States – is a founding member.

The first formal agreement between any of the Communities and Canada was the Euratom–Canada agreement on nuclear cooperation signed in 1959. A further agreement on nuclear materials was signed in 1991 and in 1991 the EC agreed to pursue cooperation on controlled nuclear fission. In overall terms, the EC/EU has managed its relationships with Canada through the 1976 non-preferential trade and economic cooperation agreement which was supplemented in November 1990 by the Transatlantic Declaration. Overall cooperation was further elaborated in the 1996 Joint Political Declaration and Joint EU–Canada Action Plan. The action plan was followed by a decision in 1998 to launch the EU–Canadian Trade Initiative – designed to improve trade cooperation in a number of areas including services, government procurement, intellectual property rights, cultural cooperation and business to business contacts.

Actors, instruments, legal bases and decision-making procedures

The Commission is the major actor in the relationship. The Council, particularly the Presidency, has the potential to play an important part in the relationship as the 1990 Transatlantic Declaration provides for the President of the Council and the Commission and the Prime Minister of Canada to meet annually and for EU foreign ministers to meet twice yearly with their Canadian counterpart. In practice the Commission has taken the lead even in the Summits, with the 2000 Summit held in Portugal notable for its absence of Council representatives. In addition a 15-member European Parliament delegation meets regularly with representatives of the Canadian Parliament to discuss matters of mutual interest. The instruments are the trade and related agreements which operate under the provisions of Articles 133 (ex 113) and 308 (ex 235) of the EEC Treaty, Article 101 of the Euratom Treaty and Article 6 of the European Coal and Steel Community Treaty.

EUROPEAN UNION RELATIONS WITH AUSTRALIA AND NEW ZEALAND

European Union relations with Australia and New Zealand have developed in a somewhat parallel manner although, because of New Zealand's comparatively less powerful economic and political status, it has had less room to manoeuvre in its negotiations with the EU than has its near neighbour. Many of the important issues in the Union's relationship with Australia and New Zealand have, however, been negotiated outside the bilateral frameworks and, instead, within the multilateral negotiating rounds of the GATT.

As with Canada, *security and defence* have not been major issues in the relationship with these two states. The EU has sometimes expressed rhetorical interest in utilising Australia as a gateway into the Asia-Pacific region but this expression of interest has not so far translated itself into effective political action – despite occasional meetings with both Australia and New Zealand which include discussions on international political issues. Until 1997, when a wide-ranging Joint Declaration was signed with Australia and 1999 when a similar declaration was signed with New Zealand, the focus of relationships had been almost entirely on *trade* matters, most importantly in respect of agriculture and minerals. Agriculture has caused the most conflict, with Australia forming the Cairns group of 15 agricultural exporting countries in 1986 to protest EC protectionism caused by the operation of the common agricultural policy. Some improvements in the often conflictual relationship with Australia took place towards the end of the Uruguay Round negotiating process – in 1992, for instance, an agreement on Australian wine exports was signed. The EU remains keen to exploit Australia's mineral deposits and in 1981 signed a 30-year agreement on uranium and the transfer of nuclear material to the EC.

New Zealand benefited from a special arrangement to preserve market access for its agricultural products to European markets after British accession to the Community in 1973 – managing to maintain some preferential treatment although its favourable dairy and sheepmeat quotas were gradually being whittled away by the 1990s.

The 1997 Joint Agreement with Australia covered bilateral cooperation in the areas of environment, employment, education and training, refugees, agriculture, and scientific and cultural issues. It remains to be seen whether the full potential of this framework for cooperation will be fulfilled. A scientific and technical agreement, mainly on agricultural and environmental issues, was signed between the EC and New Zealand in 1991. A number of minor sectoral arrangements have been agreed; for instance, in the 1997 agreement on trade in live animals and animal products. The 1999 Joint Declaration on relations between the European Union and New Zealand provides a broad framework for further consultations and anticipates that these discussions will include political matters. *Devel-*

opment cooperation and *interregional cooperation* were not areas of direct mutual interest.

Actors, instruments, legal bases and decision-making procedures

The Commission is again the major actor in policymaking and implementation in relationships with both Australia and New Zealand. There exists a 16-member European Parliament delegation to both Australia and New Zealand which meets annually and successively in Australia, New Zealand and the EU. The instruments are trade-related and the legal basis for relationships is provided by Article 133 (ex 113) of the EEC Treaty. Annual ministerial talks were formalised in the 1997 Australia Agreement and the 1999 New Zealand Agreement as were the regular meetings between officials.

THE UNITED STATES AS KEY PARTNER: SHAPING EU FOREIGN POLICY CHOICES?

By far the most important foreign policy relationship that the EU has with its OECD allies is with the United States. This relationship shapes, facilitates and constrains the general direction and practice of EU foreign policy in many more areas than issues of direct bilateral concern. The EU–United States relationship, which is much more harmonious in the early twenty-first century than it was for most of the second half of the twentieth, continues to help shape EU policies elsewhere in the world – in both the pan-European, post-Communist world, and also in relations with the South. The conflicts and the commonalities of EU/US policies abroad and their effects on the Union's decisions and actions are reviewed in the next three chapters.

Guide to Further Reading for Chapter 5

A useful source of data is from the very accessible publications produced by the Community. See for instance the annual *General Report on the Activities of the European Communities*, particularly the sections on 'external relations'. These give details of Community/Union activity in regions, specific countries and international organisations. Perhaps of more relevance to most students is the Commission's excellent external relations website, divided into six sub-topics, which can be found on http://www.europa.eu.int/comm/dgs_en.htm. The six topics are titled: the common service for external relations, development, enlargement, external relations, humanitarian aid office (ECHO) and trade.

On the broad background to US/EC relations during the Cold War see Fred Halliday, *The Making of the Second Cold War* (London: Verso, 1986). For a readable, if not self-reflective, participant view on US/Europe relations see George P. Shultz, *Turmoil and Triumph: My Years as Secretary of State* (New York: Charles Scribner's Sons, 1993). For an excellent overview of the Atlantic alliance which within that context discusses US/West European relations see William Park, *Defending the West: A History of NATO* (Brighton: Wheatsheaf, 1986). On US/EU relations Simon Nuttall, *European Political Cooperation* (Oxford: Clarendon, 1992) in general is again a useful source of data while Roy H. Ginsberg, *Foreign Policy Actions of the European Community: The Politics of Scale* (Boulder: Lynne Rienner, 1989) provides a theoretical framework. For a comprehensive discussion of the beginnings of Euro–Arab relations see David Allen and Alfred Pijpers (eds), *European Foreign Policy and the Arab-Israeli Conflict* (Dordrecht: Martinus Nijhoff, 1984). A detailed and useful account of US and West European approaches to the 1981 Polish crisis, the 1983 Grenada invasion and the 1986 bombing of Libya can be found in an unfortunately difficult to access source. This is Neil Winn, 'European Crisis Management in the 1980s', a paper prepared for the annual conference of the British International Studies Association (BISA), York, December 1994. For an extensive discussion of United States/European Community differences on Central America see Hazel Smith, *European Union Foreign Policy and Central America* (London: Macmillan, 1995). John Peterson provides detail and analysis of relationships with reference to both the Bush and Clinton administrations in his *Europe and America* (London: Routledge, 1996). Michael Calingaert has useful data and analysis in *European Integration Revisited: Progress, Prospects and US Interests* (Boulder: Westview, 1996). On the relative roles of the United States and its allies in the Bosnia peace agreement see Pauline Neville-Jones, 'Dayton, IFOR and Alliance Relations in Bosnia', in *Survival*, Vol. 38 No. 4, Winter 1996–97. *The New Transatlantic Agenda* (internet) can be obtained through documentation available on the internet from either the European Commission or the United States government. For an introduction which includes useful discussion of the trade issue-area see Kevin Featherstone, 'The EC and the US: Managing Interdependence', in Juliet Lodge (ed.), *The European Community and the Challenge of the*

Future, second edition (London: Pinter, 1993). See also Kevin Feath-erstone and Roy H. Ginsberg, *The United States and the European Union in the 1990s: Partners in Transition*, second edition (New York: St Martin's Press, 1996). Although more opinion than analysis, there is some useful background information on trade and monetary relations in Peter Coffey, *The EC and the United States* (London: Pinter, 1993). For analysis of systemic differences between the EU and the US vis-à-vis trade and related market access issues see Stephen Woolcock, *Market Access Issues in EC–US Relations: Trading Partners or Trading Blows?* (London: RIIA/Pinter, 1991). For an accessible political economy approach see Peter Holmes and Alasdair Smith, 'The EC, the USA and Japan: The Trilateral Rela-tionship in World Context', in Mehmet Ugur (ed.), *Policy Issues in the European Union* (London: Greenwich University, 1995). On EC–Japanese relations see Clemens Stubbe Østergaard, 'From Strategic Triangle to Economic Tripolarity: Japan's Responses to European Integration', in Ole Nørgaard, Thomas Pedersen and Nikolaj Petersen (eds), *The European Community in World Politics* (London: Pinter, 1993). See also the 1995 Commission report *Europe and Japan: The Next Steps*, Com (95) 73 final, Brussels, 08.03.1995. There is little in the way of extended treatments of EU relations with Canada, Australia and New Zealand. The best source of infor-mation is either the Commission documentation (annual reports of external activities, etc.) or via the internet to the homepages of the foreign ministries of the countries concerned.

6 The European Union and the Neighbouring South

European Union policy towards the Mediterranean and the Middle East – its nearest southern neighbours – sometimes called the 'proximity policy' – has been shaped by political and economic security concerns. The Union wants to protect major sources of its oil supplies in the Middle East and it also wants to prevent political violence spilling over into the European Union. There are three distinct sub-regions for EU policy in this region – respectively the Maghreb (the Southern Mediterranean), the Mashreq (the Eastern Mediterranean) and the Gulf states.

In the wake of the 1990/91 Gulf War, the EU's policy towards the Mediterranean overlapped considerably with its Middle East policy as the Israel–Palestinian conflict brought a strong reaction from Arab publics and their governments. Relations with the Mashreq and Israel therefore provided a constant theme of Union foreign policy. The EU had had considerable historical involvement with the political problems of the Middle East although much of this involvement was conducted in fora outside the geographical framework of Mediterranean-based agreements, most importantly in its post-1973 'Euro–Arab' dialogue with the Arab League. On the other hand, not all EU foreign policy towards the region has been concerned with the Arab–Israeli conflict. Relations with the Maghreb in the 1990s, for instance, were dominated by security which included the issue of Libyan relations and, to a lesser extent, Algerian political violence.

The Gulf region is obviously not part of the Mediterranean Basin but the political and economic security priorities that have shaped European Union policy towards this area are precisely the same as the political and economic concerns which shape the overall relationship with the Eastern Mediterranean and Middle East region. Union relations with the Gulf are, therefore, also evaluated in this chapter. Following European Union practice, the discussion of Union relations with Albania, Cyprus, Malta, Turkey and former Yugoslavia is framed within the context of EU relations with the 'New Europe' and is, therefore, left to Chapter 8.

The chapter opens with a discussion of the Union's attempts to develop a comprehensive approach towards the Mediterranean. It then evaluates sub-regional policies towards the Maghreb, the Mashreq and the Gulf region via the issue-areas of security and defence, trade, development cooperation and interregional cooperation. Given that this chapter focuses on relations with extra-European actors, enlargement as an issue-area is inapplicable although, of the states discussed in this chapter, Morocco once applied for membership – in 1987 – but was turned down on the basis that it was an extra-European state. Again following the structure already established, the relevant actors, instruments, legal bases and decision-making procedures involved in each issue-area are evaluated.

A GLOBAL MEDITERRANEAN POLICY?

The first signs of a Mediterranean policy appeared even prior to the date when the EC became able to 'speak with one voice' with the implementation of the common external tariff in the late 1960s (see Chapter 2). From its inception the EC responded to demands from its closest geographical neighbours (outside the eastern Communist bloc) for some regularisation in trade, aid and, at least implicitly, political relations. The EC offered a series of bilateral initiatives that included association with Greece in 1961, Turkey in 1963, Morocco and Tunisia in 1969, Malta in 1970 and Cyprus in 1972. In addition, non-preferential trade agreements were signed with Israel in 1964 and Lebanon in 1965. Another bilateral non-preferential agreement was signed with Yugoslavia in 1970 and again in 1973 and preferential trade agreements were signed with Spain and Israel in 1970, and Egypt, Lebanon and Portugal in 1972.

The EC attempted a more 'global' response to the Mediterranean basin from the mid-1970s onwards but, in practice, political attention prioritised two distinct geographical parts of the region: the first the European candidate states and the second the volatile Middle East. After the two enlargements of 1981 and 1986, when first Greece, and then Spain and Portugal joined the Community, the EC again attempted to reformulate a comprehensive strategy towards the Mediterranean but, at the same time, it continued to differentiate both between different regional groupings and within regional groupings. The Union conceives of the countries of Algeria, Libya, Morocco and Tunisia and, to a lesser extent, Mauritania as having a collective Maghreb regional identity. There were also attempts to 'regionalise' policy towards the Mashreq – comprising Egypt, Jordan, Lebanon and Syria – and Israel and the Palestinian territories.

As part of the effort to establish a 'global' Mediterranean policy, the Community adopted a 'New Mediterranean Policy' in 1990 and initiated a policy of 'Euro–Mediterranean partnership' in November 1995 at the Barcelona conference. The conference brought together European Union member states with Maghreb (not including Libya), Mashreq, Israeli and Palestinian representatives as well as Turkey, Cyprus and Malta in a multilateral process whose aim was to facilitate peace and stability in the region. Numerous obstacles have, however, worked against its fulfilment. One is the continued violence and lack of a real peace settlement between Israel and the Palestinians. The second is the unwillingness of Israel, and still to a certain extent the United States, to allow the EU an independent and influential role in this highly strategically sensitive region. The third is that, since the Maastricht Treaty (see Chapter 3) the Union is only able to develop institutional links with states that accept the principles of the market economy, political pluralism, rule of law and respect for human rights. For the EU, this ruled out Ghadaffi's Libya, particularly while Libya was the subject of United Nations Security Council sanctions in the aftermath of the Lockerbie disaster when two Libyan nationals were accused of planting a bomb on a United States airliner which had exploded over Scotland. (One suspect was found guilty and another acquitted by a Scottish court sitting in the Netherlands.) Reservations were also expressed about Algeria, Syria and both the Palestinian Authority and Israel on some of the above counts. In addition, because the Barcelona initiative started out as a way to support the Middle East peace process rather than as a forum where all Mediterranean security issues could carry equal weight, until that process came to fruition, it arguably was not a forum in which it was likely that a comprehensive foreign policy strategy and programme towards the Mediterranean could be developed.

Nevertheless the EU continued to reaffirm region-wide objectives and in 1995 reiterated that it would support the Mediterranean states with economic transition, achieving a better socioeconomic balance and regional integration. In pursuit of these objectives the EU would work towards a Euro–Mediterranean free trade area, support the private sector in the Mediterranean and encourage private European investment in the region. The means included the negotiation of a series of bilateral agreements and, at the same time, the organisation of thematic 'forums' on energy, industry, banking, private investment, governance etc. that have sought to bring together representatives of governments and 'civil society'. In addition follow-up conferences of foreign ministers involved in the Euro–Mediterranean partnership were held.

By the mid-1990s, therefore, the Union's Mediterranean policy had evolved as a multilateral umbrella for the promotion and implementation of regional *as well as* bilateral initiatives. By 2000 the Euro–Mediterranean partnership initiated at Barcelona in 1995 comprised the 15 member states of the Union and 12 Southern partners. These were Morocco, Algeria, Tunisia, Egypt, Israel, Jordan, the Palestinian Authority, Lebanon, Syria, Turkey, Cyprus and Malta. From 1999 onwards, after the lifting of United Nations Security Council sanctions, Libya was permitted to participate in the partnership as a 'special guest'. The major political regional initiative remained that of support for the Middle East peace process – mainly through financial assistance but also through the promotion of a free trade area between the Union and the Mediterranean partners as well as the rather amorphous-sounding 'area of peace and stability'.

By 2001, however, the Euro–Mediterranean partnership seemed to have run out of steam. One factor in the inability to advance was the slow progress in the Middle East peace process – signified in summer 2000 by the breakdown in talks between the Palestinians and the Israelis and the escalating violence in 2001. Another factor was that the Union conducted its most important negotiations with three of the Mediterranean partners – Cyprus, Malta and Turkey – through the framework of accession negotiations. In response to this rather desultory progress, in 2000 the European Council launched a 'common strategy' (see Chapter 3) on the Mediterranean designed to reinvigorate the Barcelona process. A common area of peace and stability was still to be promoted, as was free trade between the partners. The common strategy also was designed to increase cooperation in justice and home affairs – with the focus on migration-related issues including visa procedures, illegal immigration, border controls and the treatment of overseas residents within the Union. What was also new was the statement by the Union that it would make use of the evolving common European policy on security and defence to work with the Mediterranean partners to achieve 'cooperative security' in the region.

Actors, instruments, legal bases and decision-making procedures

The European Council is responsible for the strategic direction of Mediterranean policy but it is the external relations directorate general of the Commission which has so far been the most important actor in Union policy towards the Mediterranean – taking responsibility for implementing the Euro–Mediterranean partnership and for promoting the Euro–Mediterranean Free Trade area. It represents the Union – as does the Council – in the Middle East peace process. The Commission also manages the MEDA programme – the main financial instrument used to implement the Union's Mediterranean policy. MEDA is an acronym designed to signify 'financial and technical measures to accompany the reform of social and economic structures in the Mediterranean non-member countries'. MEDA funds constituted about 3.5 billion of the 4.6 billion Euros that were provided to the region between 1996 and 2000 from Union funds. In addition the European Investment Bank provided 4.6 billion Euros-worth of loans in the same period. Bilateral Euro–Mediterranean association agreements provide another instrument of cooperation as do the cooperation agreements still extant from the 1970s (for details on individual countries see sections below). For bilateral aid to be disbursed, there must first be concluded a financing framework convention. The legal bases for the common strategy include both Title V of the Treaty on European Union (the CFSP procedures) along with Community-based competencies and Title VI of the Treaty on European Union. The MEDA programme is based on the 1996 MEDA regulation.

EUROPEAN UNION RELATIONS WITH THE MAGHREB (SOUTHERN MEDITERRANEAN)

All five Maghreb states had some form of colonial experience with EU member states. Prior to independence in 1962, Algeria was treated as a French overseas *département* and therefore legally part of the Community (as specified in Article 299 ex Article 227 of the treaty establishing the European Community). Morocco, Tunisia and Mauritania had been French colonies. Libya had been a former Italian colony and, in the postwar period, was subject to British political and economic influence. (The disputed area of the Western Sahara which gained its independence from Spain in 1975 but which has still to fully establish its sovereignty does not have direct links with the Union.) The two EC enlargements of the 1980s provided a watershed for EC/EU–Maghreb relations. The north Africans feared trade diversion and isolation and conversely the EC/EU became concerned at the risk of instability on its now extended southern flank. New impetus was given therefore to trying to provide some form of relationship that could prevent or ameliorate any growth in tensions for these or other reasons. The defining political aspect of the relationship was Union reluctance to include Libya in partnership arrangements.

Security and Defence

The EU has repeatedly expressed concerns about internal Maghrebi developments which its sees as posing problems in terms of 'security and social stability'. The 1992 Lisbon declaration on the CFSP for instance stated that Maghrebi stability 'is of important common interest to the Union' and this stability is threatened by 'population growth, recurrent social crises, large-scale migration, and the growth of religious fundamentalism and integralism'. The violence in Algeria, after the government cancelled the second round of the general elections in 1992 because of the victory of the Islamic Salvation Front (FIS) in the first round, elicited regular condemnation from the EU whose reaction was also to maintain economic aid to Algeria at the same time as calling for talks between all parties. In general the EU's response to Maghrebi political instability has been to attempt to encourage economic development by promoting trade and aid links with Algeria, Morocco and Tunisia and by continuing to work with Mauritania within the framework of the Lomé and Cotonou conventions (see sections on trade and development cooperation below). Specifically, the Union has welcomed the more liberal government which came to power in Morocco in 1997. It maintained political and economic relations with Algeria, despite the continuing massacres, the human rights abuses and the closure of the Commission delegation between 1994 and 1998 because of concerns for the safety of staff.

By far the most direct security issue, however, has been in respect of relations with Libya. The EU supported the United States which, particularly since the 1980s, argued that Libya promotes terrorism internationally and thus should be treated as an 'outlaw' state. To this end the US imposed diplomatic and economic sanctions on Libya and tried to encourage its allies to do the same. While the EU has never been as enthusiastic in support for economic sanctions as the United States, partly because its own commercial interests would be endangered, member states have supported the United States because of their own grievances with Libya. The United Kingdom is the most prominent of these because of the killing of a British police-woman by a shot fired from the Libyan embassy in London in 1984, the alleged supply of arms and money to the IRA and suspected Libyan involvement in the 1988 Lockerbie bombing. There is therefore a certain ambivalence within the EU on Libyan policy. This was demonstrated in 1986 when the UK was the only member state to support President Reagan's bombing of Tripoli although all EU states agreed to impose sanctions. From the early 1990s onwards, France joined with the United Kingdom in ensuring that the EU maintained a tough policy and in 1992 limited United Nations Security Council sanctions were imposed on Libya. European Union sanctions were lifted in 1999, after Libya complied with the terms of the UN Security Council resolutions, except for the embargo on arms exports, and a European Union troika visited Tripoli in March 2000 as it tentatively began to try to re-establish relations between the two sides.

Actors, instruments, legal bases and decision-making procedures

Within the institutions of the EU it is the Council that has been the most significant actor in respect of security aspects of policy towards the Maghreb. More specifically it is Britain, with respect to Libya, and France, in relation to the rest of the Maghreb, that has provided policy direction. The provisions of the CFSP and so-called 'pillar one' competencies have been used to implement policy with diplomatic *démarches* underpinned by the economic sanctions available under Article 301 (ex Article 228a). The European Parliament has a 22-member Parliamentary Delegation to the Maghreb countries and the Arab Maghreb Union which has met with counterparts from Algeria, Morocco and Tunisia. It has discussed economic relations as well as political issues such as the Western Sahara dispute and human rights. Intergovernmental procedures have been used to make diplomatic interventions but the mechanisms of the Community have been used to implement the economic agreements seen as essential to help stabilise the Maghreb.

Trade

The EU's balance of trade with Morocco and Tunisia is positive but negative with Algeria from which it imports oil and gas and

Mauritania from which it imports iron ore and fish. The EU has been anxious to maintain open trade relations with the Maghreb because of the importance of energy imports from both Libya and Algeria. Libya provides Italy, for instance, with about 50 per cent of its oil requirements. Frictions in the trade relationship have been caused because of Union import restrictions on 'sensitive' goods such as textiles and clothing – with Tunisia and Morocco particularly affected. In the mid-1990s one dispute, which caused delays in the negotiations in respect of an EU/Morocco association agreement, was that over EU fishing rights in Moroccan waters. The agreement resolving this dispute, signed in 1995, expired in 1999, however, and negotiations will again take place to try to prevent a reoccurrence of conflict in this area. Tunisia has also called for liberalisation of the Union's protected agricultural markets – particularly so that it can sell its olive oil in Europe.

In 1976 the EC had signed non-preferential economic coopera-tion agreements with Algeria, Morocco and Tunisia which were updated in the late 1980s after the accession of Spain and Portugal to the Community. Renegotiated 'Euro–Mediterranean' association agreements subsequent to the Barcelona conference aimed to strengthen ties to allow for political dialogues as well as economic and financial cooperation within the context of eventually estab-lishing free trade. The Euro–Mediterranean association agreements with Tunisia and Morocco came into force in, respectively, 1998 and 2000. Although negotiations have taken place with Algeria to extend the country's 1976 cooperation agreement into a Euro–Mediter-ranean association agreement, these were suspended by the Algerian government in 1997 and resumption only agreed for 2000. The most important economic links with Mauritania, one of the most aid-dependent states of all the 71 African, Caribbean and Pacific (ACP) states, is through the Cotonou convention. However, the EU has also signed sectoral trade agreements with Mauritania – for instance the 1996–2001 fisheries agreement that permitted increased EU fishing in Mauritania's waters – allowing compensation of 267 million ECU for this privilege.

Actors, instruments, legal bases and decision-making procedures

The Council and Commission were both active but the southern Mediterranean member states, particularly Spain, Italy and France, were heavily involved in shaping policy. The European Parliament has also sometimes played a part in trade relations. Under the provisions of the 1987 Single European Act, for instance, the European Parliament must give assent to the financial protocols and in 1992, because of human rights considerations, the Parliament delayed agreement to the Moroccan financial protocol for ten months. Trade cooperation agreements provided the major instrument of policy, until these were replaced by the Euro–Mediterranean association agreements. The association agreements are structured around regular ministerial meetings in an Association Council as well as meetings of officials in an Association Committee. The legal foundation of the agreements with the Maghreb was provided by Article 310 (ex Article 238).

Development Cooperation

All the Maghreb states except Libya were entitled to development aid. Programme aid for Algeria, Morocco and Tunisia was allocated via the financial protocols of the cooperation agreement and for the latter two, after the signing of the Euro–Mediterranean association agreements, by way of the accompanying conventions. Financial assistance totalled just over 2.5 billion ECU in a combination of grants and loans between 1976 and 1996. Between 1978 and 1996, Morocco received 1,091 million – with 574 million from the Community budget and 518 million from the European Investment Bank compared to Algeria's 949 million – with the rest allocated to Tunisia. Post-1996, the MEDA programmes allocated financial support with committed funds for Morocco between 1996 and 1998 of 630 million Euros and for Tunisia of 458 million. Algeria was allocated 250 million Euros under the MEDA programme for 1996 to 1998. Development aid priorities have changed since the mid-1990s. Prior to the introduction of the MEDA programmes, the sectoral priority, particularly in Tunisia and Morocco, was for the support of agriculture and rural development. Since the mid-1990s, assistance is directed towards the creation of 'efficient' and 'open' economies with support for structural adjustment forming the core of Union development efforts. Algeria, Morocco, Tunisia and Mauritania have also benefited from food aid and Algeria has received humanitarian aid for refugees and as a response to natural disasters.

Aid for Mauritania was channelled through the Lomé conventions. Between 1976 and 2000, Mauritania received some 630 million Euros assistance from the Community. Since the mid-1980s, the Union prioritised road infrastructure, rural development and health for development aid. During the late 1990s, priorities shifted slightly in that urban and rural infrastructure continued to receive support as did rural development and the environment – new priorities, however, included the strengthening of institutions and the rule of law and support for structural adjustment. Mauritania has also received compensation for lost export earnings through the STABEX scheme.

Actors, instruments, legal bases and decision-making procedures

The Commission is responsible for monitoring and implementing development aid and another important participant has been the European Investment Bank (EIB). Over half the total of aid allocated via the financial protocols to the cooperation agreements was accounted for by EIB. Instruments utilised include the financial protocols, humanitarian and emergency aid including food aid. The EU distributes large proportions of humanitarian aid via the World Food Programme (WFP) and UNHCR. It also uses as instruments of cooperation large numbers of non-governmental organisations. The legal base and decision-making procedures are the same as for the trade matters (see above) in respect of Algeria, Morocco and Tunisia. The EU generally makes policy towards Mauritania, however, within the context of the Lomé procedures and institutions – now the Cotonou agreements (see Chapter 7).

Interregional Cooperation

The European Union has been ambivalent about the benefits of interregional cooperation in its relations with the Maghreb. On the one hand the EC/EU has maintained its policy preferences for region to region cooperation schemes – supporting institutional links with the Mediterranean as well as wider links with the Arab League through the Euro–Arab dialogue (see below – the section on the Mashreq). On the other hand, despite Maghreb efforts both to constitute a regional association – the Arab Maghreb Union (AMU) – and to use the AMU as a negotiating partner with the EU, the EU's response has been lukewarm and sometimes inconsistent. The EC/EU imposed sanctions on Libya from 1986 and the conundrum for policymakers was how to manage some form of relationship with this regional organisation in order to reap the perceived benefits of region to region partnership at the same time as maintaining Libya in diplomatic isolation. The EC supported the establishment of the AMU in 1989, but because of the Libyan issue it only ever showed signs of engaging with the AMU in the period of the 1990/91 Gulf

War when EC leaders became concerned at the strength of Maghreb public opinion against allied intervention and were worried that energy imports might be jeopardised. In 1990 the Commission floated the possibility of a cooperation agreement but, in the aftermath of the war, the Union forsook the multilateral approach and renewed its bilateral approach to the Maghreb in the context of moves towards Mediterranean region-wide partnership (see section on the global Mediterranean policy above).

The same Gulf War pressures led to two other, eventually aborted, multilateral initiatives: the Conference on Security and Cooperation in the Mediterranean (CSCM) (1990/91) and the so-called 'Five plus Five' dialogue (1990/91). The CSCM, which would have included all Mediterranean countries and the Palestinians, was actively promoted by France, Italy and Spain. Its remit would have been to cover arms control, arms proliferation, socioeconomic inequality and migration but talks fizzled out after opposition from some Arab opinion which feared an over-preponderant role for Israel and because of lack of EU enthusiasm at the end of the Gulf War. The Five plus Five arrangement which brought together four member states – France, Italy, Portugal and Spain – plus Malta and the AMU states (called collectively the Western Mediterranean Group) was a Mitterand initiative and was meant to provide a forum for improved dialogue with the Maghreb. Working-groups on issues including debt, culture, transport and communication, food self-sufficiency and immigration were established. The dialogue petered out, however, after opposition from northern EU states who resented the possibility of paying for policies decided outside Union fora and also because of fears of intra-EU political division, particularly over the inclusion of Libya.

The pressures from powerful member states to isolate Libya had an important consequence for European Union foreign policy towards the Maghreb in that it was impossible for the EU to negotiate with the Maghreb countries as a collectivity. In the Maghreb, therefore, the Union was unable to follow its preferred foreign policy strategy towards the developing world – which was to promote regional integration and multilateral links with the EU. Attempts at promoting sub-regional cooperation and interregional cooperation were therefore eventually abandoned and subsumed into global interregional cooperation efforts with the Mediterranean region as a whole.

Actors, instruments, legal bases and decision-making procedures

Attempts to achieve interregional cooperation were not successful despite a multiplicity of actor involvement. Unlike many other examples of interregional cooperation when the Commission is the most significant actor with support from the Parliament, the Council and the member states, particularly the southern EU states, have played an important role. This is because moves to any form of inter-regional cooperation that involve Libya were politically sensitive. EC foreign ministers met with their AMU counterparts, for instance in November 1990 and November 1991, and the troika visited Libya in March 1991 to discuss, *inter alia*, the possibilities of interregional cooperation. The Commission has followed the Council's line in the Maghreb and only attempted to pursue the possibilities of interregional cooperation during the Gulf crisis.

EUROPEAN UNION RELATIONS WITH THE MASHREQ AND MIDDLE EAST (EASTERN MEDITERRANEAN)

The Mashreq states (Egypt, Jordan, Lebanon and Syria) and Israel and Palestine have all been subject to British and French colonial rule but it was contemporary political and economic rather than historical factors that forced the Union to give foreign policy priority to the region. EU policy towards the Eastern Mediterranean has been shaped by efforts to support, and sometimes initiate, proposals for resolution of the conflict between Israel and the Palestinians and Israel and her Arab neighbours – Jordan, Lebanon and Syria. It has had to take account of the priority given by the United States to the region and this has occasionally pitted EU interest in maintaining good relations with the Arab world in order to help secure its energy imports, against the necessity to retain a harmonious partnership with its major ally, the United States (see Chapter 5). Although the 'Euro–Arab dialogue' strictly speaking involved Arab states from outside the 'Eastern Mediterranean' region, it is discussed below because it evolved as a result of the Union's efforts to deal with the Arab–Israeli conflict.

Security and Defence

The Middle East has been a foreign policy priority for the Union since it was first able to act as a (more or less) coherent international actor. In 1970 the newly created European Political Cooperation mechanism (EPC) concerned itself with just two issues: the first was the Conference on Security and Cooperation in Europe (CSCE) and the second was policy towards the Middle East. During the 1967 Arab–Israeli 'Six Day War' each of the six member states had taken different positions in terms of who they would support, exposing the wide areas of political disagreement between them and their lack of a common foreign policy. During the October war of 1973, although some tentative rapprochement had been achieved, the now nine member states remained divided and were treated differentially by the Arab states. The Arab states instigated an oil embargo against those member states that supported Israel – principally the Netherlands – and at the same time instituted an oil price hike and production cut-back that affected every member state. EC leaders recognised that the lack of an effective policy towards the Arab–Israeli conflict could have extraordinarily deleterious repercussions for member-state economies and it is this that has since propelled Middle East policy to its position as centrally important to the security concerns of Union foreign policy. The Arab oil embargo eventually petered out but EU efforts to develop a credible Middle East policy continued through the 1970s with various statements issued that repeatedly stressed both Israel's right to security and the Palestinian right to some form of self-determination. The EC and the Arab League initiated the Euro–Arab dialogue subsequent to the December 1973 Copenhagen Summit where discussions had taken place between the EC Heads of State and Government and a delegation of Arab foreign ministers (see interregional cooperation below). The Euro–Arab dialogue continued to provide a sometimes sporadic forum for multilateral political and economic consultation up until the mid-1990s. It did not provide, however, a base for Union initiatives within the Middle East conflicts – partly because of Israeli and US opposition and partly because of internal disagreement as to what that role should be. European attempts to play a political role in the search for peace were also sidelined by the unexpected Camp David process in which President Sadat of Egypt first visited Jerusalem in 1977 and then signed a peace agreement with Israel in 1979 under the auspices of the United States government. Considerable Israeli, United States and Egyptian pressure was placed on the EC to both support Camp David and to desist from any unilateral intervention.

The EC more or less accepted its subordinate position, although it did issue what became a famous statement of principles in the 1980 Venice Declaration, which reiterated the EC's commitment to a

settlement of the conflict through adherence to the relevant UN resolutions by all parties, and which restated the EC belief that both
Israel's right to security and Palestinian rights to self-determination
should be met in a process in which the Palestine Liberation Organisation (PLO) would be 'associated with the negotiations'. The EC
also promised a new political initiative in the peace process but in
practice were unable to offer much of substance given US and Israeli
hostility. Instead the EC found itself reluctantly continuing to
support US initiatives and gave its backing in 1981 to the decision
of France, Italy, the Netherlands and Britain to send troops as part
of a US-led deployment of a Multinational Force (MFO) whose
objective was to ensure the Israeli military withdrawal from the Sinai
agreed under the Camp David process. The EC continued to make
diplomatic *démarches*, for example after the 1982 Israeli invasion of
Lebanon, which also resulted in agreement to delay signing the
Financial Protocol with Israel. In general, however, the EC failed to
play a significant part in securing amelioration of the conflict or in
making any significant contribution to peace.

The subordinate position of the Union as an actor in the international politics of the Middle East was confirmed after the 1990/91
Gulf War. The United States was the unquestioned major power in
the region as it led the postwar peace process between the Palestinians and Israel and the Arab states and Israel. Although the EU made
the peace process the subject of a CFSP 'joint action', in practice, it
had to settle for providing humanitarian and economic assistance,
particularly to the newly established Palestinian territories as well as
providing technical and financial assistance in the 1996 Palestinian
elections. This does not mean that the economic issues in which the
EU continued to play a full role were not of immense strategic
importance for both the EU and the states of the region. The EU's
policies and activities on trade, investment and future water
resources and its contribution to creating a possible Middle East free
trade area and market (see trade and interregional cooperation
sections below) – providing some political settlement can be
maintained – are crucial for both maintaining that settlement and
helping to secure EU objectives including the maintenance of peace
and stability in the region. More detailed objectives are to try to
persuade Israel to change its policies on settlements in the Occupied
Territories and to encourage the Arab countries to refrain from trade
boycotts of Israel. The EU also declared its intention, in April 1996,
to produce a 'European plan' for the reconstruction of Lebanon after

the break-out of armed conflict with Israel earlier that year. It also welcomed Israeli withdrawal from southern Lebanon in compliance with UN resolutions in 2000.

Security concerns also led the Union's approach to Syria, with the United Kingdom insisting on an arms sales boycott and some diplomatic sanctions because of alleged support by the Syrian state for international terrorism. The Union also complained that Syria was not doing enough to allow the full expression of human rights domestically. In 1992, for instance, the European Parliament delayed giving assent to the Syrian financial protocols to protest human rights conditions in Syria. It was because of these overriding security concerns that, although Syria was a participant in the Barcelona process, it remained difficult for the Commission to include Syria in the wave of bilateral negotiations it conducted with the other states involved in the Euro–Mediterranean dialogue. It was only in 1997 that the Commission could suggest that negotiations should be opened with Syria to try to produce a 'Euro–Mediterranean' agreement with discussion continuing through 2000.

Actors, instruments, legal bases and decision-making procedures

The major actors were the member states in the Council with the French and the British playing key roles. Different foreign ministers holding the Presidency have engaged in active diplomacy in visits to the region for instance in the wake of the Venice Declaration in 1980 and 1981. Different troikas have subsequently attempted active intervention, for example with a visit to the region in April 1996 in an attempt to broker a cease-fire between Lebanon and Israel. A special envoy to the Middle East, whose brief was to coordinate Union activity to facilitate the peace process, was first appointed in 1996. The Parliament sent an 18-member Parliamentary delegation to the Mashreq countries and the Gulf states and has issued several opinions on the Middle East conflicts. Instruments ranged from the decentralised use of the military through the four member states (operating in the Sinai) – to active and declaratory diplomacy – to aid, sanctions and trade-related inducements. Member state military forces in the Sinai operated under national flags although EPC 'cover' was provided in the diplomatic statement of support for the action.

The CFSP mechanisms provided a framework for Middle East policy with the October 1993 Brussels European Council agreeing that the proposed Joint Action in the Middle East (agreed in April 1994) should use political as well as 'economic and financial means provided by the Union in support of a comprehensive peace plan'. The legal bases for Union activity and the ancillary decision-making procedures are located within 'Title V' clauses of the Treaty on European Union although Community competencies provide the legal foundation for the economic instruments utilised to support security objectives. Article 310 (ex 238) provides the basic enabling framework.

Trade

In 1998 Israel was the Union's eighteenth most important export market (around the same level of importance as South Africa and Singapore). None of the Mashreq states were in the top 20 of importing or exporting states to the Union – with Egypt closest at trading partner number 39 in terms of Union imports and placed at 25 in terms of its value as a recipient of exports. The EC signed a free trade agreement with Israel in 1975 and trade agreements with Egypt, Jordan and Syria in 1977 and Lebanon in 1978. The Israeli agreement guaranteed free trade in the industrial sector and it was accompanied by a financial protocol guaranteeing economic aid in the form of loans. In 1978 the agreement was supplemented by an ancillary protocol on industrial, scientific and agricultural cooperation. The Mashreq agreements were similar to those forged with Maghreb states in that they included trade concessions and aid codified in accompanying financial protocols.

In the wake of the new 'Euro–Mediterranean' policy concluded at the 1995 Barcelona conference, the EU focused on trying to negotiate Euro–Mediterranean agreements with Israel, Egypt, Jordan and Lebanon. Trade policy is integral to the Union objective of creating a Euro–Mediterranean zone of peace and stability as the promotion of an ever-widening and deepening free trade area is seen as a crucial underpinning element for political stability.

Israel was the first to sign a Euro–Mediterranean agreement, in June 1995, but ratification was delayed, partly because of French and Belgian concerns over lack of progress in the peace process, and the treaty did not enter into force until June 2000. Jordan signed an agreement in 1997 while negotiations with Egypt were concluded in 1999. In addition the EU signed a 'Euro–Mediterranean Interim Association Agreement' with the Palestine Liberation Organisation (PLO) representing the Palestinian Authority in the West Bank and the Gaza Strip in February 1997, the agreement coming into force in July 1997. Economic and trade clauses were accompanied by commitments to political dialogue. Negotiations have also taken place with

Syria but were partly delayed by the unwillingness of President Assad to sign up to the EU's version of democracy, human rights and the rule of law – a prerequisite of the Euro–Mediterranean accords. These may accelerate in the wake of President Assad's death in 2000 although there still remain differences of political culture and system between the Union and Syria which could mitigate against a speedy improvement in trade relations.

Actors, instruments, legal bases and decision-making procedures

The Commission takes the lead on trade policy towards the region although it has worked closely with the Council given the inextricably interwoven 'high' and 'low' politics of the Middle East. Similarly to the Maghreb, trade cooperation agreements provided the major instrument of policy, until these were replaced by the Euro–Mediterranean association agreements. Also as with the Maghreb, association agreements are structured around regular ministerial meetings in an Association Council comprising ministers and an Association Committee made up of officials. The legal foundation for trade agreements is Article 310 (ex Article 238).

Development Cooperation

Aid to the Mashreq and Israel, similarly to the Maghreb, was initially channelled through the financial protocols to the trade agreements. Renegotiated agreements with Israel and the Mashreq states after Spanish and Portuguese accession brought increased financial aid so that the Mashreq states received in total just under 2.5 billion ECU in grants and loans up until 1996. Israel was allocated 133 million ECU in the same period. Between 1995 and 1999 a further 4 billion Euros were allocated to Egypt, Jordan, Lebanon, Syria and the West Bank and Gaza – with just over 2 billion as grants from the Union's budget and the balance provided through European Investment Bank loans. By far the biggest tranche of assistance from both the Community's own budget and from the EIB went to Egypt – 40 per cent and 54 per cent, respectively. Regional projects were allocated the next biggest slice of Community funding at 20 per cent, but with nothing for regional projects from the EIB. Syria received the least benefit from the financial protocols – being allocated just 4 per cent of the Mashreq share of financial assistance between 1995 and 1999 and nothing from the European Investment Bank.

The West Bank and Gaza have, since 1995, received around 600,000 million Euros in grants and loans. Israel has not benefited from the MEDA programme and therefore from the main source of European Union assistance since the mid-1990s – according to the Union because its level of economic development is so high that it does not qualify. Israel is entitled, however, to participate in regional aid through the MEDA programme and does benefit from small-scale assistance through the Union's Investment Partners scheme – designed to encourage small and medium-sized enterprises.

Apart from development aid, the sub-region has also benefited from humanitarian and emergency assistance. The West Bank and Gaza have been major recipients of food aid and humanitarian assistance. In addition, the Commission also makes an annual contribution to UNRWA of just under 50 million ECU for Palestinian refugees. Egypt, Lebanon and Jordan have also received food aid, with Egypt and Jordan being allocated specific assistance in the aftermath of the 1990/91 Gulf War when they had to cope with absorbing returning workers from Iraq and Kuwait and, at the same time, assist in the general refugee crisis precipitated by the war. In total, from September 1990 to the end of 1991, the EC foreign ministers agreed an expenditure of 1.5 billion ECU to assist Egypt, Jordan (and Turkey) – the neighbouring states most affected by the Gulf War.

Actors, instruments, legal bases and decision-making procedures

Actors, instruments, legal bases and decision-making procedures are similar to those involved in relations with the Maghreb. The Commission is responsible for monitoring and implementing development aid along with the European Investment Bank (EIB). The European Parliament has been visible in that it used the competencies first given to it by the Single European Act to make political points in the case of both Israel and Syria; in the case of the former the EP delayed ratification of the 1988 agreement and in the case of the latter the 1992 agreement on financial assistance. In respect of Israel the Parliament was trying to secure fairer treatment for the Palestinians. In the case of Syria the Parliament argued that the Syrian state did not respect human rights. In addition to the distribution of humanitarian aid through the World Food Programme (WFP) and UNHCR, the EU also channels aid through the United Nations Relief and Works Agency for Palestine Refugees in the Near East (UNRWA). Non-governmental organisations are also important partners for the EU in the distribution of aid in the region. During the 1990/91 Gulf War the EC and the member states worked closely together with two-thirds of the aid agreed derived from member states' budgets and one-third from the Community budget. Instruments utilised are the financial protocols, humanitarian and emergency aid including food aid. The legal base and decision-making procedures follow the trade agreements and the ancillary protocols.

Interregional Cooperation

There has been no real attempt at promoting regional association among the Mashreq states and, although there have been attempts to develop economic interrelationships between the Arab states and Israel post the Madrid peace process, there are no immediate possibilities of regional integration. The nearest that the EU has come to interregional cooperation with the states of the Mashreq (excluding Israel) is in the Euro–Arab dialogue that started in 1973.

The Euro–Arab dialogue (EAD) involved the EU in cooperation links with all the states of the Arab League but its political focus was that of the Arab–Israeli conflict, most particularly the Palestinian–Israeli conflict. The EC foreign ministers first met Arab League leaders at the December 1973 Copenhagen summit of the Community Heads of State and Government but the institutionalised dialogue between them started in 1975. EC interest in the dialogue was motivated by worries about access to Arab oil exports but the Arab side insisted on political linkage between the Arab–Israeli conflict and economic issues. The EC attempted to handle these alternative emphases by organising economic dialogue through Community and treaty-based competencies and political statements through the mechanisms of EPC.

In practice, however, the EC was propelled into a political position on the conflict which separated it from the United States and Israel in favour of a more conciliatory position towards the Palestinian claims for self-determination (see Chapter 5). In 1975 for instance the EC accepted from the Palestinian Liberation Organisation (PLO) a formula that would allow participation in the Euro–Arab Dialogue (EAD) – at the time an immensely controversial decision. The EAD remained reasonably active in the 1970s in respect of discussions over economic cooperation but virtually ceased to operate after the beginning of the Camp David process in 1979 that split the Arab League. The assassination of Egypt's President Sadat in 1981 consolidated the divisions in the Arab world and progress within the EAD remained slow throughout the 1980s. President Mitterand attempted to reactivate the dialogue in 1989 and an agreement was made to pursue new economic, social and cultural projects. The agreed restructured EAD did not materialise, however, as the outbreak of the 1990 Gulf War radically changed the international and regional environment. The United States became the unquestioned leader of Western policy towards the Middle East and, in the wake of the war, continued to set the terms of reference for international political and economic cooperation with the Middle East. The EAD was then subsumed by the EU into the new 'Barcelona process' that attempted to develop a pan-Mediterranean partnership with the EU (see above).

Actors, instruments, legal bases and decision-making procedures

Both Commission and Council have been active in the Euro–Arab Dialogue. The EAD established a General Committee to oversee the dialogue – which was supported by a series of working-groups, specialised committees and a coordination committee. The political instruments were those of diplomatic *démarches*. No trade or economic agreements were concluded. Legal bases reflected the respective competencies of treaty and EPC/CFSP modes of operation with the consequent mix of both intergovernmental and supranational decision-making procedures.

EUROPEAN UNION RELATIONS WITH THE GULF REGION

The EU developed a regional approach to the Gulf states and their neighbours in that it has promoted interregional cooperation as a mechanism of policy implementation, particularly with respect to its main concern in the region which is the security of oil supplies. Interregional dialogue with the Gulf Cooperation Council member states of Saudi Arabia, Kuwait, Bahrain, Oman, Qatar and the United Arab Emirates is accompanied by bilateral institutional arrangements with Yemen. Relations with Iraq and Iran have not been institutionalised and have remained conflictual. *Security and defence* concerns have been dominant in the EC/EU's relations with the Gulf and these are in turn inextricably tied up with the EC/EU's concern to maintain the security of its *trade* in terms of energy supplies from the Gulf region. *Development cooperation* is not a priority given the wealth of the Gulf states although Yemen is the exception as an aid recipient and some humanitarian assistance has been given to Iran and Iraq. *Interregional cooperation* has been utilised as a mechanism of maintaining dialogue in respect of Union security concerns and has been organised via institutional cooperation established with the Gulf Cooperation Council (GCC) in 1979. Given the dominant security motivation for EU policy in this region there remained a significant overlap between all issue-areas and, therefore, the actors, legal bases and decision-making procedures utilised in each issue-area. This overlap is mirrored in the structure of the following sections. The four issue-areas are discussed separately but – given the interrelationship of policy implementation – the subsidiary sections on actors, instruments, legal bases and decision-making procedures are combined and amalgamated.

Security and Defence

British colonial dominance of the Gulf region ended with British Prime Minister Harold Wilson's decision to withdraw 'east of Suez' in the early 1970s. Subsequently, during the Cold War, both the US and the USSR attempted to wield influence but, post-1989, the US remains the most important world power in the Gulf and US interest remains high given the importance of Gulf oil imports for the US economy. Within the Gulf, security issues have been characterised by jostling for regional dominance by Iraq, Iran and Saudi Arabia with the additional tensions caused by the persistent Arab–Israeli conflicts making for a backdrop of permanent tension. The Union has not seriously challenged US pre-eminence in the Gulf. It has been prepared to play an ancillary role to the US in respect of security issues, even if it has not always reacted with the alacrity that the US might have wished. In the 1979/80 Iranian hostage crisis, for instance, when over 60 US citizens were held hostage in Teheran by the revolutionary guards, the EC only reluctantly agreed to join the US in implementing sanctions on Iran and then, because of domestic opposition within the member states, had problems in implementing the limited measures agreed.

The two major security issues with which EC/EU members were directly involved were handled outside EC/EU fora. The first was the 1987/88 mine-clearing operation in the Gulf in which British, French, Italian, Dutch, Belgian and German navies (with some financial support from Luxembourg) contributed to safeguarding oil tankers – organised and coordinated by the WEU. The second was the 1990/91 Gulf War – formally led by the UN if in practice by the United States. In the aftermath of the war the EU and the member states continued to support the UN embargo on exports to Iraq – with some exceptions made for humanitarian aid supplies.

The EC imposed limited sanctions on Iran after the taking of the US hostages in 1979 but in 1991, after Iran condemned Iraq's intervention in Kuwait, it restored high-level diplomatic contacts. In 1992, it attempted an independent initiative towards Iran when it experimented with what it called 'critical dialogue' in the hope of safeguarding trade relations at the same time as exerting some diplomatic influence. However, following the findings by German courts in 1997 that the Iranian authorities had been involved in acts of individual terrorism the Union suspended the dialogue, and instituted diplomatic sanctions against Iran. It suspended ministerial visits to and from Iran, agreed not to supply visas to Iranian military and intelligence personnel and attempted to exclude Iranian personnel from entry to Europe. It also confirmed an EU ban on arms sales to Iran. The EU has also engaged in diplomatic representations to Iran – for example in its repeated condemnation of the death sentence imposed by *fatwa* on the British author, Salman Rushdie.

Relations improved again in the late 1990s after the election of President Khatami in 1997, and in 1998 troika meetings at the level of deputy minister started to take place with Iranian counterparts. Political discussions take place in the context of the troika meetings and Iran has requested that the relationship be intensified in the form of a cooperation agreement. Union policy was to argue that if further 'reform' takes place in Iran, a cooperation agreement might be possible.

Trade

European Union trading interests in the Gulf region relate mostly to oil and energy products and are therefore of immense strategic and security importance for EU member states. Only the Gulf Cooperation Council states and Yemen, however, have contractual trade relations with the Union – leaving Iran and Iraq out of the Union's global network of cooperation and association agreements. Because of the high demand for oil and gas in the Union, the lack of contractual relations has not prevented trade in those products. Even trade with Iraq, which suffered international sanctions since the 1990/91 Gulf War, has increased in recent years. Trade between the two virtually ceased between 1991 and 1996 but subsequent to the easing of restrictions in 1997 trade restarted so that by 1998 the Union imported 2.28 billion Euros-worth of Iraqi exports – almost all of this being oil. Exports to Iraq also rose but not to the same levels so that in 1998 the Union sent exports worth just under half a billion Euros to Iraq. In addition, despite the political frictions with Iran, it remains an important source of the Union's oil and natural gas.

The Gulf Cooperation Council states – that is Bahrain, Kuwait, Oman, Qatar, Saudi Arabia and the United Arab Emirates – have much more regular trade relations with the Union than either Iran or Iraq. They provide 23 per cent of total Union oil imports and in addition remain the Union's fifth largest export market – worth around 27 billion Euros in 1999. Exports are composed of machinery, transport equipment, other manufactured goods and food. Frictions persist in the relationship, however – one persistent and unresolved bone of contention being restrictions on access to EU markets for Gulf petrochemical products. The Union has tended to make concessions when precipitated to do so by security imperatives (in 1987/88 at the climax of the Iran/Iraq war and in 1990 during the Gulf War) but once these security crises have been resolved, the EC has pulled back from these concessions.

Perhaps the least security-related of the Union's trade relations with Gulf states are those with Yemen which were institutionalised in a commercial, development and economic cooperation agreement which came into force in 1998. The agreement was concluded in 1998 and provides a framework for trade relations which in 1998 comprised 600 million ECU of exports to Yemen from the Union at the same time as the Union imported about 100 million ECU-worth of Yemeni products.

Development Cooperation

Given the wealth of most of the Gulf region, development cooperation has not been a major feature of the relationship although humanitarian aid, for instance, was donated to Iran in the wake of the March 1997 earthquake. Iran has also been provided with assistance designed to help with its 2 million refugee population. Yemen and Iraq are, however, the major recipients of aid in the region. Prior to the comprehensive agreement of 1998, the Union had signed a development cooperation agreement with the former (North) Yemen Arab Republic in 1984. This agreement was consolidated in an exchange of letters in March 1995 after North and South Yemen came together to form the Republic of Yemen. It has received food aid and has also received development cooperation financing. Between 1977 and 1998 Yemen received around 180 million ECU which financed some 59 development projects – the most important of which are those designed to improve food security.

Since 1991, the Union has provided Iraq with 242 million Euros-worth of humanitarian aid. This assistance has been provided outside the 'oil for food' facility where the United Nations has allowed Iraq to sell oil to buy food. The Union recognised that this facility has not helped to respond to the basic needs of those suffering from the breakdown of health and social services in Iraq. A Commission document pointed out that 'the end of the embargo is a prerequisite to a solution of the problem it has created'. In 1999 the Commission responded further to these humanitarian concerns by allocating 2 million Euros to supply essential medicines, to help children's institutions and to help provide basic sanitation in Baghdad.

Interregional Cooperation

The Union chose to develop interregional cooperation with the Gulf Cooperation Council states because these countries are important sources of oil and gas supplies – containing 45 per cent of global oil reserves. As the Union, particularly after the Maastricht Treaty, was legally obliged to promote human rights and liberal democratic principles, it would be very difficult for the Union to develop bilateral relations with Saudi Arabia – the most important of the GCC states – because of its problematic human rights record. The Union has attempted to act independently of the United States so as to maintain a distinct and discrete presence as a 'reliable partner' for the Gulf states and to do this has sought an institutionalisation of interregional cooperation with the Gulf Cooperation Council (GCC).

The EC encouraged the Gulf states to form a regional organisation. The GCC was established in 1981 and was dominated by Saudi Arabia which sought to consolidate its regional hegemony in the wake of the start of the 1980–88 Iran/Iraq war. Both Saudi Arabia and the five small emirate states which were the other founder members agreed to exclude Iran and Iraq and the two Yemens – partly because of the then Marxist influence in Yemen but arguably also because Yemen remained poor and undeveloped compared to the rich oil-producing GCC states. All six GCC members were anxious to build an institution that could help prevent insurrectionary 'spill-over' from the post-1979 Iranian revolutionary state. The US which, after the 1979 Soviet invasion of Afghanistan, wanted to find ways to buttress Saudi Arabia, the last remaining US ally of any size and strategic significance in the Gulf region, also supported the formation of the GCC.

It was not until 1988, however, that the GCC–EC agreement was signed – allowing for economic cooperation in agriculture, fisheries, industry, energy, science, technology, investment and trade. The agreement, concluded in 1989, did not contain any resolution to the petrochemical dispute. In practice, however, the substantive achievement of the dialogue for GCC states was not in the economic clauses of the agreement. Not only did the EU continue to protect its own petrochemical industries against Gulf exports but, in the early 1990s, proposed a carbon/energy tax which GCC states considered would directly reduce demand for their oil, thus damaging their export interests. The GCC/EU dialogue remained, however, a useful venue for the discussion of joint security concerns. The Union, for instance, welcomed the GCC initiative to develop joint security arrangements with Egypt and Syria in 1991 at the end of the Gulf War. The dialogue also provided a forum for exchange of views on security issues in the wider Middle East – for example, the Palestinian issue, Lebanon, the European claims against Libya in respect of the Lockerbie bombing, and instability in north Africa.

Actors, instruments legal bases and decision-making procedures

The initial proposal for EC dialogue with the Gulf region in 1979 came from Hans-Dietrich Genscher the then German foreign minister. Subsequently, both Council and Commission have been involved in their respective spheres of influence – that is in terms of issuing diplomatic *démarches* (the Council) and negotiating the 1988 cooperation agreement (the Commission). There is a Parliamentary delegation to the Mashreq and the Gulf states and the Parliament has occasionally made its views known on issues pertaining to the Gulf, although it has not been a major actor in EU policy towards the region. EU–GCC trade negotiations are carried via the framework of the GCC agreements and political dialogue is undertaken through regular ministerial meetings between EU and GCC foreign ministers. EU–GCC negotiations are conducted via the joint cooperation council set up by the 1988 agreement. EU–Yemeni relations are carried out via the joint EC/Yemen committee in which the EU is represented by a senior official from the Directorate General responsible for external relations. The instruments used have ranged from the diplomatic *démarches* to the use of sanctions (with Iraq and Iran) to aid (to Yemen). The legal base for the 1988 cooperation agreement with the GCC is provided by Article 133 (ex 113) and Article 308 (ex 235). For the Yemen agreement, the legal bases are provided by Article 133 (ex 113) and Article 300 (ex 228).

SECURING OIL AND SECURING PEACE

The objectives of EU foreign policy have been dominated by the twin requirements of securing oil supplies and economic markets, and trying to help bring peace to the region. The Union has more or less accepted its subordinate political role to the United States in this region but that has not prevented it intervening to further its own political and economic interests as far as possible. Policy has been carried out through a range of competencies and different actors have taken key roles depending on the exigencies of policy and circumstance.

Guide to Further Reading for Chapter 6

For a detailed and authoritative work on the aid dimension of EU policy towards the South, which discusses some of the countries mentioned in this chapter and the next, see Enzo R. Grilli, *The European Community and the Developing Countries* (Cambridge: Cambridge University Press, 1993). For a detailed tabulation of EC foreign policy activities from 1958 to 1985 which includes specific reference to agreements entered into with the countries discussed in this chapter and the next see Roy H. Ginsberg, *Foreign Policy Actions of the European Community* (Boulder: Lynne Rienner, 1989).

For a useful review of early EC Mediterranean policy see Kevin Featherstone, 'The Mediterranean Challenge: Cohesion and External Preferences', in Juliet Lodge (ed.), *The European Community and the Challenge of the Future*, first edition (London: Pinter, 1989). For a more theoretical look at the same period see the chapter on 'EC-Mediterranean Basin Relations' (Chapter 5) in Roy H. Ginsberg, *Foreign Policy Actions of the European Community* (Boulder: Lynne Rienner, 1989). For a very comprehensive exposition and analysis of relations with the Arab world see Yousif Maloud Mohammed Shakona, 'The Arab Regional Organizations' Relations with the European Community', University of Kent (unpublished doctoral thesis, 1996). For a review of EU–Mediterranean relations which more or less avoids the stale CFSP/external relations distinction see Richard Whitman, 'Towards a Zone of Stability and Security in the Mediterranean? The EU and the Development of an EMEA', paper presented to UACES research conference, University of Birmingham, September 1995. A thorough background on EPC discussions of the

Middle East can be found in Simon Nuttall, *European Political Cooperation* (Oxford: Clarendon, 1992). See also David Allen and Alfred Pijpers (eds), *European Foreign Policy-Making and the Arab–Israeli Conflict* (The Hague: Martinus Nijhoff, 1984). For a comprehensive review of post-Gulf War EU involvement in the Middle East peace process see Esther Barbé and Ferran Izquierdo, 'Present and Future of Joint Actions for the Mediterranean Region', in Martin Holland (ed.), *Common Foreign and Security Policy* (London: Pinter, 1997). For a detailed discussion of the 1987/88 European/WEU intervention in the Gulf see Ian Gambles, *Prospects for West European Security Cooperation* (London: IISS/Adelphi papers 244, 1989).

The Commission issues a wide range of documentation on relations with countries and regions of the South. These range from the reviews of generic programmes including food aid and humanitarian assistance through to special reports on individual countries and regions. The Parliament also issues documentation in the form of reports on various subjects to its external economic relations, foreign affairs (formerly political affairs) and development cooperation committees. The internet sources are invaluable and can be obtained from the Commission's external relations, development and trade sites. Comprehensive access can be found through http://www.europa.eu.int/comm/dgs_en.htm. For one example, on humanitarian assistance to Iraq, quoted in this chapter, see www.euromed.net/eu/iraq_en.htm.

7 The European Union and the Distant South

The European Union has had a series of extensive links with poorer countries separated from it by large distances and with which it has had little direct security and political interest. In geographical fact and in political interest this is the 'distant South' for the European Union. Many Union policies have been development led – most particularly in relation to the African, Caribbean and Pacific (ACP) states but also in relation to the poorer states of Asia and Latin America. Policies towards the more prosperous Asian states and towards most of Latin America have been, in the main, driven by trade imperatives. This does not mean that at different times there has not been a very strong security dimension to EU policy in respect of the distant South – simply that security has not been the overriding concern, by contrast, for instance, to relations with the neighbouring South.

This chapter first evaluates European Union relations with its longest established partners in the South – the African, Caribbean and Pacific (ACP) states, followed by relations with Asia and Latin America. A noticeable trend, apparent from the mid-1990s onwards, was the change in European Union policy to all these countries – from one which only very cautiously intervened in the internal affairs of partner states – to one where, at least for most countries, political and economic conditionality provided the *sine qua non* of all of European Union foreign policy, including development and trade relations.

EUROPEAN UNION RELATIONS WITH THE AFRICAN, CARIBBEAN AND PACIFIC (ACP) STATES

European Union links with the ACP group of states comprise its oldest and largest region-to-region link. Its antecedents lay in the founding Treaty of Rome and the commitment to consolidating 'special' relations with ex-colonies and dependent territories. EC policy had originally been driven by French concerns to maintain privileged links with overseas territories, colonies and ex-colonies (see Chapter 2) and at the same time to find a way to ensure that other member states – particularly Germany – helped to fund these ex-colonial commitments. France continued to ensure that EU policy towards the ACP received some level of priority – insisting, for instance, that a clause be inserted in the Maastricht Treaty committing the Union to support for the ACP states irrespective of claims from other developing countries (Article 179 – ex 130w).

The first institutionalised links with these territories were the two Yaoundé conventions of 1964 and 1971 (see Chapter 2). These were renegotiated after British accession to the EC in 1973 and the consequent incorporation of British former colonies and dependencies in an expanded agreement known as the Lomé convention, after the Togolese capital in which it was signed in February 1975. Subsequently three further Lomé conventions were signed, in 1979, 1984 and 1989 – the last having a duration of ten years, as opposed to the previous five-year terms. The Cotonou agreement, signed in Benin in 2000, replaced the Lomé convention, and was designed to last for 20 years with provision for revision every five years.

The first Lomé convention brought together the associated African, Caribbean and Pacific (ACP) states into an institutionalised ACP grouping. The successor Lomé conventions consolidated the ACP as a group, given the necessity for the ACP states to negotiate collectively with the EC/EU. By 2000 the ACP states had grown to 71 in number – 48 from Africa, 15 from the Caribbean and eight from the Pacific.

The EU's overall policy approach to the ACP shifted from the 1970s through to the early twenty-first century – moving from a non-interventionary approach to one which, although formally abhorring conditionality, in practice made assistance conditional on the fulfilment of agreed political and economic criteria. Economic criteria involved WTO compatibility for trade schemes, conventional structural adjustment criteria including fiscal balance (reducing public sector subsidies) and debt sustainability combined with poverty reduction targets. Political conditionality included explicit insistence on ACP adherence to human rights and democratisation policies prior to the disbursement of aid.

European Union policy towards the ACP states has not been directly concerned with *security and defence*, at least as far as the Union's own security is concerned. On occasion, however, the Union and its member states have been moved to intervene diplomatically and militarily in respect of intra- and inter-state conflicts within and between ACP states and non-ACP states and, more commonly, to offer humanitarian aid to victims of military conflict. The Union has sought to sustain and expand *trade* links but the core of the relationship is based on *development cooperation*. Relationships were extensively institutionalised in a network of formal and treaty-based arrangements and these are discussed in the section on *interregional cooperation*. Given the large numbers of states involved, there is no attempt to summarise every single Union activity and policy towards the ACP states. Instead the following sections discuss the most significant of EU policies and activities in respect of ACP states themselves and in respect of the ACP as a regional grouping.

Security and Defence

The Union has had no significant or sustained direct security and defence interests in the ACP states. It has never developed a comprehensive security policy to this very disparate group of states and has not seen the need to do so. The EU became involved in security-related problems in individual ACP states although not because it was concerned about direct threats to the security of the EU and the member states. Instead the EU has tended to become involved as a response to political conflicts that have engaged the attention of the international community as a whole and where it has seen itself as playing a part in an international effort at mediation or conflict resolution. The most prominent of these international crises, within or directly affecting what are currently ACP states, were the internal conflicts in southern Africa and the October 1983 invasion of tiny Grenada (population 100,000) by the United States.

The most notorious of the African crises was the long-running conflict in South Africa which saw the majority Black population fight White Boer governments to try to attain human rights denied to them by the apartheid regime and which was only resolved in the early 1990s with the release of Nelson Mandela from prison, the abolition of apartheid and the installation of a democratically elected government. The EC's strongest response towards the apartheid regime had been its 1977 decision to impose a *Code of Conduct* on EC firms operating in South Africa but, on the whole, its reaction was muted. It applied only limited economic sanctions, in 1986, and supplied economic aid to the victims of apartheid but it was constrained in its ability to take stronger action because of internal dissension within the Council, between the member states, as to what might be an appropriate response to the apartheid government. After the abolition of apartheid, the Union maintained some involvement in South Africa, however, committing itself to a 'joint action' within the terms of the Common Foreign and Security Policy provisions in December 1993 in support of the first democratic elections in South Africa. Further support for the transition period was given through the extension of the Union's 'Special Programme for Assisting the Victims of Apartheid' – previously allocated through the churches and NGOs – to government as well as to non-governmental partners.

Other internal conflicts in Africa in the 1970s involved the struggles for independence against the last of the colonial regimes in southern Africa – in Angola, Mozambique, Zimbabwe and Namibia. From the late 1980s onwards, the nature of internal conflicts moved from that of battles for independence to an emphasis on the nature and legitimacy of governments. Authoritarian regimes were less tolerated by the major global powers and internal movements for democratisation gained powerful allies from abroad. The Union was, however, a cautious international actor on these issues. The pattern set was that of humanitarian assistance with sometimes the application of sanctions, occasionally accompanied by diplomatic interventions, particularly in respect of individual human rights abuses. The Union demonstrated these political concerns with the adoption of a number of common positions including those on Rwanda (1994 and 1999), Burundi (1995), Angola (1995), Nigeria (1995), Angola (1998), Ethiopia and Eritrea (1999) and the Democratic Republic of Congo (1999). Joint actions adopted included those on Nigeria (1998), Mozambique (1999) and the Great Lakes area (2000). The Union also implemented policy in respect of support for democracy and human rights by utilising measures open to it through the aid programme. In 1994, for example, eight ACP states, all of which were located in Africa, had had aid suspended or restricted for political or security reasons. These states were Gambia, Equatorial Guinea, Liberia, Nigeria, Somalia, Sudan, Togo and Zaire. In addition the EU increased its diplomatic, and sometimes economic and technical support for electoral processes, as demonstrated in presidency statements on Sierra Leone (1996), Gambia (1997), Liberia (1997) and Cameroon (1997).

Another EU intervention, expressly designed to deal with the security problems engendered by collapsed state institutions, was its operation in Somalia. This changed from a supporting role to that of the lead participant in the international effort for restoration of order and the provision of humanitarian assistance. In 1993 an EC special envoy, whose functions included leading the international community's aid and reconstruction effort through the Somalia Aid Coordination Body (SACB), was appointed to Somalia. By 1995, after the departure of the second UN mission to Somalia, the special envoy was effectively acting as the shaper and director of international conflict resolution and democratisation efforts. The EU encouraged the evolution of transitional functional authorities to oversee the provision of essential services such as health and education. It also gave institutional support to representatives of the Somali leadership on constitution-building around forms of decentralised power. By the mid-1990s, the UN, the United States and even the historical colonial powers – Italy and Britain – seemed content to allow the EU to maintain and consolidate its leadership of international efforts to bring stability to Somalia.

Outside Africa, probably the most high profile EC intervention in respect of an ACP state occurred in 1983, with the imposition of economic sanctions on the rump New Jewel Movement government in Grenada after the murder of Prime Minister Maurice Bishop. There was less harmony in respect of a collective reaction when the United States invaded Grenada in October 1983. Although EC leaders were angered by this unilateral use of force and the EC refrained from statements condemning US action, individual EC leaders including, from opposite ends of the political spectrum, France's socialist President Mitterand and Britain's conservative Prime Minister Margaret Thatcher, publicly expressed their disapproval of the United States. In the 1990s Haiti became the ACP Caribbean state of significant political concern and was the subject of two CFSP common positions – in May and later in October 1994. The first imposed limited economic sanctions and the second ended trade restrictions.

Actors, instruments, legal bases and decision-making procedures

The European Council, the Council of Ministers and the Presidency have all made various diplomatic interventions in respect of security concerns. The Commission has also done so to the extent that its reasons for suspension or restrictions of aid have been overtly political. This was also the case with the Commission's financial support for the victims of apartheid. The Parliament has passed numerous resolutions and presented reports on issues of broad concern such as the apartheid regime as well as on the political situation in various individual ACP states. In the specific case of South Africa, additional actors were the 307 EU election observers employed for the duration of the 1994 South African elections. In Somalia, the EC special envoy became an important actor in the formation and implementation of EU policy. The legal bases for EU policy have derived from both the mechanisms and procedures of EPC/CFSP. Insofar as security-related policy was implemented through the provisions of the Lomé convention, particularly with respect to suspension of aid, competencies were derived from Article 310 (ex 238).

In the particular case of South Africa, the CFSP mechanisms were utilised in support for democratisation – the subject of the Council's third joint action in 1993 – while the CFSP procedures relating to common positions were also utilised. The Joint Action was implemented directly through the Commission with DG1A managing the EU's electoral mission in South Africa. Instruments have included diplomatic statements, economic sanctions and humanitarian and development aid. Again in the specific case of South Africa, the finances expended have been significant. The Commission found 12 million ECU for Union support for the 1994 elections. The special programme to support victims of apartheid – later renamed the European Programme for Reconstruction and Development (EPRD) and extended to development work with the post-apartheid government – was allocated just under 1 billion Euros between 1986 and 1998.

In Somalia, the lead institution since 1993 was the Commission. The Commission faced legal and institutional problems in its intervention in Somalia because, although it drew its legal competencies from the Lomé conventions, the Somali state collapsed before it could ratify the fourth Lomé convention, and EU activity therefore remained on a shaky institutional foundation. Nevertheless the Commission financed 105 projects in Somalia between 1994 and 1996 – spending some 38 million ECU – and allocated 47 million ECU for the period between 1996 and 1998.

Trade

The development of increased trade between ACP states and the Union was one of the major objectives of the first Lomé convention and this objective increased in importance so that by the mid-term review of the fourth Lomé convention in 1994, both partners were insisting that trade must be at the heart of future EU–ACP cooperation – arguing that all the instruments provided by the convention should be used to improve ACP trading performance. Yet by the end of the century, when the fourth Lomé convention expired, the ACP countries' share of the Union's market had actually decreased – from 6.7 per cent in 1976 to 3 per cent in 1998. The picture is even more dismal if the comparison is made with the trends in the share of EU trade for non-ACP developing countries. Despite the lack of access to similar sorts of preferences to the ACP states, non-ACP developing states increased their share of EU trade. At the same time, the ACP share in Union imports from all developing countries decreased.

It could have been expected that the Lomé convention, which institutionalised preferential trading arrangements between the Union and the associated states in the ACP group, would have led to increased trade between the two partners. Unlike the Yaoundé agreements, which had demanded reciprocal preferential access between the EC and the associated states, the Lomé conventions had offered trade preferences to ACP states without expecting a two-way commitment. These trade preferences, combined with measures to subsidise ACP exports, trade promotion efforts and financial assistance, were specifically designed to promote increased trade with the Union and to contribute to economic development in what were, and are, some of the poorest countries of the world.

Trade preferences failed to meet EU and ACP objectives for a number of reasons. One is that although the EU argued that Lomé convention arrangements implied benefits because of duty- and quota-free access for nearly all ACP exports, these benefits were in fact diluted by broader EU trade policies. Something like 50 to 60 per cent of ACP exports, for instance, such as oil from Nigeria and Gabon, would have entered the EU duty-free irrespective of their point of origin. In addition, although the ACP states received preferences as against other developing countries for about another 10 per cent of their exports, they were not preferred over EU domestic producers who have clear marketing and access advantages. Where the ACP states have had some advantage is in the provision of tropical beverages and some fruit, particularly bananas. The conventions have supported certain agricultural exports to the EU very directly. In Lomé IV, special protocols served to maintain protected markets for sugar, bananas, rum, beef and veal. The sugar protocol was particularly important for sugar exporting ACP states in that it offered guaranteed prices for agreed quantities of exports.

Theoretically the ACP states also received preferential treatment on their exports of manufactured goods to the EU. Only a tiny part of ACP exports, however, mainly textiles and clothing from the Ivory Coast, Mauritius and Madagascar, qualified as manufactured goods. Even these preferences were not as favourable as might have been imagined given the additional preferential treatment to other developing countries under the Generalised System of Preferences scheme. They were also subject to hidden restrictions applied by the EU which refused to allow preferential treatment to ACP manufactures that included much more than 50 per cent non-local content. Given that ACP manufacturers relied almost by definition on non-local inputs because of the lack of industrialisation in their home states, the effect of such provisions was to create barriers to ACP exports of manufactured goods. In addition, the Commission placed ceilings on 'sensitive' ACP exports such as textiles. Lomé IV did little to alter these restrictive practices – allowing ACP products to contain 10 per cent of non-local content (as opposed to 5 per cent under Lomé III).

Some attempts were made in the Lomé IV convention to encourage trade diversification, towards for instance developing tourism as a source of export earnings. In addition the 1990 convention argued for the institution of a comprehensive trade strategy with an emphasis on market research, product identification, personnel training and marketing. The convention set aside funds for ACP attendance at trade fairs if part of an overall trade programme and also allocated 70 million ECU for regional trade promotion. Articles 124–138 of the Lomé convention emphasised these trade promotion strategies as being necessary to promote ACP trade with the Union, intra-ACP trade, ACP trade in international markets and improved regional cooperation in trade and services.

The inadequacies of the conventions combined with global trends towards trade liberalisation eroded the value of ACP preferences, to the extent that the negotiations on a new partnership – which ended with the signing of the Cotonou agreement of 2000 – accepted that new trade arrangements would be in conformity with WTO provisions and would be based on liberal trade principles. The new agreement phased out preferential treatment, albeit with a transition period up to 2008 and with continued assistance promised for the poorest countries. The essential nature of the Union's trading arrangements with the ACP countries irrevocably changed, from the preferential schemes of the 1970s to arrangements for the twenty-first century that were firmly based on competitive liberalism.

Actors, instruments, legal bases and decision-making procedures

The Commission has been the major actor in EU trade policy with the ACP status although the Council maintained its overall oversight of relations and the Parliament contributed its views via the institutional mechanisms established by the conventions (see section on interregional cooperation below). The instruments used include trade preferences and some financial support for trade promotion. Relations with the ACP countries are based on Article 310 (ex 238). Decision-making procedures in respect of the conventions are delineated in the section on interregional cooperation below.

Development Cooperation

Although the EU tried to push trade as the centrepiece of EU policy towards the ACP states, in practice it is the development cooperation aspects that have assumed the most significance. Without the incentive provided by the substantial sums of money provided as a means to implement the development cooperation aspects of the Lomé conventions, the ACP states would have had little reason to meet, coordinate and negotiate with the EU. Development cooperation policy is the cement that holds the edifice of EU–ACP policy together. It would also not be too much of an exaggeration to say that without the financial assistance component of the conventions, the ACP as a group would cease to exist.

Changes in EU priorities: from Lomé to Cotonou

As demonstrated above (see section on trade) the principles underlying EU development policy towards the ACP states changed over time – from those where equality and non-interference in the internal affairs of sovereign ACP states provided the distinctive *sine qua non* of policy – to that where political and economic conditionality are considered appropriate and necessary features of development assistance. In the 1975 Lomé agreement, both partners had heralded the convention as providing a new model of relations between developed and developing countries, the reason for this statement being that the ACP states were supposed to be left to decide their own development priorities without donor interference. By 1985, when the third convention came into operation, objectives were much more realistic, recognising the need to 'consolidate and diversify relations in a spirit of solidarity and mutual interest'. The reasons for this change in attitude were rooted in the changing bargaining power of ACP states. In the mid-1970s the ACP states and the EC had been aware of the seeming success of oil producers in their demands for a fairer price from the West for their exports. ACP states, and to some extent the EC also, thought that developing country producers of other commodities might be able to force higher prices from the West. By the 1980s, however, it had become apparent to all parties that not only had ACP states little negotiating power but that they were increasingly dependent on the West, including the EC and EC member states, for sources of supplementary finance, part of which was necessary to pay interest rates on debts accumulated during the 1970s.

EU policy also changed in respect of which sectors should be targeted for development assistance. Support for transport and communication, rural production, education and training, health, water, urban infrastructure, housing, trade promotion, industrialisation, emergency aid and subsidies to provide stability in export earnings (STABEX) have all remained central to ACP programmes but over the years emphases changed and new areas of cooperation were introduced. Expenditure on transport and communication, for instance, decreased in percentage terms while the priority given to the encouragement of rural production increased. Lomé II introduced a System for the Promotion of Mineral Production and Exports (SYSMIN) while additional sectors targeted for support within Lomé III included regional cooperation, and cultural and social cooperation. Lomé IV shifted emphasis further towards the more conventional focus of multilateral aid agencies (such as the World Bank) with its insertion of a budget line into the financial protocol that offered support for 'structural adjustment'. The fourth convention also included a specific budget line for aid for refugees. Other areas targeted for expenditure in Lomé IV were 'disasters' and the battle against AIDS. Lomé IV also introduced political conditionality in that, from the mid-term revision of 1995, human rights were conceived of as an 'essential' basis of cooperation such that aid could be suspended if human rights were violated in the recipient country.

The Cotonou agreement of 2000 attempted to develop a 'global' strategy which placed poverty reduction at the centre of development efforts and which also encouraged private sector and non-state actor involvement in drawing up national development programmes. Poverty reduction strategies laid heavy emphasis on supporting the private sector to promote economic development in ACP countries. They also envisaged a mix of policies to include support for economic, social and human development as well as regional cooperation and integration. Three cross-cutting themes – designed to influence all aspects of the development programme for each ACP country – were also included as development priorities. These were gender equality, environmental sustainability, and institutional development and capacity building.

STABEX and SYSMIN

Another major change from Lomé to Cotonou was the move away from specific instruments to compensate ACP states for instability in export earnings – the dedicated instruments of STABEX and SYSMIN – to a more general facility which would provide assistance only if macroeconomic stability was threatened. Both STABEX and SYSMIN had been highly valued by ACP states because they brought an element of predictability and security to export earnings and because the financial assistance given was non-reimbursable. STABEX had been designed to provide insurance to those states which were dependent on income from agricultural commodities and this was particularly important for some of the very poorest states that remained dependent on exports of just one commodity to provide the majority of their export income. STABEX funds amounted to 380 million ECU under Lomé I, 660 million ECU under Lomé II, 1,449 million ECU under Lomé III and 1,600 million ECU under Lomé IV.

SYSMIN was similarly valued in that it was an instrument designed to compensate ACP mining sectors for losses in income due to falls in the price of copper, cobalt, phosphates, manganese, bauxite and alumina, tin and iron ore, with Lomé IV extending the range of minerals to include uranium and gold. Under Lomé II and III, the SYSMIN facility amounted to 230 million ECU and 253 million ECU, respectively (Lomé I did not include support for mining), with these amounts being repayable but under very concessional terms. Lomé IV, however, provided 480 million ECU of SYSMIN support in the form of non-reimbursable aid. The SYSMIN approach was not put into place entirely from altruistic motives. It had served EU interests in that it helped guarantee supplies of minerals to EU consumers.

Financial support

The last Lomé convention was agreed for a ten-year duration (1990–2000) and its initial financial protocol of 12,000 million ECU was designed to last from 1990 to 1995. The European Development Fund (EDF) provided 10,800 million ECU of the total while the remaining 1,200 million ECU consisted of European Investment Bank (EIB) loans. The largest sums within this total were allocated for subsidies (7995 million) including 1,150 million ECU for structural adjustment and 280 million ECU for interest rate subsidies. Other budget lines included 1,500 million ECU for STABEX, 824 million ECU for risk capital and 480 million ECU for SYSMIN. Of these amounts only EIB loans and risk capital needed to be repaid – the rest was provided in the form of outright grants. The financial protocol agreed for the second half of the convention (1995–2000) amounted to 14,625 million ECU – with the EDF providing 12,967 million ECU and the EIB 1,658 million ECU.

Although the Cotonou agreement was concluded for 20 years, it was also agreed that it could be revised every five years and that the financial protocols, as with Lomé IV, should cover five-year periods. For the period 2000–05, the financial allocation through the European Development Fund is 13.5 billion Euros while an additional 1.7 billion Euros will be found from European Investment Bank resources. In addition, because of the problems that the Union has in actually disbursing development cooperation, some 10 billion Euros were left over from previous allocations which the Union also intended to commit to the ACP countries under the new Cotonou protocols.

Humanitarian and food aid

ACP states have been allocated substantial amounts of humanitarian assistance – including food aid. ACP states received 2,156 million ECU-worth of humanitarian assistance between 1986 and 1998 – compared to the largest single recipient of humanitarian aid – former Yugoslavia – of 2,222 million ECU in the same period. The main areas targeted for humanitarian assistance have been Rwanda and Burundi, Sudan, Angola, Somalia and Ethiopia – where over half of the funds allocated between 1986 and 1998 have been spent. The EU has also channelled some funds for rehabilitation of production and infrastructure and assistance for the return of displaced people and refugees.

Between 1986 and 1998, the ACP states also received some 2,643 million Euros-worth of food aid – compared to 1,269 million Euros allocated to the next largest recipient group – the newly independent states of the former Soviet Union. These overall figures, however, mask the changes in direction of food aid so as to give ACP countries a lower priority at the end of the 1990s compared to their position in the mid-1980s. In 1989 for instance the ACP counties received 248 million ECU of food aid and were the largest recipient group. In 1998, ACP states received 138 million ECU of food aid – compared to 400 ECU allocated to the Russian Federation alone.

Evaluating the record of cooperation

EU development cooperation policy and practice has been criticised for creating dependency in the ACP states and for not helping to achieve the development objectives set by itself and its partners. In addition EU aid has been criticised by the ACP states themselves as being insufficient in quantity and worth progressively less in value and in per capita terms. In the first Lomé convention, for example, 46 states with a population of 250 million received 3,462 million ECU (in 1976 figures) to cover a five-year period. The fourth Lomé convention allocated 12,000 million ECU (in 1990 figures) which had to initially cover 68 states with a population of 493 million also for five years. The Cotonou agreement covers 71 states – with an initial allocation of 15.2 billion Euros, also for five years.

Measuring effectiveness of aid programmes is, however, notoriously difficult given the multifarious domestic and external factors that determine development outcomes and it remains difficult to judge to what extent EU aid programmes have made a difference. A nuanced judgement might be that the EU has carried forward development policy in such a way as to serve its own interests – for instance in respect of securing sources of mineral supplies – but at the same time it has helped to assist some of the poorest states of the world when those states have had few alternative sources of support.

Actors, instruments, legal bases and decision-making procedures

The major actors in EU development cooperation in respect of the ACP are the same as those involved in trade. Additional actors include the European Investment Bank (EIB) and non-governmental organisations. The EU works in partnership with major intergovernmental organisations. For instance SYSMIN operations have been co-financed with the World Bank and the African Development Bank. The EU routinely implements emergency aid programmes in conjunction with NGOs and intergovernmental organisations – for instance a six-month EU-funded programme in Angola in 1994 involved 20 NGOs, the International Red Cross, UNHCR and the

World Food Programme. In the same year the EU worked with the same organisations in the Sudan, Burundi and Rwanda, among others. The European Community Humanitarian Office (ECHO) plays an important part in the implementation of emergency aid programmes – coordinating agencies and programmes both in Brussels and on the ground. One innovation by ECHO, for instance, was the installation of an air transport system, based in Kenya, to provide support for the humanitarian agencies operating in Somalia, Sudan and Rwanda.

The main instrument available to the EU is financial assistance provided mostly by the conventions but additionally through the Community's own budgetary resources including support via food aid, NGO co-financing and humanitarian assistance budget lines. The majority of the financial assistance provided for in the protocols is channelled through the EDF whose funds are generated through fixed and special quotas contributed by the member states. The EIB, on the other hand, generates its funds from commercial operations, mainly from floating loans on international capital markets. The link between the two is close, however, as although EIB loans to ACP states are supposed only to be made to commercially viable projects, the risks are offset by the possibilities of EDF interest rate subsidies which are available in the form of grants. The sums of money allocated to the ACP were made explicit in the accompanying financial protocols to each convention. The legal bases for EU development cooperation financed under the Lomé conventions arise from Article 310 (ex 238), supplemented by the provisions of the Lomé conventions themselves. Decision-making procedures are outlined in the section on interregional cooperation below.

Interregional Cooperation

EU relations with ACP states were framed around the Lomé treaties and currently are shaped by the Cotonou agreement. Instruments available through the treaties are used to implement security, trade and development policies. More recent additions to the agenda of interregional cooperation include cultural and social cooperation, and human rights – issues inserted as objectives and principles of EU and ACP cooperation in the third Lomé convention and further emphasised – particularly human rights – in the fourth convention. The treaties of 1975, 1980, 1985, 1990 and 2000 progressively brought together around half the world's developing countries including some of the poorest. The ACP states include all of sub-Saharan Africa – again including some of the poorest states in the world.

EU policy has been to maintain institutional links with the ACP states out of economic and political interest. The EU is concerned to maximise its access to markets, even if these are sometimes very small, and is anxious to maintain privileged access to commodities that are not obtainable within the EU. At the same time, the EU has considered itself since 1973 at least (see Chapter 3) as a global foreign policy player and institutional links with the ACP states comprise a part of the armoury of EU foreign policy influence worldwide. These links are highly formalised and involve all major institutions of the Union. EU interregional policy has been successful in that it has been able, by and large, to retain privileged political and economic access to ACP states. On the other hand, ACP states have also judged the relationship worthwhile, with a continuing demand for membership – so that the ACP grew from 46 countries in 1975, to 58 in 1980, to 65 in 1985 and 68 in 1990 – with Namibia, Eritrea and South Africa joining in subsequent years to take the total to 71. It remains to be seen, however, because of the Union's clear and increasing priority to Eastern and Central Europe and because the new agreement explicitly abandons preferences, if the relationship will remain important for both partners during the 20-year span of the new Cotonou agreement.

Actors, instruments, legal bases and decision-making procedures

Although the Commission engaged in much of the negotiating, the Council, with (since the Single European Act) the assent of Parliament, concludes the conventions – under the legal competencies provided by Article 310 (ex 238). The three most important of the institutions engaged in managing EU policy within the context of the conventions are the ACP–EU Council of Ministers, the Committee of Ambassadors and the Joint Assembly. The Council is the general oversight body that sets policy objectives and resolves conflicts arising out of the application of the conventions. It meets at least once a year and is composed of members of the Council of the Union, the Commission and a member of the government of each ACP state. The Presidency of the Council is held alternately by a member of the EU's Council of Ministers and an ACP government member. The Committee of Ambassadors supervises the implementation of the treaties and is composed of the permanent representative of each member state, a representative from the

Commission and the ACP Heads of Mission based in Brussels. It meets at least once every six months. The Joint Assembly is a consultative body, meeting twice a year – in the Community and in an ACP state. It is composed of a parliamentary representative of each ACP state and an equal number of members of the European Parliament. An innovation of the Cotonou agreement is the decision to decentralise administrative and financial competencies so that the Delegation *in situ* in the country concerned can make decisions in respect of certain development projects. The most significant instruments are the financial provisions of the protocols which, at the same time as providing inducements, can also be used as a source of sanctions should the EU decide to suspend aid in the pursuit of specific policies towards specified states. Once in place, the conventions themselves provide a legal framework for EU policy towards the ACP states. The conventions also set up a delineated and formal decision-making and consultation process.

EUROPEAN UNION RELATIONS WITH ASIA

Asia had not, until as recently as the mid-1990s, been an important target of European Union foreign policy. With the accelerating importance of China as a trading partner and the increasing significance of the Asian international political economy for the world economy, Asia has become much more important for the EU. The Union attempted some regionalisation of its policy towards Asia – helping to initiate the first Asia–Europe Meeting (ASEM) in 1996. ASEM was designed to bring together the major states of east Asia in a continuing (although non-institutionalised) dialogue on a variety of issues of mutual importance (see section on interregional cooperation below).

EU practice, however, has tended to divide the region into four different although not mutually exclusive spheres of interest. The first is China, in both the narrowest sense, relating to the People's Republic of China (PRC) but also since the 1997 British handover of Hong Kong to Chinese sovereignty, the wider China – including Hong Kong as well as Macao (itself becoming part of the PRC in 1999) and Taiwan. The second is the Association of South-East Asian Nations (ASEAN) comprising Indonesia, Malaysia, the Philippines, Singapore, Thailand and, from 1984, Brunei, joined in 1995 by Vietnam, Laos and Myanmar in 1997 and Cambodia in 1999. The third area of Union activity is southern Asia – including Afghanistan, Bangladesh, Bhutan, India, the Maldives, Nepal, Pakistan and Sri

Lanka and to a lesser extent Indo-China, including Cambodia, Laos, Mongolia, Myanmar and Vietnam. Southern Asia and Indo-China combine the poorest parts of the continent. Consequent on the incorporation of the states of Indo-China into ASEAN, however, it seems inevitable that policy towards these states will be subsumed into the interregional framework of EU–ASEAN relations, leaving southern Asia as a distinct region possibly attracting a more targeted and sustained EU policy. The fourth target of EU foreign policy in Asia is the Korean peninsula – including the Republic of Korea (south Korea) and less directly with the Democratic People's Republic of Korea (north Korea).

The EU treats the former Soviet republics of southern Asia, because of their continuing connections with Russia through the Commonwealth of Independent States (CIS) in the context of its pan-European strategy and, for this reason, EU policy towards these new states is discussed in Chapter 8. Union policy towards Japan is also developed in a 'non-Asian' context in that it is framed as part of policy to the OECD 'West' (see Chapter 5).

Security issues have been minimal in terms of EU relations with Asia with two exceptions. The first was in the specific case of the Soviet invasion of Afghanistan in December 1979 and the second in the context of the EU's anxiety to support ASEAN as a bulwark against the spread of Communism in South-east Asia. Much more dominant have been *trade* imperatives with *development cooperation* leading policy direction in southern Asia and Indo-China. The most visible and arguably the most successful aspect of policy towards the region has been the long-running *interregional cooperation* with the ASEAN.

Security and Defence

The EU's most high profile involvement in the region did not result in a successful outcome for its foreign policy when, in the wake of the 1979 Soviet invasion of Afghanistan, the EC's Council of Ministers, led by the then British foreign minister Lord Carrington, proposed that Afghanistan be declared neutral territory in an attempt to create the conditions for Soviet disengagement and respect for subsequent Afghan non-alignment. The Soviet Union unceremoniously rejected the proposal and the EC was left to play second fiddle in the battle between the superpowers – the USSR and the US – over the future of Afghanistan.

By comparison, a less obvious security-related involvement was the EC's decision to establish formal cooperation arrangements with the ASEAN in 1980. The ostensible purpose of the agreement was to pursue economic cooperation. The underlying objective, however, was to contain potential Vietnamese hegemonic aspirations in the South-east Asian region, given that the end of the Vietnam war in 1975 had resulted in both a historic defeat for the United States and increased regional credibility for alternatives to capitalist-free market modes of development. ASEAN states were concerned to prevent the spread of domestic Communist-nationalist movements and looked to the EC to lend legitimacy to free market alternatives that were not tainted by the legacy of US napalm and saturation bombing in the region. France, Britain and the Netherlands, the former colonial powers, were helped in their efforts to slough off their colonial heritage behind the mediation of an EC initiative towards the ASEAN led by Hans Dietrich Genscher, the powerful foreign minister of the Federal Republic of Germany – a state without a colonial past in the region.

The EU has also intervened diplomatically on a number of issues in the region. These have included interventions related to specific incidents such as the Vietnamese occupation of Cambodia in the late 1980s and Indonesia's occupation and suppression of nationalist movements in East Timor. The EU also made numerous statements about human rights in respect particularly of China, Myanmar and Vietnam but also in relation to the rest of the continent, and expressed its support for democratisation regionwide. The EU suspended Myanmar's access to its system of trade preferences in 1995 – on the grounds that Myanmar employed forced labour to produce its exports. It also insisted that unless Myanmar's human rights record improved, it would not approve an automatic accession of Myanmar to the EU–ASEAN cooperation agreement, even after Myanmar joined ASEAN. One result of this failure to agree on the status of Myanmar in the cooperation process was the postponement, in 1999, of the scheduled ministerial meeting in March 1999 between the two partners. The Parliament has also been active in this region – highlighting the conflict in Tibet and arguing for negotiations between the Tibetan religious leader, the Dalai Lama, and the Chinese government.

After the Korean nuclear crisis of 1994 that resulted in a decision by the United States, south Korea and Japan to fund the Korean Energy Development Organisation (KEDO), the European Union also joined KEDO, in 1997. The Union argued that it intended not only to support the peaceful use of nuclear energy on the Korean peninsula, but also to facilitate a political settlement in Korea. The troika mission to the DPRK in 2001 – headed by the Swedish Prime Minister and supported by Javier Solana and Chris Patten – which was designed to support the peace process on the Korean peninsula, formed an integral part of this approach.

There are some signs that the European Union is attempting, albeit tentatively, to increase its profile on security issues in Asia at the beginning of the twenty-first century. China and India join the select few states with which the European Union holds regular bilateral summits in which regional and global security issues are discussed. The Union also envisages itself playing a central role in the ASEM process – in which security and economic issues are routinely discussed.

Actors, instruments, legal bases and decision-making procedures

The key actors in what has been an issue-area of low policy salience have included the Council, and to a lesser extent the Commission and the Parliament. The Council issued *démarches* on various topics and the Commission has provided back-up, in the form of channelling trade and development cooperation towards those states seen as appropriate regional partners – either for security reasons, or more commonly out of a mix of security, economic and development rationales. The Council engages in regularised political dialogue on security issues with all its major Asian partners – including China, ASEAN, India and the Republic of Korea (ROK). Council presidencies have also used UN fora, including the General Assembly and the Human Rights Commissions in Geneva, to raise the question of Indonesia's violent occupation of East Timor (ended in 2000) and the associated abuses of human rights. The Parliament occasionally acted to draw attention to security issues through asking parliamentary questions, visits to the region and the production of parliamentary reports. The mechanism of political cooperation (EPC) and CFSP have been used to issue various statements on security issues – sometimes in combination with Community instruments. In 1996, for example, the EU agreed a Joint Action in respect of policy towards the Korean nuclear issue. It also agreed to use the competencies provided by the Euratom Treaty to conclude an agreement with KEDO. The Union has also used CFSP and Community procedures and instruments to implement policy towards Myanmar – using the procedures and instruments of the Community to effect sanctions in 1995. In 1996 the EU adopted a common position on Myanmar, reinforcing the policy in 2000, and using CFSP procedures and Presidency statements repeatedly called for the government to enter into dialogue with the leader of the opposition, Ms Aung San Suu Kyi.

Trade

The EU made some attempts to create a global Asian policy but in practice trade policies have been differentiated in respect of the four sub-regions – the wider Chinese area, ASEAN, Southern Asia and Indo-China – the least developed states of the continent – and the Korean peninsula.

China markedly increased in importance for EU trade policy throughout the 1990s. In 1991 it was the EC's eighth most important supplier but did not feature at all in the list of the EC's top 20 export markets. By 1997 China ranked as the EU's fourth most important export and import partner. China's main exports were foodstuffs, chemicals and ores while the Union exported technology, industrial plant, electrical goods, steel goods, chemicals and transport equipment. China's importance was not just in respect of its own trade potential for the European Union but because, with the incorporation of Hong Kong into the People's Republic of China (PRC) in 1997, it significantly expanded its economic capacity and attraction to foreign investors and traders. This was because Hong Kong was a viable international economic entity in itself. In 1991, for instance, Hong Kong, was already, as an independent entity from China, the EC's nineteenth most important supplier and fourteenth most important market. In 1993, the value of EU trade with China amounted to 31,000 million ECU. The analogous figure for Hong Kong was 17,818 million ECU. A trade deficit with China for that year of around 8,000 million ECU was matched by a surplus with Hong Kong of 5,000 million ECU.

The EU is particularly concerned that in the global competition for markets the United States has managed to increase trade with China at a much faster rate than the EU. The EU sees Hong Kong as its natural gateway into Chinese markets – not least because of the comparative advantage provided by the European presence prior to the handover. In 1997, for instance, of the 2,068 foreign companies which had regional headquarters in Hong Kong, 597 were based in the European Union – compared to 501 based in Japan and 344 in the United States. Post the handover, Hong Kong retained an autonomous trading capacity – supported by Beijing – which wanted to take advantage of Hong Kong's access to international markets. European Union trading relations remained strong and EU policy was to consolidate Hong Kong's trading autonomy. In 1999, Hong Kong remained the European Union's tenth largest trading partner – with the Union continuing to account for its trade with Hong Kong separately from its trade with China.

The Union had signed a trade cooperation agreement with Macao in 1992. For the EU, the Macao agreement provided a further avenue into future intensified cooperation with China. The Macao agreement was formulated in the context of the impending transfer of Macao's sovereignty to China in 1999 and the joint cooperation projects established – for example in training public administrators – were explicitly designed to facilitate the transfer.

The EC first signed a trade and economic cooperation agreement with China in 1978 – three years after establishing official relations. China was permitted access to the GSP in 1980. In 1985 the EC replaced the 1975 agreement with a more wide-ranging economic agreement which incorporated a non-preferential trade component and identified industry and mining, energy, transport, communications and technology as sectors on which cooperation should take place. Trade cooperation was disrupted, but not ended, by the 1989 Tiananmen Square killings, with only minor sanctions imposed including an embargo on arms sales and military cooperation.

The Commission took a very proactive stance towards China in the 1990s. It argued, against United States objections, that China should be permitted conditional entry to the World Trade Organisation (WTO). In addition, in 1995 it introduced a new long-term strategy towards China, designed 'to maintain stability in foreign and security relations, to integrate China into the world trading system, to support sustainable development, to help alleviate poverty, and to promote the rule of law'. The Union has supported a China–Europe International Business School based in Shanghai, an EU–China Legal and Judicial Cooperation Programme, environmental and industrial cooperation activities and has held three conferences on EU–China energy cooperation.

Taiwan remained outside the network of EU institutionalised exchange and was also excluded from access to the GSP. In addition Taiwanese exports have been heavily discriminated against with quotas, 'voluntary' export limits and tariffs used to prevent them obtaining access to the EU. Despite these constraints, in 1997, after Japan and China, Taiwan was the European Union's third most important single trading partner in Asia – with a total two-way trade amounting to 28 billion ECU. An agreement on market access was signed between these two trading partners in 1998 although the European Union and Taiwan have no diplomatic relations with each other.

EC representatives had started to make contact with *ASEAN* states as early as 1972 with ministerial meetings taking place from 1978. The EC–ASEAN Economic and Commercial Cooperation Agreement was signed in 1980 and renewed and extended in 1986 and 1990. There were, however, problems in the negotiations for a renewed agreement because of EU reservations about the human rights record of Indonesia in East Timor. EU trade policy towards ASEAN had initially been somewhat desultory – links with ASEAN were ostensibly designed to improve economic cooperation between the two yet, in practice, their primary significance was to provide international political support in the battle against Asian communism. By the mid-1990s, the principal erstwhile Communist adversary – Vietnam – was now a member state of ASEAN. The new dynamic shaping EU policy was how to find ways to take advantage of the long-standing relationship with ASEAN in order to retain and consolidate a privileged place at the centre of an economically dynamic Asia. This new Asia was increasingly shaped by sub-regional organisations – with ASEAN being at the hub of a number of interregional and intraregional cooperation efforts.

In 1997 total two-way trade between the EU and ASEAN states amounted to 94 billion ECU. The Asian financial crisis of the late 1990s had, however, a major impact on EU–ASEAN trade with Union exports down 40 per cent in 1998 from their previous year's level of 46 billion Euro, with this trend continuing into 1999. ASEAN is unusual in terms of its variation from the usual pattern of EU 'North–South' trade – which is for the EU to import commodities and to export technology and capital goods. By contrast, important ASEAN exports to the EU include electrical machinery, textiles, clothing and automobiles (from Malaysia) – although ASEAN still does export primary commodities to the EU such as palm oil, manioc and rubber.

Trade is organised on a non-preferential basis although ASEAN states were being permitted access to the GSP until the late 1990s when Thailand and Indonesia were excluded from the GSP scheme as was Singapore because of its relative level of prosperity. ASEAN states, particularly Malaysia and Thailand, had taken advantage of the GSP scheme more than most developing countries, but it is debatable as to the extent of their contribution to EU–ASEAN trade. The GSP is notoriously underused, partly because of the complexity of the scheme and partly because its utility is limited by quotas. ASEAN states have only utilised the GSP to about half its potential and ASEAN exports have benefited more from global GATT rules (the most-favoured nation – MFN clause) as from the EU's GSP. European Union policies did not practically contribute to the growth in the ASEAN states' capacity to effectively export to the European Union. The Union, for instance, actively discriminated against key ASEAN exports through preferential tariffs offered to ACP states, for example cocoa and palm oil, and also obstructed access for those agricultural commodities that were directly competitive with EU products such as rice, sugar and tapioca.

Southern Asia and Indo-China are of negligible trade importance for the EU and policy towards these states is led by development priorities (see below). Institutional links, however, do exist. Bangladesh, Pakistan and Sri Lanka have commercial agreements with the EU. India, the 'giant' of the region, has been linked to the EC through a Commercial Cooperation Agreement since 1974. It has also signed a number of trade agreements with the EC with reference to specific products such as jute. More comprehensive EC–India cooperation agreements were made in 1981 and 1992. The former combined trade and aid provisions and the latter broadened the cooperation agenda to include human rights and the promotion of the private sector.

Policy towards Vietnam, Cambodia, Laos and Myanmar looked likely to be subsumed into a generalised policy towards ASEAN after those states acceded to the sub-regional organisation although there remains resistance from the EU to the idea of allowing Myanmar to receive benefits from the EU cooperation agreement with ASEAN. Individual non-preferential cooperation agreements were signed with Vietnam and Nepal in 1995, and with Laos and Cambodia in 1997 – although the Cambodia agreement was reconsidered in the light of the coup against Prime Minister Hun Sen in 1997. Afghanistan, Bhutan, the Maldives and Myanmar do not have contractual trade relations with the European Union.

EU trade with the *Korean peninsula* is primarily trade with the ROK (south Korea). Some trade with the Democratic People's Republic of Korea (DPRK) in the north has taken place but there is little prospect of any major expansion until the political future of the Korean peninsula is resolved. EU trade with the ROK, however, quadrupled between the early 1980s and the early 1990s and by 1998 south Korea was the Union's ninth most important source of imports. In 1998, south Korea ranked as the Union's twenty-second most important export market with two-way trade reaching a total value of 25 billion ECU. This trade growth took place despite the discrimination practised by the EC against south Korean exports. Steel, chemical products, electrical and electronic equipment, metal flatware and footwear have all been subjected to 'voluntary' export restraints and Union shipbuilding has been heavily protected against the competitive Korean industry by way of subsidies to EU firms. Trade relations were only institutionalised in 1996 when the EU concluded a framework trade and cooperation agreement and a customs cooperation and mutual assistance agreement with the ROK. Trade relations have not been easy between the two partners with the Union concerned about market access and copyright protection among other things. The eleventh EC–Korea high-level consultations on trade that took place in 2000, for instance, raised a query about copyright enforcement measures on European brands. Chanel, champagne and the 'BBC's teletubbies' were picked out by European Union negotiators as being trademarks that were particularly infringed.

Actors, instruments, legal bases and decision-making procedures

The Commission has played a primary role in the development of trade strategy towards Asia. The Parliament has made its views known on human rights issues and has also issued more general parliamentary reports on the region. Instruments include the provision of bilateral and multilateral agreements and access to the GSP. The legal bases for the trade and economic cooperation agreements with China and with ASEAN are provided by Articles 133 (ex 113) and 308 (ex 235). The GSP is founded on Article 133 (ex 113). The agreement to join KEDO was founded on Article 101 of the Euratom treaty.

Development Cooperation

Asia has not been the subject of an elaborated and comprehensive EU development aid strategy – partly because the sheer size of the potential target population (2 billion in China and one billion in India) and the scale of underdevelopment has precluded an EU intervention that could make anything other than a nominal impact. The EU has focused its development cooperation policy and instruments either on discrete projects designed to meet specified sectoral objectives or as a complement to broad politico-economic objectives. An example of the former is EU support for the dairy industry in India and, of the latter, the use of development cooperation as part of its policy of 'constructive engagement and cooperation with the Chinese authorities and with Chinese society'.

Financial and technical assistance for development to Asia (and Latin America) has only been available on a systematic basis since 1976 when the Community introduced a budget line for non-associated developing countries, designed to benefit the non-ACP states and those not covered by the financial protocols attached to the agreements with the Mediterranean countries. The division of assistance between Asian and Latin American (ALA) states in the period 1996–98 meant that Asia received about 49 per cent of the total available to 39 per cent allocated to Latin America. The sums involved are very small, however, and wholly insufficient in terms of making any substantial contribution to development. The entire Asia budget for 1998 amounted to just 617 million ECU, with India, Bangladesh, China, Afghanistan and north Korea the top five recipients in the period 1996–98. The figures are equally derisory in terms of the humanitarian aid budget. Asian states were allocated just 123 million ECU in 1998 for humanitarian aid, out of a global budget of just over 936 million ECU. Afghanistan, Bangladesh, Cambodia, Vietnam and Pakistan were the chief beneficiaries. In terms of food aid, Asia, particularly India, had been the major recipient until the early 1980s, receiving up to two-thirds of global allocations. By the late 1980s, however, sub-Saharan Africa had replaced Asia as the largest recipient and by the late 1990s the former Soviet Union was the largest recipient of food aid. In 1998, Asia received 81 million ECU-worth of food aid – divided between Bangladesh, China, north Korea and a small amount for India – compared to 400 million ECU-worth of food aid for the Russian Federation.

Development cooperation with *China* is of relatively recent provenance – only starting in the early 1980s and increasing in size as China became more significant for the Union's global foreign policy, with food aid projects closely tied in to overall EU foreign policy objectives. Economic and technical cooperation funds are channelled into human resource development, business cooperation, environmental cooperation, and economic, social and legal reform and poverty alleviation. The EU states that the objective of financial assistance to China is to promote 'social reform, good governance and the rule of law'. Development projects are targeted at specific provinces – including the poorest and those that are inhabited by minority ethnic groups, for instance in Yunnan province. Tibet has also become a focus for development cooperation with the EU planning a combined health, education, environment and agricultural programme for the politically controversial province. Development projects agreed for Macao are also geared very specifically to supporting EU macro policies towards China. Priority areas are training and human resource development, culture and education, but with the core project for both sides being identified as the promotion of business cooperation. China has received some humanitarian assistance, for instance, in the provision of food, blankets and drugs for Tibetan herdsmen. Some of China's food aid has been spent on supporting the expanding dairy industry – particularly in terms of milk production.

Development cooperation with *ASEAN states* has not been a major issue-area of Union foreign policy (the more recent and poorer members notwithstanding – see below) and what aid has been allocated has also been geared towards support for the Union's overall foreign policy objectives – including the promotion of increased trade between the two regions and democratisation. In the early 1990s, for instance, the Philippines and Malaysia benefited from aid for the management of forestry resources; the Philippines from rural development schemes; Thailand from projects designed to improve infrastructure; and Indonesia received assistance to promote trade and financial cooperation. All ASEAN states are eligible for humanitarian assistance with Indonesia and the Philippines, for example, receiving help in the aftermath of typhoons, earthquakes and floods. Food aid has also been allocated to these states with both Thailand and Malaysia having benefited from this facility.

Of the states of *southern Asia and Indo-China*, India, Bangladesh and Pakistan were the preferred recipients of external cooperation (development aid and humanitarian, including food assistance) – in the period 1986–98 receiving, respectively, 1,228 million Euros, 935 million Euros and 367 million Euros. Although the poorest in per capita terms, Cambodia (267 million Euros), Laos (101 million Euros), Myanmar (24 million Euros) and Vietnam (287 million Euros) received less support. Available funds from a very restricted budget have therefore been assigned to ideologically friendly states – not the Communist or anti-Western regimes of Indo-China. With the incorporation of Indo-China into ASEAN in the late 1990s, it is likely that the Union's policy may reconsider development cooperation policy towards these states in terms of an ASEAN regional context.

Between 1986 and 1998, Afghanistan, Bangladesh, Vietnam and Cambodia received the majority of humanitarian assistance in Asia – at respectively 244 million Euros, 112 million Euros, 91 million Euros, 74 million Euros and 58 million Euros. Not surprisingly, southern Asia and Indo-China were also major recipients of food aid. Again between 1986 and 1998, Bangladesh received food aid valued at 364 million Euros, India 101 million Euros and Pakistan 68 million Euros. Food aid has been famously used in India to fund a development project which, through the sale on local markets of EU-supplied skimmed milk powder and butteroil to provide counterpart funds, finances the development of the Indian dairy industry. One further source of Union assistance has been access to a STABEX scheme that since 1987 has benefited Nepal, Bangladesh and Myanmar.

Although the sums have been small, European Union relations with Bhutan and the Maldives are almost entirely based on development and humanitarian criteria. Between 1991 and 1997 the Union allocated 33 million Euros to Bhutan, and 1.6 million Euros to the Maldives between 1993 and 1995.

As a member of the OECD, the Republic of Korea is not a target for European Union development cooperation. Its northern neighbour, however – the DPRK – benefited from EU food aid and humanitarian assistance in the late 1990s and early 2000s as it tried to cope with the food crisis caused by structural economic collapse compounded by natural disasters.

Actors, instruments, legal bases and decision-making procedures

The Commission has been the major actor in this area although the Parliament has maintained a strong interest in development cooperation with Asia. The EIB has been permitted to operate in Asia since 1992 – financing its first project in China, for instance, in 1995. The Commission has worked extensively with non-governmental organisations in the provision of development aid in Asia and, at the same time, cooperates with the UN system. Humanitarian aid to north Korea, for example, is supplied indirectly through EU funding of the World Food Programme at the same time as assistance is directed through small European NGOs. Instruments are diverse – including the financial and technical aid provided from the Community budget, support for NGOs, humanitarian and food aid, and access to STABEX. The legal bases for development cooperation with Asia are provided by Article 308 (ex 235) along with the Council framework regulation (EEC) No. 443/92 on financial and technical assistance to and economic cooperation with the ALA countries of February 1992. Humanitarian aid is provided under competencies derived from Articles 37 (ex 43), 133 (ex 113) and 300 (ex 228). Decision-making procedures are those established by the treaties and therefore have a supranational element.

Interregional Cooperation

Asia is the site of three cooperation ventures – the first with ASEAN and one of the oldest of the EU's interregional experiments – the second the incipient relationship with the South Asian Association for Regional Cooperation (SAARC) – and, thirdly, the much looser and much more recent region-to-region link with East Asia known as the Asia–Europe Meeting (ASEM). The first and the last of these ventures are the most important for the Union and have spawned numerous intra- and interregional offshoots, involving both state and business organisations – in the process serving a number of different facets of EU policy. ASEAN and ASEM have provided fora in which security issues can be discussed with the Union's key Asian partners, a means by which the EU can distinguish its own international identity, interests and policies from those of the United States and a way to promote trade and commercial links between the European Union and Asia.

The 1980 EC–ASEAN Cooperation agreement marked the institutionalisation of relations that had been evolving on an informal basis since 1972 when ASEAN had established a mission in Brussels. Formally, the subjects of cooperation include trade, economic cooperation, cooperation in science and technology, energy and rural development, refugee relief and drug prevention, treatment and rehabilitation as well as environmental protection. In practice the EU has been as concerned with the larger strategic and political issues including, during the Cold War, the prevention of the spread of communism in Asia, and post-Cold War, in ensuring a bridgehead into what EU leaders feared could become an exclusionary Asia-Pacific region dominated by the United States. EU relations with ASEAN have also provided a forum whereby the Union can, at the same time, cooperate with the United States and East Asian states on security matters. EU representatives meet regularly with ASEAN foreign ministers and the foreign ministers of all of ASEAN's dialogue partners – including the United States and Japan, Australia and New Zealand – in what is termed the Post-Ministerial Conference (PMC) to discuss regional security. Since 1994 these states and the EU have met in the more formalised ASEAN Regional Forum (ARF) which was expressly designed to consider post-Cold War security issues. By 2000 the ARF included all the major powers of the region including India, as well as external powers including the United States, Canada and Russia.

SAARC brings together India, Pakistan, Bangladesh, Sri Lanka, Nepal, Bhutan and the Maldives and was founded in 1985. It has attempted to encourage trade liberalisation between its members – ratifying the South Asian Preferential Trade Arrangement in 1995. The Union has not developed extensive cooperation with SAARC although it has given some assistance to help develop SAARC institutions.

ASEM is of much more recent origin, the first meeting taking place in Bangkok in 1996, the second in London in 1998 with the third taking place in Seoul in 2000. ASEM brings together the EU and the member states, ASEAN states and China, the Republic of Korea and Japan. Although not formalised in the sense of creating permanent institutions, the political and economic dialogue was regularised through both an agreement to meet every two years at the level of Heads of State and the establishment of supporting networks, designed to consolidate and strengthen Asia–Europe links. Heads of State have also agreed to work towards a possible Asia–Europe Cooperation Framework.

Actors, instruments, legal bases and decision-making procedures

The major actors in both EU–ASEAN and ASEM have been the Council and the Commission. The Parliament has taken some interest in SAARC and is involved with ASEAN to the extent that it meets with the ASEAN Interparliamentary Organisation (AIPO) on a regular basis but, in overall terms, it has played a secondary role in terms of policy implementation and development in respect of interregional cooperation with Asian organisations. In respect of ASEAN, an EU–ASEAN Joint Cooperation Committee, comprising senior officials, manages the link in between the annual ministerial meetings. In addition organisations promoting sectoral interests have met, such as the ASEAN–EC Business Council. ASEM has spawned a number of various offshoots including the important

Senior Officials Meeting on Trade and Investment (SOMTI), a working-group on investment promotion and an ASEM Business Forum. Projects include an Environmental Technology Centre in Thailand, an Asia–Europe University Programme, and an Asia–Europe Forum – the last based in Singapore and established in 1997. Instruments of policy range from the *démarche* issued through the CFSP mechanisms to the panoply of instruments provided by the treaties including particularly the competencies underlying trade promotion and, in some instances, development cooperation (see sections above). The legal basis for the EU–ASEAN agreement is provided by Articles 133 (ex 113) and 308 (ex 235). Agreements are concluded between the EU and ASEAN partners by consensus and this is a pattern that is followed in ASEM.

EUROPEAN UNION RELATIONS WITH LATIN AMERICA

Until the 1970s, Latin America was not very high on the foreign policy agenda of the European Union. Formal agreements were few and limited in their scope, being based around fairly narrowly defined economic objectives and none of them included political concerns. EC economic policy towards Latin America was also weak and incoherent. The EC only became systematically involved in Latin America subsequent to its intervention in Central America in the 1980s, after which it inaugurated new institutionalised relationships with Latin American sub-regional and regional groupings. By the end of the 1990s every state in Latin America, except Cuba, was involved in some form of regional institutionalised partnership arrangement with the EU.

In October 1994 the EU reformulated policy towards Latin America, offering a nuanced approach that attempted to marry economic and political objectives with appropriate instruments in a way that could accommodate policy requirements towards the differing socioeconomic and political status of the different groups of states in Latin America. The policy involved a tripartite approach. The emphasis was on aid and economic development in respect of the poorer states of Central America and Bolivia. Secondly, the middle income developing states of the Andean Community were to be incorporated in a more extensive cooperation agreement than hitherto. The real change, however, was in the new approach to the 'emerging states' of Mexico, Chile and the Southern Cone Common Market (MERCOSUR) member states of Argentina, Brazil, Paraguay and Uruguay. In a significant shift in policy, the EU decided to move towards some form of associated status with Mexico, Chile and MERCOSUR. Hitherto associated status had been reserved for those states that either for historical reasons (the ex-colonial states of Lomé) or political reasons (the near abroad of East and Southern Europe) had been considered a foreign policy priority.

Mexico is important for the EU because it is a founder member of the 1994 North American Free Trade Area (NAFTA) which unites Mexico, Canada and the United States. Mexico could also be an interlocutor for the EU, in both the Asia-Pacific Economic Cooperation Forum (APEC) of which it is an active member and the Association of Caribbean States which it has also joined. In addition Mexico is at the heart of a growing number of bilateral and multilateral free trade agreements in Latin America. These include, most importantly, the 1994 'Group of 3' accord between Mexico, Colombia and Venezuela to create a free trade zone between themselves, and the agreements with Chile (1991), Bolivia and Costa Rica (1994) to move towards free trade. Mexico has also signed an economic complementarity agreement with all five Central American republics (1991) with the intention of extending the provision to a free trade accord. In addition, the EU is concerned that were the Mexican elites to exclude or curtail EU trade they would have the legal economic powers to do so given that Mexican operative tariffs are well below those required by the World Trade Organisation (WTO).

The EU regards Chile in a similar manner to Mexico, particularly as a potential gateway to NAFTA since President Clinton stated that Chile was the next likely NAFTA member. Chile too is emerging as the core of a network of economic agreements – signed with Argentina and Mexico (1991), Bolivia, Colombia, Venezuela (1993) and Ecuador (1994). MERCOSUR also is important to the EU because it brings together the strongest of Latin American economies – Brazil and Argentina – in a functioning and rapidly accelerating project of economic integration. Like Mexico and Chile, MERCOSUR has an active linkage policy with its neighbours – formalising association agreements with Chile and Bolivia in 1996.

The European Union's *security and defence* considerations in Latin America are almost non-existent, although there was a period when the EC was very involved in security matters in Latin America – during the Central America crisis of the 1980s. *Trade* concerns were minimal until the 1990s and *development cooperation* with Latin America was never as high a priority as compared to the EU's links with other regions of the world. *Interregional cooperation*, initially spontaneously developed as a response to the Central American crises of the 1980s, proved useful as a base on which to manage rejuvenated EU–Latin American relations in the 1990s and early twenty-first century.

Security and Defence

By the mid-twentieth century, despite the fact that modern Latin America was created through a fusion of European colonialism and indigenous tradition, it was the United States that dominated the security and defence agenda of the sub-continent. In the immediate postwar period, the West Europeans more or less consented to United States hegemonic status with, for instance, both Britain and France supporting the US-sponsored invasion of Guatemala in 1954. The late 1950s saw a slight move away from unquestioning support for the US when the trade-oriented Europeans did not join the US embargo against Cuba after the 1959 revolution. France also agreed to sell arms to Cuba and it was France again that voted against the United States in the United Nations Security Council after the 1965 US invasion of the Dominican Republic.

The EC demonstrated a significant political interest in Latin America on only two occasions. The first was in respect to the Chilean coup led by Pinochet against the democratically elected President Allende in 1973, although EC protestations at Pinochet's human rights abuses in the 1970s and 1980s stayed at the level of the occasional diplomatic *démarche* rather than taking the form of a sustained policy. The second time that the EC became politically involved in Latin America (as opposed to Central America) was in 1982 when EC member states collectively implemented sanctions on Argentina (though they only maintained that cohesion for just under two months) in support of Britain in the Falklands/Malvinas War.

In the wake of the 1979 Nicaraguan revolution, however, the EC became an active political player in the eventually successful attempt to find a peaceful means to resolving the decade-long Central American regional wars that killed a quarter of a million people (out of a total population of 30 million), left 2 million as refugees and economic devastation to the tune of some $5 billion. Apart from working directly with the Central American and Contadora states (Colombia, Mexico, Panama and Venezuela) to develop a peacefully negotiated settlement, the EC both redirected development aid in support of the peace process and actively campaigned against United States policy. The United States had hoped to internationally isolate and delegitimise the Sandinista government and had tried to force them from office by military means through the financing and training of counterrevolutionaries, or contras as they were widely known. The EC and all member states (including Mrs Thatcher's Conservative government) had refused to go along with the military option. They had feared a domestic political backlash in Europe because of the widespread unpopularity of US Central American policy and, more importantly, were concerned that the US was escalating a regional conflict to something that could have international repercussions in respect of an extension of Cold War hostilities. The United States argued that the Central American conflicts stemmed from the 'Moscow–Havana' axis and were the result of Communist instigation. The Europeans argued that the conflicts stemmed from indigenous roots and were caused by deep-seated poverty and socioeconomic deprivation. Domestically, US policy towards Central America was finally discredited in 1987 when the Iran/contra hearings in the United States revealed that governmental representatives had illegally armed the contras with the proceeds from clandestine negotiations with Iran to try to release US citizens held hostage in the Middle East. Internationally the US had never, despite its greatest efforts, managed to persuade its allies to support its Central American policy. Its most important allies, the EC and its member states, not only launched a diplomatic effort against US policy, but also acted as a legitimating force for Latin American plans for peace which were developed contrary to US foreign policy aims.

Once the Central American peace process achieved momentum after 1987 and the Sandinistas were defeated at the polls in 1990 and replaced by a government more acceptable to the US, the Group of 8 (the Contadora group plus Argentina, Brazil, Peru and Uruguay) and the EC institutionalised their annual meetings in the 1990 Rome agreement. The meetings were transformed into a forum for wider political and economic cooperation with an expanded Latin American membership which included the Group of 8 – minus Panama (because of the then difficulties in respect of Panama's democratic credentials) but plus Bolivia, Chile, Ecuador and Paraguay. Discussions in the 1990s, however, did not revolve around security issues – instead trade and economic relations provide the pivot for the Union's policy towards the region.

Actors, instruments, legal bases and decision-making procedures

The Commission and the Parliament took most of the initiatives in support of the Central American peace process. The Council initially played a supporting role to the Commission, although both Hans-Dietrich Genscher the West German foreign minister and Claude Cheysson (as French foreign minister and later as European Commissioner) played high-profile roles in the setting-up of institutionalised political and economic dialogue with Central America. The primary instruments of policy were development aid (financial assistance, humanitarian aid and food aid), the diplomatic *démarche* and active diplomatic intervention in international organisations such as the UN and bilaterally, for instance through negotiations with the United States Secretary of State. The Commission used the competencies of the treaties to offer development aid to Central America as a way of providing inducements to the Central American states to participate in the peace process. The Council presidencies participated in active diplomacy (through visits to the region and through diplomatic interventions with the United States and other participants in the conflict). These diplomatic interventions were carried out under the aegis of the EPC mechanisms. Because the Commission was such an important actor in the process and the Community treaties were used as a basis to supply foreign policy instruments, decision-making was predominantly undertaken within the Community procedures, not within EPC decision-making channels. In the Falklands/Malvinas crisis, the Council took the initiative (led not surprisingly by Britain). EPC decision-making procedures were used but the instruments adopted, economic sanctions, were implemented by each member state separately, not within the context of Community procedures.

Trade

Latin America has frequently been hailed as of 'potential' interest to the Union but both the continuing low overall trade volumes and structural limits to trade growth militate against EC interest in strengthening links with Latin America. In 1999 Latin America provided just 4.7 per cent of Union imports with a value of 36.4 million Euros and took just 6 per cent of Union exports with a value of 45.5 million Euros. Within this small percentage, Brazil and Argentina benefited disproportionately. In 1999 imports from Brazil amounted to over a third of the Union's total imports from Latin

America (13 million Euros) while its share of the Union's export markets in Latin America amounted to just under a third (14 million Euros). In 1999, Brazil was the Union's fifteenth most important supplier of imports, compared to say Canada as the thirteenth-ranking import partner. It was also the thirteenth most important individual country export market for Union goods and services – compared to say Russia at ranking number twelve.

There were specific structural limits to trade between the EC and Latin America. Latin America's businesses find it much easier to penetrate Japanese and United States markets than those of the European Union. One important reason for the poor performance of EU–Latin America trade was because of EU protectionism. The Union's preferential trading arrangements with the Lomé countries, many of whose exports were similar to those produced by Latin American exporters, were one source of discrimination. In addition, the Generalised System of Preferences (GSP) that had been available to Latin America since 1971 did not allow Latin American exporters to compete with 'sensitive' EC exports such as textiles and steel, precisely those export sectors in which Brazil, Mexico and Argentina, for instance, would have been competitive. The most serious of the structural limits to trade, however, was the active discrimination against Latin American exports as a result of the common agricultural policy (CAP) which both dumped subsidised Union agricultural commodities abroad and imposed barriers to trade on those competitive Latin American exporters which could produce more efficiently and cheaply than EU producers.

The Union has signed a number of trade agreements with Latin America, however. The most important of the early agreements were the cooperation agreement with Argentina (1963), the agreement on the peaceful use of nuclear energy with Brazil (1965), the three non-preferential trading agreements with Argentina (1971), Uruguay (1973) and Brazil (1973) and the non-preferential economic and commercial agreement with Mexico (1975). In the 1970s the EC also signed a number of bilateral agreements in respect of trade in handicraft products and textiles with Bolivia, Chile, El Salvador, Ecuador, Honduras, Panama, Paraguay, Peru and Uruguay and with Brazil, an exchange of letters on trade in manioc. The agreements of the 1990s, by contrast, attempted to achieve political and economic objectives and were meant to try to provide a gateway into Latin American markets in the context of their new importance at the nexus of the United States and Asia. The agreement with

MERCOSUR was formalised in 1995. The June 1996 Florence European Council agreed a similar arrangement with Chile and at the same time the EU agreed to negotiate a political, commercial and economic agreement with Mexico. The Mexican Agreement on Economic Partnership, Political Co-ordination and Co-operation was signed in 1997 and was due to come into force in 2000. In order to persuade the Latin American partners of their serious intentions the EU proposed that at an unspecified future date a selected few of the Latin American states could achieve 'associated' status – symbolically of more significance than the 'non-associated' nature of previous relationships.

Actors, instruments, legal bases and decision-making procedures

The Commission has been the most important actor in the direction of trade relationships with Latin America, although Parliament has maintained an interest, periodically issuing reports on the state of EU–Latin America trade relations. The instruments used included financial and technical assistance, the GSP and the International Investment Partners (IIP) facility – designed to encourage joint venture investment in Latin America (and Asia, the Mediterranean and South Africa). The legal base for the trade agreements of the 1990s was provided by Articles 300 (ex 228) and 308 (ex 235).

Development Cooperation

Latin America became eligible for financial and technical assistance only in 1976 when this facility was extended to non-associated developing countries. EU aid to Latin America has been small in volume terms but significant in terms of its political impact in that it was used to support a major political intervention in Central America in the 1980s. The countries of Central America and Bolivia and Peru, the poorest of the non-Lomé mainland South American countries, received the largest proportions of EU aid to the region. Between 1976 and 1988 Central America received just under 400 million ECU and the Andean Pact countries (Bolivia, Colombia, Ecuador, Peru and Venezuela) just over 300 million ECU, out of total aid to Latin America of just under 970 million ECU. Between 1986 and 1998, Latin America received 4,301 billion Euros – of this 1,426 billion Euros were allocated to Central America. Priority areas include rural development, environmental protection and the fight against drugs – all of which are pursued in the context of encouraging the process of regional and sub-regional integration and, increasingly, 'good governance' in Latin American countries.

Humanitarian aid to Latin America amounted to 432 million Euros between 1986 and 1998 – with Nicaragua, Guatemala, Cuba and El Salvador receiving around two-thirds of the total between them. In the same period, Latin America received 453 million Euros-worth of food aid with just three states – Peru, Nicaragua and Bolivia – being allocated around two-thirds of the total.

Actors, instruments, legal bases and decision-making procedures

The Commission is the most significant actor in the development aid relationship, with the Parliament maintaining an active interest through the production of parliamentary reports and visits to the region. The Parliament was instrumental in 1976 in the introduction into the Community's budget of an appropriation for financial and technical assistance for Latin America (and Asia). In 1993 the EIB was permitted to extend its operations to Latin America and has financed two projects – in Peru and Costa Rica. The EU also channels its aid through non-governmental organisations – particularly when it does not want to give credence to the governments of certain countries or the government does not control all of its territory (El Salvador for part of the 1980s is an example of both these cases). Instruments include the financial and technical aid provided from the Community budget, support for NGOs, humanitarian assistance and food aid.

The same legal bases and decision-making procedures that apply to relations with Asia underpin development cooperation relationships with Latin America. The legal bases are provided by Article 308 (ex 235) along with the Council framework regulation (EEC) No. 443/92 on financial and technical assistance to and economic cooperation with the ALA countries of February 1992. Humanitarian aid is provided under competencies derived from Articles 37 (ex 43), 133 (ex 113) and 300 (ex 228). Decision-making procedures are those established by the treaties.

Interregional Cooperation

The EU has heavily promoted the development of regional integration in Latin America and at the same time has endeavoured to consolidate interregional relations through institutionalisation of region-wide and sub-regional links. The EU works on a Latin America region-wide level with the Latin America Economic System (SELA), the Latin American Integration Association (ALADI) and the Rio Group. It has also developed links with the sub-regional groupings of MERCOSUR and the Central American Common Market (CACM).

Attempts at interregional cooperation started after an approach by the Latin American Economic System (created in 1975) to request consultation mechanisms. Meetings took place in Brussels with the Group of Latin American Ambassadors (GRULA) and the EC's Committee of Permanent Representatives (COREPER) but did not achieve much of substance. Links with the Group of 8 (the Rio Group) grew out of both partners' attempts to find a peaceful solution to the Central American crises. These links were institutionalised in the 1990 Rome accord and in 1991 the EC formalised relations with the Latin American Integration Association. The Central America link had been formalised in 1984 when the Community had agreed to meet annually at ministerial level to discuss political and economic issues with their Central American counterparts. The Central American relationship, known as the 'San José process' after the city where the inaugural meeting had taken place in 1984, was formally renewed in 1996. In 1992 the Commission reactivated long-standing (since 1983) but hitherto rather desultory relations with the Andean Community, comprising Bolivia, Colombia, Ecuador, Peru and Venezuela, with the agreement coming into force in 1996. In December 1995 the European Council agreed the new interregional cooperation agreement with MERCOSUR. Given that Guyana, Surinam and Belize were associated with the EU via the Lomé treaties, this meant that by the 1990s every Latin American state – bar Cuba – was incorporated into a formalised working relationship with the EU (except French Guiana which is an overseas *département* of France – literally part of French territory).

Actors, instruments, legal bases and decision-making procedures

The Commission and the Parliament have been active in the promotion of interregional links. The Council agrees broad policy direction although the Commission takes the lead in decision-making in the development and implementation of regional integration projects. EU foreign ministers meet more or less annually with their counterparts in the Rio Group. This was also the pattern for the Central America relationship until policy was reviewed in 1996, when meetings changed to a biannual basis. The MERCOSUR agreement empowers EU and Latin American ministers who together form the Joint Cooperation Council to meet 'periodically and whenever circumstances require'. They are supported by a Joint Cooperation Committee and a Subcommittee on Trade – both comprising officials who, it was envisaged, would meet once a year. The MERCOSUR agreement also envisages a meeting between MERCOSUR heads of state and the 'highest authorities of the European Union' on a regular basis to discuss political matters of mutual interest. Similarly to the relationship with Asian regional organisations, instruments include both the diplomatic *démarche* and those provided by the treaties – particularly development cooperation instruments (see section above). Regional integration agreements are underpinned by Articles 133 (ex 113) and 300 (ex 228). Article 177 (ex 130u) – on development cooperation – was also used to support the agreement with MERCOSUR. Agreements are concluded by consensus.

DIFFUSE RELATIONS AND DIVERSE INTERESTS

The European Union's links with the distant South have been shaped by trade and development cooperation considerations. Security issues have only impinged upon the Union' foreign policy agenda in a one-off ad hoc manner, for instance in the sustained involvement in Central America in the 1980s. The Commission has made much of the running-on policy towards this rather diffuse group of states – with the Council and the Parliament operating, for the most part, as subordinate actors. Relations with the ACP states have become more politicised as the EU has sought to encourage democratisation abroad while relations with the wealthier states – in Asia and Latin America – are primarily relations of trade. The United States and the Union are economic competitors in this region – particularly in Asia and Latin America.

Guide to Further Reading for Chapter 7

A useful short survey of EC policy towards the ACP is Adrian Hewitt, 'Development Assistance Policy and the ACP', in Juliet Lodge (ed.), *The European Community and the Challenge of the Future*, second edition (London: Pinter, 1993). The discussion of the notorious 'banana' debate can be found in Christopher Stevens, 'Trade with Developing Countries', in Helen Wallace and William Wallace (eds), *Policy-Making in the European Union*, fourth edition (Oxford: Oxford University Press, 2000). An extremely useful and detailed discussion on aid policy in respect of the ACP is located in Enzo R. Grilli, *The European Community and the Developing Countries* (Cambridge: Cambridge University Press, 1993). A review of the negotiations and outcome of the fourth Lomé mid-term review can be found in David Lowe, 'Keynote Article: The Development Policy of the European Union and the Mid-Term Review of the Lomé Partnership', in Neill Nugent (ed.), *The European Union 1995: Annual Review of Activities* (Oxford: Blackwell, 1996). For an authoritative guide to EU policy towards South Africa see Martin Holland, *European Union Foreign Policy: From EPC to CFSP Joint Action and South Africa* (London: Macmillan, 1995). For detail on CFSP activity in South Africa see also Martin Holland, 'The Joint Action on South Africa: A Successful Experiment?', in Martin Holland (ed.), *Common Foreign and Security Policy: The Record and Reforms* (London: Pinter, 1997). A useful summary of the implementation of the post-Maastricht CFSP procedures that makes reference to EU policy towards South Africa, Burundi, Rwanda, Angola and Nigeria is Roy H. Ginsberg, 'The EU's CFSP: The Politics of Procedure', in Martin Holland (ed.), *Common Foreign and Security Policy: The Record and Reforms* (London: Pinter, 1997).

There are few useful secondary sources on EU–Asian relations. One of the reasons for this is the speed, scale and scope of expansion and development of EU–Asia, and particularly EU-China links, in the 1990s, which has simply not allowed the time for considered evaluation. A good introduction, however, can again be found in Enzo R. Grilli, *The European Community and the Developing Countries* (Cambridge: Cambridge University Press, 1993). A collection of short essays can be found in Richard Grant, *The European Union and China: A European Strategy for the Twenty-first Century* (London: Royal Institute of International Affairs, 1995). Relations with ASEAN are discussed in Manfred Mols, 'Cooperation with ASEAN: A Success Story', in Geoffrey Edwards and Elfriede Regelsberger (eds), *Europe's Global Links: The European Community and Inter-Regional Cooperation* (London: Pinter, 1990). ASEAN trade with the EC is reviewed in Jayshree Sengupta, 'The Effect of Project 1992 on the ASEAN', in Sandro Sideri and Jayshree Sengupta (eds), *The 1992 Single European Market and the Third World* (London: Frank Cass, 1992). A short discussion of EU–India relations can be found in Jørgen Dige Pedersen, 'The EC and the Developing Countries: Still Partners?', in Ole Nørgaard, Thomas Pedersen and Nikolaj Petersen (eds), *The European Community in World Politics* (London: Pinter, 1993).

Political and economic interregional cooperation between the EU and ASEAN and its offshoots is extremely well covered by the annual *Strategic Survey* published by the International Institute for Strategic Studies (London: Oxford University Press, 1994 onwards). A useful overview of the various intra- and interregional Asian networks is Richard Higgott, 'Shared Response to the Market Shocks', in *The World Today*, Vol. 54 No. 1, January 1998.

There is very little secondary material on EU policy towards Latin America. See Hazel Smith, 'European Community Policy towards Central America in the 1980s' (London School of Economics, doctoral thesis, 1993) for a discussion on EU policy towards South America. See also Hazel Smith, *European Union Foreign Policy and Central America* (London: Macmillan, 1995). See also Hazel Smith, 'Actually Existing Foreign Policy – or Not? The European Union and Latin America', in John Peterson and Helene Sjursen (eds), *A Common Foreign Policy for Europe* (London: Routledge, 1998). An excellent survey of the reorientation of EU policy towards Latin America in the 1990s is in Catherine Flaesch-Mougin and Joël Lebullenger, *Les relations contractuelles de l'Union Européenne avec les pays et groupements Latino-Americains* (Rennes: Centre de Recherches Européennes de Rennes, undated but 1996). The classic discussion of the EC's reaction to the Falklands/Malvinas conflict is Geoffrey Edwards, 'Europe and the Falklands Islands Crisis 1982', in *Journal of Common Market Studies*, Vol. XXII No. 4, June 1984. The EU-funded Institute for Europe–Latin America relations (IRELA) based in Madrid produces some useful material. As with the previous chapter, the most useful source of data is the EU itself. The Directorate General for Development and the Directorate General for Information, Communication and Culture produce very detailed reports on EU policy and activities in respect of the ACP. For the most up-to-date information, the Union's various internet information links are invaluable. For data, speeches, documents and press statements see the 'Europa' link – the web address is http://europa.eu.int/index-en.htm.

8   The European Union in the New Europe

The European Union has been pivotal in helping to reshape the politics and economics of post-Cold War Europe. EU foreign policy now places relations with the rest of Europe at the core of its foreign policy agenda – with the central concern of ensuring political stability and economic growth. Equally as important for the EU is to promote economic growth along the right lines. The objectives are to institutionalise and consolidate free markets, political pluralism, the rule of law and liberal democracy and to help prevent the threat of any resurgent communism.

EU policies vary as they focus on each of the very diverse political and economic circumstances and requirements of the different parts of Europe. The discussion in this chapter reflects the sub-regional distinctions of EU foreign policy. The five sub-regions are Northern Europe, Russia and the Commonwealth of Independent States (CIS) sometimes called the Newly Independent States (NIS), East and Central Europe (ECE), South-East Europe (SEE) and the three Mediterranean applicants – Turkey, Cyprus and Malta.

EUROPEAN UNION RELATIONS WITH THE NORTHERN EUROPEANS

European Union foreign policy towards this region up until the end of the Cold War was focused on its trade relations with the member states of the European Free Trade Association (EFTA). These states included the Scandinavians – Finland, Iceland, Norway and Sweden – and the 'Alpines' – Austria and Switzerland, with Liechtenstein joining EFTA in 1995. In the wake of the Cold War and Austrian, Finnish and Swedish accession, Union policy continues where possible to integrate its domestic and external policies with non-EU EFTA joiners – Iceland, Liechtenstein, Norway and Switzerland.

Security and defence have not been major concerns for the EU in this relationship apart from in the immediate aftermath of the Cold War when the position of Russia in respect of Baltic state independence was uncertain and there was some concern about the potential spill-over of conflict into the EU. Major issues in the relationship have been the management of *trade* and economic links between the two partners. Given the high level of economic development in this area, *development cooperation* policy does not form a significant part of EU foreign policy towards this sub-region. *Interregional cooperation* provided a core strategy and instrument of European Union foreign policy prior to the 1995 Scandinavian *enlargement*.

Security and Defence

Four related issues have informed the security aspects of EU relations with its Northern neighbours. The first is the neutral stance of many of these countries in foreign policy and the second is an understanding that the management of strategic relations with Russia, formerly the Soviet Union, remains an important foreign policy priority for many of these countries. The third is the sensitivity of the EU to its long-standing Nordic member state, Denmark, which has consistently viewed security as more properly the concern of the nation-state (or of NATO), not that of the EC/EU whose competencies, it feels, should primarily remain in trade and straightforwardly 'economic' areas. The fourth is simply the absence of major security and defence problems in the area since the creation of the European communities in the 1950s.

Prior to the end of the Cold War, overt security issues were not of primary importance in European Union relations with these states. If security issues were considered, it tended to be in the context of the commitments to either official neutrality or the policy of neutralism on the part of Austria, Finland, Sweden and Switzerland. Although neutrality precluded EU enlargement northwards in the context of Cold War politics, neutral states on the Union's eastern borders helped provide a convenient buffer between Western capitalist states and the Cold War antagonist, the Soviet Union. Post the Cold War, however, neutralism became a non-issue as there was no longer a world characterised by superpower rivalry and therefore no rationale for neutrality in the face of a non-bipolar international system.

Even after the dissolution of the Soviet Union in December 1991, security concerns did not become a major factor in EU relations with the northern European states. EU member states which were also members of NATO tended to leave the institutional and strategic aspects of security and defence to the latter organisation – involving, as they did, very large strategic questions relating to the overall shape of the Western alliance's relationship with Russia. Inevitably, such major strategic issues involved the United States as the major alliance partner as well as the Union and its member states. For non-NATO EU member states, particularly the Nordics, other channels of institutional deliberation and cooperation were available – including the Western European Union, the OSCE, the Nordic Council, the Council of Baltic Sea States and the Parliamentary Conferences on Cooperation in the Baltic Sea Area. In addition, the Barents Euro-Arctic Council was established in 1993 – providing an institutional forum for cooperation with Russia – and whose members were the EU states of Denmark, Finland and Sweden as well as the European Commission along with Iceland, Norway and Russia.

Actors, instruments, legal bases and decision-making procedures

The primary security forum for the major strategic concerns of member states in this area, namely relations with Russia, continues to be NATO. The WEU provides a potential security forum for Union relations with many of the northern neighbours as, institutionally, the WEU brings together NATO and non-NATO European Union member states as well as non-EU NATO members with European Union member states. Austria, Finland, Ireland and Sweden (non-NATO members) have observer status in the WEU and Norway and Iceland (non-EU but NATO members) have associate membership of the WEU. The 1993 Maastricht Treaty declared that the 'Western European Union was an integral part of the development of the Union'.

The institutional links with the northern neighbours operate mainly on an intergovernmental basis with efforts made to achieve consensus between the various states involved in each institution. The EU also maintains bilateral links with individual states through the Common Foreign and Security Policy mechanisms. The Swiss for instance are kept informed about CFSP priorities. Regular patterns of interaction with the Norwegian foreign ministry have existed since 1973 when Norway first rejected EC membership and was therefore ineligible to be a member of EPC. From 1988, meetings between the then EPC Presidency were formalised and Norway remains close to the CFSP process – although, as a non-EU member, not part of it.

Trade and Interregional Cooperation

The interrelated questions of trade and economic interpenetration and the institutional management of these relations have dominated

EU relations with the northern neighbours. Union objectives have been to try to maintain open access to EFTA markets. The move to 'ever-closer' relations with the northern neighbours is founded on complementary trade and economic links although it is by no means confined to those areas. The environment, for instance, is a significant area of mutual concern between the European Union and its northern neighbours in the early twenty-first century.

Prior to the 1995 enlargement that brought Austria, Finland and Sweden into the EU, the primary vehicle for interregional cooperation was through the link with the European Free Trade Association. This link was institutionalised in the creation of the European Economic Area (EEA) in 1993. The link was further consolidated when three more EFTA states, Austria, Finland and Sweden, joined the EU in 1995 (following on from former EFTA states – the United Kingdom which joined in 1973 and Portugal which had joined in 1986).

Trade

EC/EU trade with the EFTA countries grew in importance over the 1970s and 1980s so that by 1988, over 25 per cent of exports from the then EC/12 found their destination in EFTA countries – then comprising Austria, Finland, Iceland, Norway, Sweden and Switzerland. The percentage of EC imports from this area also grew in importance – from 17 per cent of all imports between 1977–79 to 23 per cent in 1991. Switzerland and Norway remained important trading partners for the EU after the 1995 enlargement. In 1998, Switzerland was the EU's second most important export market – and the third most important source of imports. Norway, with a population of only 4.5 million, was the Union's fifth most important market for both exports and imports in 1998.

For the EU, there have been minor irritations in the trade relations between itself and individual EFTA countries – particularly over fisheries policy. EU relations with Iceland, for instance, which obtained half of its export income from the fishing industry in 1995, have been marred by a series of disputes as Iceland has battled to maintain control over its 200-mile fishing limits. Fisheries disputes have also spilled over into key 'high politics' concerns with, for instance, EU attempts to improve access for Spanish and Portuguese fishing fleets, as part of the 1993/94 enlargement negotiations, arousing hostility from the Norwegian public and contributing to the 'no' vote in the November 1994 referendum.

On the whole, however, the Union has attempted to consolidate, institutionalise and, as far as has been possible, to harmonise trade relations with the EFTA states – both before the 1995 enlargement and after – to the extent that by the beginning of the twenty-first century, the remaining EFTA states are treated very similarly to EU member states. The main difference is that EFTA states remain outside the formal decision-making structures of the EU. One of the reasons, therefore, that EFTA states attempted to create more intensive institutional relationships with the EU, particularly as the Union has become a more important trading and political power since the 1980s, is to maximise involvement in rule-making within the EU on issues of direct relevance to the EFTA states. Given the close trade linkages between the two groups of states, were the EFTAns not to acquire some form of institutional relationship with the EU, they could be in the position of having trade rules imposed upon them. European Union impetus to greater cooperation comes from the attempt to chart a middle course – recognising a necessity to permit some EFTAn input but at the same time guarding the privileges of decision-making for the member states of the Union.

Interregional cooperation

The now very long-lasting interregional cooperation arrangements between the Union and EFTA were initiated by the UK and Denmark in 1973. Both states had been committed to establish a free trade area in industrial goods incorporating EC and EFTA member states after their 1973 accession to the EC and withdrawal from EFTA. In 1973 therefore, the EC entered into bilateral arrangements for free trade agreements (FTAs) with each EFTA member state. The EC retained a dominant position in the relationship – as the hub at the centre of a network of 'spokes' with the agreements not requiring and not leading to much of a multilateral relationship until 1984 when EFTA member states met with EC member states for the first time in a multilateral framework in Luxembourg to discuss enhancing and improving cooperation. Claude Cheysson, the then president of the Council of Ministers envisaged the creation of a vast internal market as well as cooperation in international relations. Cheysson also introduced the idea of an EC/EFTA 'European Economic Space' – transmuted into a more formalised plan for a European Economic Area (EEA) by Jacques Delors in 1989.

European Union negotiations with EFTA prioritised market integration measures with initial agreements made on common transit procedures and on the simplification of EC/EFTA trade administration in 1987. The moves towards the EEA intensified the process of harmonisation of single market rules and procedures with EFTA countries. The EEA covered free movement of goods, services, capital and persons but did not create a customs union between the two partners nor did it include EFTA in the common agricultural policy or the common fisheries policy. It was agreed that both partners would develop common policies on taxation and financial issues, although not to the extent of including EFTA states in the common currency. In addition to economic clauses, the EEA also included coverage of research and development, education, consumer policy, social policy and the environment.

EFTA states, however, remained disadvantaged in that they committed themselves to adopting EU rules and norms without a concomitant say in the decision-making process that elaborated those rules. The increased realisation that the EEA could not be a substitute for full membership provided a major impetus for European Union membership applications from Austria, Sweden, Finland, Switzerland and Norway. Thus, by the time the EEA came into force in 1993, EFTA was being denuded of important states. In addition, the Swiss voted in 1992 not to ratify the EEA, thus excluding the most important EFTA economy from participation in the intended vast single market. Although the EU eventually negotiated a bilateral agreement with Switzerland in 1998 which effectively achieved many of the EEA objectives, EU priorities were now elsewhere. Relations with Eastern Europe assumed centre stage and relations with the four remaining EFTA states, never a high priority except perhaps in the early 1990s, receded to the back of the European Union foreign policy agenda.

Actors, instruments, legal bases and decision-making procedures

The Commission has taken the lead in the relationship with EFTA, with the Parliament playing a subsidiary role. This was not an insignificant role, however, as Parliament had to assent to the EEA, thus giving it some influence on EU/EFTA negotiations. The EEA is governed by a Joint Committee, made up of EU and EFTA officials, and an EEA Council, consisting of ministers from the EU, members of the government of each EFTA state and the Commission. The agreement also established a joint EU/EFTA parliamentary committee. The instruments used by the EU in attempting to meet its objectives have been the normal processes of negotiation – backed up by the fear of the EFTAns that their economic prosperity would suffer if they could not negotiate guaranteed market access for their exports and maintain as open an economic system with the EU as possible. The legal basis of the EEA agreement derives from Article 310 (ex 238). Decision-making procedures both in the negotiations and in the implementation of the agreement aim for consensus.

Enlargement

In the 1980s, European Union strategy to negotiate a comprehensive deal with EFTA in the creation of the EEA had been designed, to some extent, to avoid individual applications for accession. In the 1990s, however, the EU reappraised its thinking on northern enlargement because of both pressures from individual EFTA states which resented continued exclusion from the 'club' and, most importantly, because the end of the Cold War forced a rethink of foreign policy priorities.

In the post-Cold War era, enlargement to include the northern neighbours made economic and political sense for the European Union. These states were definitely geographically European, they had undisputed democratic credentials and they were economically developed. Unlike the Mediterranean enlargements, these states brought no major problems of economic 'catching up' which the EU would have had to subsidise. As important, these states could contribute to the evolution of an even bigger single market that would have domestic benefits and would enhance EU economic and political negotiating clout in the wider world. In addition, they would also be able to contribute to what had become a major strategic objective for the Union – to help guide and assist Eastern European countries to reconstruct their economies along liberal capitalist lines.

EU negotiating processes with the five applicants were remarkably rapid compared to the drawn-out negotiations of previous accessions. The earliest application was from Austria – made in 1989. Sweden applied in 1991 and Finland, Norway and Switzerland in 1992. Formal negotiations with the four states (Switzerland withdrew its application in 1992) began in early 1993 and were over by March 1994. The accession treaties were signed in June 1994. In 1995, Austria, Finland and Sweden acceded to the Union – minus Norway whose public had voted for the second time (the first time in 1972 – see Chapter 2) to reject membership.

The European Union had been anxious to prove its efficiency in the aftermath of the Maastricht Treaty negotiations that had resulted in a bad press for the EU throughout the Union – particularly in Denmark where the population had at first refused to ratify the Treaty in 1992 and only finally endorsed it in May 1993. In addition, there were some pressures to push the accession treaties through Parliament before May 1994 when a new Parliament would be elected. Parliamentary assent is necessary for accession – and a new Parliament might be perhaps less ready to go through the procedures as rapidly as an outgoing Parliament.

Enlargement served to further EU foreign policy interests in terms of the economic and political consolidation of the Union as a global actor but more specifically provided support for EU economic and political objectives and policies in its relationship with the former Communist states of East and Central Europe and Russia. Enlargement to include these three states has not significantly changed the EU's own foreign policy stance – even though all three are former neutrals. Arguably, enlargement has improved the EU's ability to deal with problems in the far north of Europe through the enhanced Scandinavian linkages into sub-regional institutions such as the Council of the Baltic Sea States (see security section above). Enlargement may also have increased EU credibility with the countries of the South – given the positive Swedish record on development assistance. Increasingly, however, the EU will have to deal with the negative effects abroad of the swing to the right in Austrian politics after the 1999 elections of the far right Freedom Party led by Joerg Haider.

Actors, instruments, legal bases and decision-making procedures

The European Commission and individual states were significant actors in EU enlargement policy and practice towards the northern neighbours. The Commission drew up the enlargement strategy which was approved at the Lisbon European Council in June 1992 but which had envisaged that accession negotiations would not start until after the problems regarding the Danish rejection of Maastricht had been resolved and the Treaty had been ratified. At the December 1992 Edinburgh European Council, the UK, however, was instrumental in pushing the timetable forward so that the Lisbon decision was overturned, enabling accession negotiations to begin immediately. The instrument of accession is the treaty that is concluded between the applicant state and the member states of the Union. The criteria for membership of the EU are set out in Article 49 of the consolidated Treaty on European Union (ex Article O). This specifies that the Council must act unanimously after consulting the Commission. The Parliament must also give its assent, by way of an absolute majority.

EUROPEAN UNION RELATIONS WITH RUSSIA AND THE NIS

EU relations with Russia remain the most important foreign policy concern in this sub-region. The Ukraine is the second most important state within this region for the EU because of its size, relative wealth and geostrategic position. The three Caucasus states of Armenia, Azerbaijan and Georgia, the five central Asian states of Kazakhstan, Kyrghyzstan, Tajikistan, Turkmenistan and Uzbekistan, and Belarus and Moldova comprise the remaining NIS.

Until the end of the 1980s, the European Union had little bilateral contact with the Soviet Union, nor did it have relations with Soviet-led multilateral organisations including the Warsaw Pact, which was organised for security and defence purposes and which disintegrated after the end of the Cold War, or the Council for Mutual Economic Assistance (CMEA), which had brought together Communist states in a trade and economic organisation. The EC recognised the independence of the three Baltic states, Estonia, Latvia and Lithuania in the summer of 1991 and, after the disintegration of the Soviet Union into the component members of Russia and the Newly Independent States (NIS) in December 1991, the EC agreed to recognise the remaining successor states. The caveat was that these states should agree to uphold treaties that had been formerly entered into by the Soviet Union and to respect human rights. Russia received recognition immediately with the remaining NIS formally recognised between January and May 1992.

Since the end of the Cold War, the Union has been increasingly concerned about instability in the former Soviet Union (FSU) and has sought to provide economic and financial assistance to encourage moves towards market economies and, towards the end of the 1990s, began to focus on encouraging the consolidation of liberal democratic models and the rule of law. It has been relatively cautious in developing relations with the FSU – especially compared to its bold and rapid moves in developing relations with the Central and Eastern Europeans. European Union reluctance to take on a more interventionary role arises because of two reasons. The first is that the scale of the problems facing FSU states means that intervention may not be successful and secondly a failure to achieve economic and political improvements would therefore associate the Union with policy failure.

Direct involvement by the EU in *security* issues has been minimal. *Trade* relations with this sub-region are increasingly important for the EU with sectors like gas and oil of both strategic and economic importance for EU/Russia/NIS relations. Policies and activities have encouraged integration in the wider liberal international political economy. The focus of EU *development cooperation* policies has been to support the construction of market economies and to promote democratisation and has complemented EU interests in the trade area. Some *interregional cooperation* has taken place, which the EU has encouraged through budgetary allocations and technical support, and the Union also recognises two groups of states as having discrete regional interests. These are the Caucasus states and the five central Asian states. In the main, however, relations with the FSU states have developed in a more or less bilateral fashion. *Enlargement* is not a policy option for the states in this region although it is sometimes conceived of as a distant goal for some of the NIS.

Security and Defence

Prior to the end of the Cold War, the EU had avoided involving itself in direct responses to the Soviet Union on security and defence issues – preferring to leave security issues to other bodies, particularly NATO. Despite pressure from the United States to become active against the Soviet Union at times of international crises, it remained a reluctant actor in security issues. It only imposed very limited sanctions on the USSR after the 1979 Soviet invasion of Afghanistan and the 1981 military coup in Poland (which the US argued was supported by the USSR).

With the break-up of the Soviet Union in 1991, the European Union became briefly involved in the security area when it engaged in shuttle diplomacy to support the independence of the three Baltic states, Estonia, Latvia and Lithuania – temporarily suspending aid to the Soviet Union as an instrument of pressure. The EU has also expressed some concerns about the massive use of military force and violations of human rights in Chechnya – although there have been criticisms that the Union has not done enough to pressure Russia in this area. In this respect, however, the EU reflected the decision of member states not to disengage from Russia – seen also in the decision in early 2000 by the Council of Europe and the OSCE to maintain 'constructive engagement'. This was despite the decision of the parliamentary assembly of the Council of Europe to suspend voting rights of the Russian parliamentary delegation in protest at the military crackdown in Chechnya.

The EU engages twice a year in direct political dialogue with Russia at the presidential level – of the Commission, the Council and the Russian Federation. This is an extremely high level of political engagement and is recognition of Russia's Great Power status – demonstrating also that the EU grants political equivalence to Russia as with the United States and Japan. Political dialogue also takes place during meetings of the EU–Russia Cooperation Councils – set up as part of the Partnership and Cooperation Agreement that came into force in 1997. The EU has also agreed cooperation on support for democratic reform and more direct security-related matters such as the retraining of army officers and the conversion of defence-related industries as part of the Action Plan for Russia adopted in May 1996.

Much European Union involvement, however, has been indirect, through links with the OSCE and through individual member-state input in NATO. Exceptions to this rule included the 1993 decision by the EU to take a 'Joint Action' under the terms of the Treaty on European Union – only the second time the procedure was used – to agree election observation at the 1993 Russian elections. For the most part, however, the Union has been content to let the OSCE take the lead in security problems in this sub-region. This is partly because this is an acceptable arrangement to Russia, the dominant power in the region, and partly because the Union has not considered that it has faced direct security challenges in the sub-region. The CSCE/OSCE is also able to call on the resources of 54 states – including the USA and Canada. The CSCE, for instance, attempted mediation in the conflict in Nagorno-Karabakh between Armenians and Azeris in 1992 and it was the CSCE again, this time with the UN, which tried to ease tensions in Georgia in 1992 in the conflict over South Ossetia and Abkhazia. Likewise, it was the CSCE that was involved in attempting to help resolve conflict in Moldova in 1993/94.

OSCE 'Missions of Long Duration' – designed for conflict prevention and crisis management – have been situated in Georgia, Tajikistan, Ukraine and Moldova – with individual EU member states involved through their membership of the OSCE but with the EU generally taking a back seat – providing finance for projects which could help to ease tensions. Examples of such support include aid for transport and energy projects in Georgia – designed to ease coop-eration with South Ossetia. The European Union has had most difficulties in Tajikistan where continuing civil war meant that Union personnel could not operate safely, and TACIS personnel were killed after being kidnapped in Dushanbe, the capital, in 1997.

Actors, instruments, legal bases and decision-making procedures

To the extent that the EU has been involved in security and defence issues, it is the member states and the Commission that have taken the lead. The Commission has played a role in EU policy towards Russia and the NIS – in 1995 using its right of initiative under Article 18 (ex J 8) to produce a report recommending that dialogue take place in the security arena. The Parliament has closely followed the relationship with Russia and the NIS – insisting, for instance, that democracy promotion be fully integrated as a key objective of Union policies. An important actor within the patchwork of pan-European security relationships is the OSCE. Since the end of the Cold War, the EU has used the classical instruments of diplomacy in its relations with the FSU and the NIS, backed up by financial and technical aid provided by the Union within the framework of various trade and development cooperation activities (see below). Security objectives have not been divorced from EU economic and political objectives including, most importantly, the promotion of market economies. EU policies have developed on an intergovernmental foundation with key decisions being made consensually. An example of this *modus operandi* was the 1993 Joint Action which was concluded under the terms of the intergovernmental pillar of the Treaty on European Union.

Trade and Development Cooperation

Prior to the end of the Cold War the Soviet Union had been an insignificant export and import market for the EC/EU. It had not been a recipient of either development or humanitarian assistance. Subsequent to the end of the Cold War, Russia and the NIS (along with East and Central Europe – see below) were transformed into a key focus of European Union trade and development policy. The demand from the new liberal capitalist economies for Western imports was a source of potential markets for EU business. Develop-ment cooperation was designed to consolidate the transformation to market economies – in the expectation that such assistance would also help to facilitate market access for EU business. In addition, the now open economies of the NIS provided potential sources of crucial strategic minerals, especially oil and gas, that the EU hoped to be able to exploit. Development aid supported these export and import objectives – not just through narrowly defined economic assistance but also through providing aid for democratisation as well as the consolidation of market economies. Humanitarian aid was also donated to Russia and the NIS – partly for its own sake and partly to help avoid further instability at times of crisis.

The Soviet Union's share of the EC's export markets had amounted to only 4 per cent in 1980, dropping to 3.5 per cent in 1990. Similarly, the Soviet Union held only a very small market share of EC imports – amounting to just 3.6 per cent in 1980 and just 2.7 per cent in 1990. EC policy had refused to recognise the CMEA as an interlocutor for trade agreements with CMEA member states as it had wanted to minimise Soviet influence over EC relations with individual Communist countries. It was not until 1988, three years after the advent of Gorbachev to power, that the two organisations entered into formal relations with each other. These multilateral relations were not developed, however, as the CMEA collapsed in 1991 at the end of the Cold War. Instead, the EC set about strengthening bilateral trade and economic relations with the Soviet Union and its successor states – at the same time as encouraging multilateral cooperation between the Soviet Union and the NIS.

In 1989, prior to the break-up of the Soviet Union, the EC signed an 'Agreement on trade and commercial and economic cooperation' with the USSR – designed to come into force in April 1990. It was of limited scope – increasing access to EC markets on the basis of the most favoured nation for only a small number of products but maintaining quantitative restrictions on the classic 'sensitive' products of textiles, coal and steel. The agreement, however, did serve to establish a negotiating relationship between the two partners and also, importantly, initiated important institutional cooperation in, among other things, customs control and nuclear safety. The agreement was also supplemented by development assistance. Food aid was sent in 1991 and technical assistance promised aimed specifically at assisting in the transition to a market economy. In addition the EU established a diplomatic presence in the Soviet Union with the opening of an official delegation in 1991.

After the creation of the Commonwealth of Independent States (CIS) in 1991, the EU ruled out the development of the kind of intensive relations that were in the process of being developed with the East and Central European countries. It did not accept overall responsibility for coordination of aid to the FSU – instead supporting member states in multilateral initiatives with the World Bank and the G7. Nevertheless, the EU recognised that basic trade and economic cooperation agreements were going to be insufficient to delineate and support future relations – particularly with Russia, still a global player despite its economic problems. Instead the concept of the 'Partnership and Cooperation Agreement' (PCA) was born – designed to intensify trade relations, promote economic coopera-tion, assist and consolidate moves towards market economies and also allow for an element of political dialogue.

PCAs took some time to negotiate – the first two being agreed with Russia and the Ukraine in June 1994, then Moldova in November 1994 – followed by Kazakhstan, Kyrgyzstan and Belarus in 1995. The EU signed PCAs with Armenia, Azerbaijan, Georgia and Uzbekistan in 1996, and Turkmenistan in 1998. Only Tajikistan, with its continuing civil war and violence, was excluded from the raft of PCAs agreed with the NIS. The signing of PCAs did not indicate an acceptance that human rights records were acceptable – after all, the US State Department issued a report in 1999 that categorised Turk-menistan's record as 'dismal' – but did reflect the anxiety to support the consolidation of market economies.

The main instrument of EU support has been the TACIS (Technical Assistance for the CIS) programme – designed to benefit the twelve NIS and Mongolia. From its inception in 1991 up until 1999, TACIS allocated around 4 billion ECU to the recipient states and was planning to spend some 4 billion more between 2000 and 2006. The EU recognised that these sums amounted to a drop in the ocean compared to the estimated thousands of billions required for economic restructuring but argued that the targeting of TACIS funds for technical assistance – as opposed to financial support or direct investment – meant that its assistance could focus on areas where it could make a difference. Thus, between 1991 and 1997, TACIS funds were heavily concentrated in specific economic sectors – nuclear safety and environment (648.5 MECU), public administration reform, social services and education (488.59 MECU), restructuring state enterprises and private sector development (478.78 MECU), energy (317.71 MECU) and agriculture (307.59 MECU) being the most important. The EU re-evaluated the TACIS programme in 1998 after some criticism that it was spending too much money on EU consultants and not enough on the NIS. Although the evaluation concluded that TACIS had on the whole been positive in its contribution to NIS development, the Union redirected policy priorities so that for 2000 to 2006 the major objectives would be the promotion of democracy and the stimulation of investment in the NIS.

In addition to TACIS, the EU utilised other sources of support for the NIS, particularly after deterioration in the Russian economy in 1998 which severely affected NIS states – which are still closely tied to Russian economic structures. The Ukraine received balance of payments support, Moldova 'macro-economic aid' and Armenia and Georgia 'exceptional financial assistance'. Rehabilitation aid for infrastructure destroyed through war or natural disaster went to Azerbaijan, Georgia and Tajikistan and support for food security programmes went to Armenia, Azerbaijan, Georgia, Kyrghyzstan and Tajikistan. Humanitarian aid – mainly food and medical assistance – went to all the NIS. Tajikistan was by far the major recipient, receiving 16 MECU in 1998 for the victims of civil war – benefiting also from the 1999 supplementary aid allocation under the TACIS programme. Even Russia had to turn to the EU for emergency assistance and, for the first time since the break-up of the USSR at the beginning of the decade, found itself an EU food aid recipient to the tune of 400 MECU in 1999.

Of the NIS, Russia still remains the state with the greatest economic interest for the EU. Its sheer size compared to the other states – with over 75 per cent of total territory of the NIS and over half the population – offers potential as an export market and source of natural resources. EU exports to Russia rose substantially after the end of the Cold War – from 6.9 billion ECU in 1992 to 21 billion ECU in 1998 – EU imports rose from 10.7 billion ECU to 23.2 billion ECU in the same period. In 1998, Russia was the Union's seventh most important export market and sixth most important source of imports. The size and the scale of investment necessary to rehabilitate and reconstruct the economy makes it difficult, however, for the EU to develop and implement a comprehensive trade, economic and development policy towards Russia. Union policy is likely to continue to narrowly target sectors in which it has both a direct interest and in which it feels it can make a direct contribution. Russia and some of the smaller states, for instance, Azerbaijan, Kazakhstan and Turkmenistan, are important actual and potential gas and oil suppliers to the Union and the Union has concentrated a significant proportion of TACIS funding in energy and transport (to Europe) projects. Targeting is to be even more fine-tuned in that the 4 billion

ECU TACIS allocation for 2000 to 2006 will fund around 100 projects – compared to 1,000 projects funded between 1992 and 1999 from a similar amount.

Actors, instruments, legal bases and decision-making procedures

The Commission played a key role in developing economic, trade and development policies with Russia and the NIS. Within aspects of the many programmes, actors were multifarious. Non-governmental organisations and international humanitarian organisations played a part in carrying out ECHO programmes. Within TACIS, apart from the Commission officials, at least seven different actors contributed to implementation. These included the TACIS national coordinator, the Coordinating Unit, the partner organisation in-country, the usually European contractor, the task manager, the EC delegation representing the Commission in the country and the monitoring team. The major instruments have been financial, technical and humanitarian, including food, assistance. TACIS funding and humanitarian aid is grant aid – and therefore an instrument of assistance that does not add to the debt burden for countries in economic difficulties.

The 1989 trade and cooperation agreement with the Soviet Union provides the legal basis for relations with the NIS. This treaty was based on Articles 133 (ex 113), 308 (ex 235) and 300 (ex 228) and forms the basis for PCAs. The PCAs themselves have the status of 'mixed agreements' as they involve both the EU and the member states. The legal foundation for the TACIS programme is in Article 308 (ex 235). Decision-making therefore involves dialogue and negotiation with all three major institutions of the Union.

Interregional Cooperation and Enlargement

The European Union does not intend to include any of the NIS in enlargement plans for the foreseeable future. This has not prevented these states, including Russia, considering at times the possibilities of membership and certainly, what the NIS states on the whole have made explicit, is their aim to build close partnerships with the Union. The EU has supported the NIS in multilateral cooperation efforts between themselves and with other international actors as appropriate. Russia, for instance, works within the Council of Baltic Sea States and the Barents Euro-Arctic Council. The latter organisation has been involved in regional and cross-border projects in areas ranging from economic development to education with a particular focus on environmental improvements. As well as encouraging intraregional cooperation the Union has engaged in a limited way with multilateral interregional activities. In 1999, for instance, the EU held a regional Summit with Armenia, Azerbaijan and Georgia.

The EU encouraged the development of both *inter*regional and *intra*regional cooperation through the TACIS programme – allocating some 40 per cent of funding to multinational projects in the 1990s with major programme areas being interstate cooperation in the fields of transport, the transit of hydrocarbon resources to Europe and environmental protection. TRACECA (Transport Corridor Caucasus Europe Asia) and INOGATE (Inter-State Oil and Gas to Europe) involve dozens of cross-national projects. Azerbaijan and Georgia, for instance, work within a TRACECA-initiated rail project while the key TRACECA objective is to provide a fast, accessible transport route from Central Asia to deep sea shipping, across the Black Sea and the Caspian Sea to EU and Western markets. Small cross-border projects also designed to facilitate interregional cooperation have included the three TACIS-funded Russian–Finnish border crossing posts.

Actors, instruments, legal bases and decision-making procedures

Much of the interregional activity promoted by the EU has been implemented through the TACIS programme with actors, instruments, legal bases and decision-making procedures therefore as set out in the section above on trade and development cooperation.

EUROPEAN UNION RELATIONS WITH EAST AND CENTRAL EUROPE (ECE)

Prior to the end of the Cold War the EC had developed limited bilateral relationships with East and Central European countries – often in the face of opposition and suspicion from the Soviet Union. In the wake of the Cold War, policy towards the ECE states became core to the foreign policy activities of the EU. From a position on the periphery of foreign policy concerns, the ECE states assumed central importance – with plans for accession being placed on the agenda for the Czech Republic, Estonia, Hungary, Poland and Slovenia. In addition the EU signalled to Bulgaria, Latvia, Lithuania, Romania and Slovakia that they would not be very far behind given further negotiations and the meeting of accession 'conditionality'.

In EU parlance, the very term 'East and Central European states' became understood as a category applying to those states based in Europe which would fairly rapidly be accepted for membership of the EU. Thus the former states of Yugoslavia were excluded from this definition (see below), apart, that is, from Slovenia which was accepted as a candidate for membership. The rationale was partly to indicate to former Yugoslav states and to outside powers with an interest in the region – like Russia and the United States – that the Union considered itself a pan-European entity and, provided European states were prepared to meet EU conditionality, there would be no long-term bar to any European state joining the Union. In addition the three Baltic states, although formed from the disintegration of the Soviet Union, were only very briefly understood by the EU as 'NIS' along with the other states of the FSU. For the EU, the Baltic states are 'East and Central European' and eligible for EU membership.

The underlying motive for the rapid intensification of European Union involvement in East and Central Europe has been the urge to prevent instability which could spill over into EU borders whether this be in the form of a vast influx of refugees and migrants or, at worst, the carrying-over of political violence. The methods chosen to respond to this strategic objective have been the promotion, development and consolidation of market democracies – thus the EU has concentrated its major efforts on support for economic reform and democratisation. The ECE countries have been encouraged to integrate their trade in the globalising world economy – to open up their internal markets to foreign trade and to modernise internally such as to make their exports competitive abroad. Thus Union *security* objectives have been underpinned by *trade* policy with *development cooperation* policy complementing both security and trade policy objectives. The EU has tried to promote *interregional cooperation* – without much success – given that the ECE countries persist in orienting their foreign policies bilaterally to the Union. In any case, interregional cooperation with the EU – the most important of all such projects for all the ECE – has been submerged under the imminent plans for *enlargement* which has provided the central focus of European Union policies towards this group of states since the mid-1990s.

Security and Defence

EU interest in security issues in ECE can be characterised as *minimal* prior to the end of the Cold War, *reasonably substantial* during the period of immediate transformation from communism to capitalism between 1990 and 1992, and *indirect* from that period onwards. Since 1992, the EU has preferred to deal with security issues indirectly, given that the relationship with Russia still provides the all-important backdrop and concerns the Western alliance as a whole. Thus NATO remains the premier organisation for dealing with security and defence issues. The EU also prefers to work within other multilateral organisations, particularly the OSCE which is seen by the EU as an appropriate forum and instrument of security cooperation, conflict resolution and conflict prevention.

Prior to the Cold War, EC relations with the ECE states were also left to NATO leadership with EC involvement only occurring in a very limited manner. The EC, for instance, after pressure from the United States, imposed minor sanctions on the Soviet Union in retaliation for the declaration by General Jaruzelski of martial law in Poland in 1981 (see section on Russia and the NIS above).

The most substantial EU involvement in the ECE in the security sphere was in the immediate aftermath of the Cold War, when the EU intervened to support Estonia, Latvia and Lithuania. The three Baltic states had declared independence from the Soviet Union in 1991 and, during the process of negotiating the terms of independence, the Soviet Union made threatening military gestures towards the three states. The EU responded with a suspension of food aid and technical assistance to the USSR. The EU also engaged in shuttle diplomacy with the major protagonists to assist in what eventually was a peaceful transition to statehood for all three states. The EU also intervened in June and July 1991 to help ward off military action by Yugoslav forces against the newly independent state of Slovenia – officially recognising Slovenia (and Croatia) as independent states in January 1992.

Potential for military conflict remained given Russian concern about the treatment of the large Russian minorities within the newly independent Baltic states. To a large extent this conflict was avoided through the mechanism of the EU-initiated 'Stability Pact' – the centrepiece of EU efforts to promote stability in the ECE and to help avoid potential military conflict and political violence through the institutionalisation of conflict resolution mechanisms.

In 1993 the French premier Edouard Balladur had proposed that the EU should contribute to the stabilisation of Eastern and Central Europe (ECE) through the organisation and implementation of a series of conferences whose focus would be the position of minorities and the consolidation of territorial borders. Eastern and Central European countries would be encouraged to resolve outstanding problems through negotiation and it was hoped that these fora would also provide the impetus for the promotion of intraregional cooperation between these countries. The EU also envisaged these conferences as enabling the ECE countries to prepare for eventual EU membership through both the resolution of outstanding political problems and encouraging habits of regional cooperation. In 1995 when the Stability Pact was finally agreed in Paris, it was also agreed that the instruments and procedures of the OSCE would be used to implement the Pact. Some of the several hundred projects developed under the aegis of the Pact are straightforwardly security oriented – in the fields for instance of de-mining and arms control. Others are broader in scope – ranging from support for the development of independent media to anti-crime and corruption measures to support for refugee return.

Stability Pact participants included the EU member states along with Canada, Japan, Russia, Turkey, the United States, and Albania, Bosnia Herzegovina, Bulgaria, Croatia, Hungary, Romania, Slovenia and the former Yugoslav Republic of Macedonia. Observers included the Czech Republic, Moldova, Norway, Poland, Slovakia, Switzerland and the Ukraine. The EU maintained quite a hefty indirect involvement as it agreed to use resources from its already existing programme to support projects in Eastern and Central Europe (PHARE) emanating from the various agreements concluded under the terms of the Pact. The OSCE, however, was left with the management of the process – with the EU member states expected to push along the process within the OSCE – thus leaving the EU somewhat distant from direct involvement in potentially conflictual security issues involving these countries.

The EU has been content to permit NATO to take the lead in the more classical concerns of security – military and defence issues – with the Czech Republic, Hungary and Poland joining NATO as full members in 1999. The remaining ECE countries – Bulgaria, Estonia, Latvia, Lithuania, Romania, Slovakia and Slovenia – are members of the NATO-led Partnership for Peace arrangement which brings together NATO member states with ECE, NIS and South-East European states in military and defence cooperation activities. An overarching multilateral forum called the Euro–Atlantic Partnership Council (EAPC) was formed in 1997, and which by 1998 had 44 members, is designed to coordinate military and political activities which bring together NATO with the partner countries.

Actors, instruments, legal bases and decision-making procedures

The Council and the Commission had been involved in security policy towards the ECE – most notably through the development of the Stability Pact. The lead actors remain NATO and the OSCE. The WEU has recognised East and Central European states, including the Baltic states, as associate partners since 1994. The Stability Pact negotiations used the classic tools of conference diplomacy while the financial instruments supplied under the PHARE programme provided a substantial means of implementation. In October 1993, the 'promotion of stability and peace in Europe' was declared an area for 'joint action' under the procedures of the CFSP underpinned by Article 13 (ex J3) of the TEU. The legal foundations for policy varied – depending on the issue being considered but also on which particular phase of specific projects was being implemented. The PHARE programme is underpinned by Article 308 (ex 235) of the treaties establishing the European Communities. As in many other areas of EU decision-making – even when the formal procedure allows for majority voting, as with the Joint Action under the CFSP, major efforts are made to achieve consensus.

Trade and Development Cooperation

Prior to the end of the Cold War, the EU had developed limited trade relations with ECE states. Since the Cold War, trade volumes have increased although they still comprise only a fraction of EU global trade. Nevertheless trade partnerships, expressed through comprehensive association agreements, have intensified to the extent that trade policy towards ECE countries forms a central focus of EU foreign policies. The importance of these partnerships is indicated by the in principle agreement to offer European Union membership to all ECE states. Trade policy has long-term objectives – designed both to increase EU export and import markets and to help in political stabilisation and the consolidation of market economies in the ECE states. EU negotiating strategy towards East Europe was to link economic concessions with progress towards political and economic pluralism. Development cooperation was channelled in support of these multifarious objectives through the mechanism of the association agreements – more commonly known as the 'Europe' agreements.

Transiting Cold War relations

Of the ECE states, Hungary, Poland and Czechoslovakia had been the most important for the EC in trade terms during the Cold War. Each of these states provided around 2 billion ECU-worth of exports and 2 billion ECU-worth of imports with the EC in 1987. The EC negotiated a number of ad hoc sectoral agreements with Bulgaria, Czechoslovakia, Hungary, Poland and Romania in the Cold War years – in agriculture, textiles and steel. Romania was given slightly preferential treatment by the EC because it was judged, along with Yugoslavia, to be more independent of the Soviet Union than the other ECE states. Romania was granted a joint committee on trade in 1980 as well as improved access to EC markets. The EC had involved itself only in a very minor way with any form of development assistance to the ECE states – with Poland receiving food aid and medical assistance after 1983.

More substantial trade agreements with ECE countries only became possible after the EC and the CMEA agreed to recognise each other in June 1988 after which EC trade and cooperation agreements with Hungary and Poland came into force in 1988 and 1989 respectively. A trade agreement had been negotiated with Czechoslovakia in 1988 – only being transmuted into a trade *and* cooperation agreement and coming into force in 1990 after elections had been held in the country. Similar agreements with Bulgaria and Romania came into force in 1990 and 1991 respectively. The German Democratic Republic (East Germany) signed a trade and cooperation agreement in 1990 – but it was overtaken by unification in 1991 and never came into force.

These early agreements were negotiated as states were on the cusp of the transition from communism to capitalism. EC negotiators took a tough line with Communist states – insisting on political reforms in return for improved access to EC markets. The rapid pace of political change in the ECE states between 1988 and 1991 was matched, however, by an accelerated implementation of EC cooperation. The hard-fought-over agreements were liberalised – particularly in relation to the abolition of quantitative restrictions on ECE exports. The EU also assumed a pivotal role in economic development of the ECE states after the Commission assumed leadership in development cooperation to the ECE on behalf of the wider international community in 1989.

Post-Cold War and the first priorities

In 1989, the Summit of the G7, the world's most prosperous nations, invited the Commission to coordinate aid from the G24 countries – the then member states of the Organisation for Economic Cooperation and Development (OECD). These were the twelve EC member states, the six EFTA states and Australia, Canada, Japan, New Zealand, Turkey and the United States. Other participants in the aid effort were the international financial institutions – including the World Bank, the IMF and, after its creation in 1990, the European Bank for Reconstruction and Development (EBRD). Initial assistance went to the areas of agriculture, access to markets, investment promotion, vocational training and environmental protection but from 1993 aid priorities shifted to nuclear safety, macroeconomic assistance and environmental protection with bilateral groups dedicated to providing a comprehensive and multi-sectoral strategy for each ECE country.

The sums of money committed through the G24, while not comprising a 'Marshall Plan' for East and Central Europe (see Chapter 2), were substantial and the majority was provided by the EU member states and the EU institutions. Between 1990 and 1996, out of a total international aid to the ECE states of some 98 billion ECU, the 15 EU member states provided some 37 billion ECU while the EU provided 11 billion ECU, the EIB nearly 5 billion and the ECSC 200 million – totalling just under 53 billion ECU. Within this overall context, however, Germany was by far the largest donor with over 17 billion ECU of aid – next in line of the member states being France with 6.5 billion ECU, followed by Austria at 4 billion ECU and Sweden at 1.5 billion ECU. By contrast in the same period the largest single donor state outside the EU was the United States at just over 11 billion ECU, followed by Japan at just over 5 billion ECU. Out of the international financial institutions, the IMF contribution amounted to just over 10 billion ECU, the World Bank just under 10 billion ECU and the EBRD around 5 billion ECU. EU aid was particularly valuable as most of it comprised grants, that is non-repayable assistance.

EU aid was allocated via the PHARE programme – designed in 1989 to aid Poland and Hungary as the countries furthest along the road to economic transformation but rapidly transformed to an instrument to assist all East and Central European states in 1990, including the then Yugoslavia. Most PHARE projects were designed to assist in the transition to market economies although PHARE regulations also permitted the funding of humanitarian assistance. Since 1994 PHARE programmes had been designed to assist in pre-accession strategies (see section on enlargement below) and there have also been continuing moves to encourage intra- as well as interregional cooperation (see section on interregional cooperation below). Between 1990 and 1996, the sector in receipt of most PHARE funding was infrastructural development at 22.1 per cent followed by private sector development at 18.4 per cent and education, health and training at 14.7 per cent. Humanitarian aid came next at 7.8 per cent.

The EU and the member states provided loans to the ECE states through the EIB, ECSC, Euratom and through an EC macro-financial assistance facility. Between 1990 and 1996, the EIB loaned just under 5 billion ECU to the ECE states (as well as Albania). These loans were focused on the areas of infrastructure, energy, telecommunications, environment and support for small and medium-sized enterprises (SMEs). Macro-financial assistance to the ECE states from 1990 to 1996 amounted to just under 3 billion ECU (again including Albania). ECSC loans have been sector specific and relatively small although the Euratom loan of 1994 (also destined for Russia and Ukraine) was reasonably large – around 1 billion ECU – and designed to support ECE nuclear safety efforts.

The EU also played a part in the establishment of the EBRD – an initiative of President Mitterand of France. At its founding in 1989/90, there was some resentment from the smaller EU member states that they had not been consulted sufficiently. However, the EBRD was eventually set up in 1990 and was created specifically to assist states in the transformation from Communist planned economies to liberal market economies *and* democratic polities through the provision of loan finance. EU member states, the Commission and the EIB held 51 per cent of shares – but the member states far outweighed the Commission and the EIB – with the community institutions holding only 3 per cent of shares each.

The trade and cooperation agreements – the so-called 'first generation' agreements – provided an inadequate and unsatisfactory vehicle through which to frame and monitor this vast expansion of EU economic activity in ECE. Even as these were coming into force, the EU started to consider how economic and political relations could be reinforced so that at the Dublin European Council in 1990, member states agreed that some form of association should be offered to eligible ECE states. Association would permit the institutionalisation of political as well as economic dialogue and would also provide the basis for a series of partnership institutions to be established which could in turn provide for more systematic cooperation between the EC and the ECE states.

The association or 'Europe' agreements as they became known were not accession agreements but instead were frameworks designed to promote free trade between the EU and individual ECE states over periods ranging up to ten years. The so-called 'second generation' Europe agreements came into force with Poland and Hungary in 1993, with the Czech Republic, Slovakia, Romania and Bulgaria in 1995, with Slovenia in 1996 and with Estonia, Latvia and Lithuania in 1998. Accession was only vaguely anticipated by these agreements and was made conditional on the ECE state fulfilling the requirements established by the EU. These agreements therefore did not represent a partnership of equals – and although trade liberal-isation in industrial products occurred, there was and remains resentment in ECE states that the EU has maintained a protection-ist agricultural policy that has restricted ECE access to EU agricultural markets. The continued pressure for accession from ECE states is to a large extent guided by the knowledge that it is only with full membership of the EU that ECE states would be able to fully benefit from both unrestricted market access and the substantial structural funds the EU allocates to EU less-developed regions.

Although trade has been growing between ECE states and the EU, it is still much more important for the former than for the latter. Total volumes of trade for the ECE states increased steadily after the end of the Cold War with a very rapid concomitant increase in total trade with the EU. By 1998 for instance only Bulgaria and Lithuania had less than 50 per cent of total imports (45 per cent and 50.2 per cent respectively) and exports (49.7 per cent and 38 per cent respec-tively) deriving from and heading for the EU. All saw large increases in a short time of their percentages of trade with the EU – with Slovakia for instance having around 25 per cent of its total trade with the EU in 1994 – rising to around half its total trade in 1998. Over two-thirds of the total trade of Hungary and Poland was by 1998 with the EU. These figures indicate that trade and economic integ-ration with the EU is already occurring as far as ECE states are concerned. For the EU, trade volumes with the ECE states are minimal and showing little sign of increasing – between 1994 and 1998 the percentage share of EU imports from all the candidate countries remained at just 3 per cent and the equivalent share of EU exports dropped from 4 per cent to 3 per cent in the same period.

Changing priorities

From 1997 PHARE priorities changed and were focused on two areas: institution-building and the financing of investment. Some 30 per cent of total PHARE funds were to be allocated to the former and 70 per cent to the latter. The budget allocation for 1995 to 1999 is just under 7 billion Euros.

Actors, instruments, legal bases and decision-making procedures

All the institutions of the Union have played important parts in trade and development cooperation relationships with ECE states. The Council and the Commission have maintained the impetus in terms of strengthening relations, with the Parliament closely monitoring developments through its various committees and delegations. The Parliament, for instance, used its co-decision rights in budgetary procedures in 1990 to increase Community aid to Hungary and Poland. The Commission has played an important internal role in terms of negotiating trade and cooperation agreements and later the Europe agreements. It has also played an important role as the coordinator of global aid to the ECE – organising and leading assistance from EU and non-EU member states including the United States.

The Europe agreements are managed by the Association Council, the Association Committee and the Association Parliamentary Committee. The Council meets once a year and comprises members of the European Council, the Commission and the government concerned – with representatives usually at foreign minister level. The Association Committee is the working body which directs the partnership and its members are Commission civil servants on the one hand and junior ministers or senior civil servants from the partner countries on the other. The Parliamentary committee, as the name suggests, brings together members of the European Parliament with parliamentarians of the partner country and it has the power to make recommendations to the Association Councils.

The PHARE programme, along with EU and EIB loans, has been the major instrument of trade and development cooperation with the ECE. PHARE has supported other programmes including the Trans-European Mobility Scheme for Universities (TEMPUS), the European Training Foundation, the Joint Venture Support

Programme (JOPP), the Programme of Local Government Cooperation East–West (Overture), Cooperation in Science and Technology with Central and East European Countries (Cost) and the PHARE democracy programme.

The trade and cooperation agreements were based on Articles 133 (ex 113), 308 (ex 235) and 310 (ex 238). The Europe agreements are based on Article 310 (ex 238) and 300 (ex 228). This has meant, among other things, that the Europe agreements had to be approved by the European Parliament, by way of an absolute majority. It also meant that the Europe agreements had to be ratified by the parliaments of the member states and the partner state. The interim agreements, which came into force to implement the trade aspects of the Europe agreements prior to ratification, were based on Article 133 (ex 113).

Interregional Cooperation and Enlargement

EU motivations for further integration were essentially political – with enlargement seen as a way of consolidating market economies, liberal democracies and political stability in the wider European space. The EU has used enlargement negotiations to promote political and economic changes in candidate countries that the EU conceives as desirable. Enlargement has been an acknowledged central focus and instrument of a European Union foreign policy designed to achieve stability and security in Europe.

The original intention had been to try to develop close relations without committing the Union to accession but this policy rapidly changed to accept enlargement as both inevitable and feasible. The EU initially made efforts to encourage interregional cooperation – for instance with its early 1992 meeting with Czechoslovakia, Hungary and Poland to discuss political issues of mutual interest such as the Yugoslav crisis. Further ad hoc meetings took place with the Czech Republic, Poland, Hungary and Slovakia but, since the mid-1990s, interregional cooperation in terms of systematic cooperation between an organised group of ECE states and an organised group of European Union states has been displaced by the overall priority of bilateral accession negotiations.

ECE states had always been reluctant to allow interregional cooperation to be used by the European Union as a delaying tactic or worse a substitute for EU membership. Since the 1993 Copenhagen Council which agreed that ECE accession could take place providing those states met the criteria for membership and the 1994 Essen

European Council where the EU took a positive decision to help prepare the ECE states for membership, interregionalism has given way to enlargement as the key policy for arranging its relations with the ECE states. Some *intra*regional cooperation continues to be supported, for instance through the PHARE programme where a percentage of the budget is set aside for the promotion of *bon-voisinage* projects between the candidate countries as well as NIS and South East European countries. The EU has also supported the formation of the Central European Free Trade Area (CEFTA) which was formed between the Czech Republic, Hungary, Poland, Romania, Slovakia and Slovenia as well as the Baltic Free Trade Area (BFTA) between the three Baltic states.

The European Union received applications for membership between March 1994 and June 1996 from ten ECE states. The Commission began working on a pre-accession strategy in 1994 and some attempts were made to engage the applicant countries with what was first termed a 'structured relationship' with the institutions of the European Union. The 'structured dialogue' that emerged from these antecedents involved, among other things, ECE leaders meeting with the European Council. Unfortunately, these meetings did not achieve their promise and were given little priority by the EU. The attempt at a multilateral focus was finally abandoned when the EU agreed a systematic programme for accession in 1997.

In July 1997, as part of its wider discussions on the future of the Union, in a paper entitled 'Agenda 2000: For a Stronger and Wider Union', the Commission recommended that accession negotiations commence with Estonia, the Czech Republic, Hungary, Poland and Slovenia. The December 1997 European Council agreed with the Commission while making clear, as had the Commission, that accession negotiations would also be opened with Bulgaria, Latvia, Lithuania, Romania and Slovakia. As soon as this latter group of countries were deemed to have met the criteria for membership they would proceed from what the Commission called 'pre-in' status to that of 'in' status. Key negotiations would be bilateral although the Union attempted to retain a supplementary multilateral forum in a 'European Conference' in which CFSP and Justice and Home Affairs issues would be discussed with all those states which had applied for membership and which had an associate relationship with the EU. The EU also registered its strategic vision of a Union that potentially includes all of Europe in that Estonia, one of the new Baltic states formed from the break-up of the former Soviet Union, as well as

Slovenia from the former Yugoslavia, are included as 'fast-track' applicants in the plans for this fifth enlargement.

The 1997 Commission 'Opinions', which found that four ECE states and Slovenia met the membership criteria and could be 'fast-tracked' into the EU and that the five remaining ECE states would have some further work to do before individual accession negotiations could commence, provide the base for subsequent Union policy. The EU opened accession negotiations with the 'ins' in a multilateral meeting of foreign ministers from the EU and the six candidate countries (five ECE plus Cyprus) in 1998 before moving to bilateral negotiating fora. The EU concluded individual accession partnerships with *all* ECE countries – both 'ins' and 'pre-ins'. The partnership agreements outlined what the candidate country needed to do to fulfil the conditions of EU membership – particularly in respect of how far the applicant state had come in adopting the *acquis* (rules, procedures and norms of the Union). The EU also used these agreements as a basis for deciding the scale and amount of PHARE funding which would be allocated in financial support for the candidate country. Since the start of accession negotiations, the Commission has researched and published annual reports on progress made towards adoption of the *acquis* by each ECE state.

In December 1999 at the Helsinki European Council the enlargement process was pushed a step further when it was agreed that the Union should be able to absorb the 'ins' – that is the first tranche of candidate states – by the end of 2002. It was also agreed that bilateral accession negotiations with the 'pre-ins' – Bulgaria, Latvia, Lithuania, Slovakia and Malta – could start in February 2000. Thus, by 2000, the EU was engaged in intense bilateral negotiations for accession with all the ECE states.

Actors, instruments, legal bases and decision-making procedures

The European Council and the Commission have both been important actors in the rapid moves towards enlargement. Strategic direction has been set by the various European Councils with Germany and the UK being particularly proactive in encouraging and supporting accession for ECE states. The Commission has also been prominent in that its 1997 Opinions and the follow-up reports have provided the foundation for EU policy on enlargement. Since the December 1994 Essen European Council, the PHARE programmes have been used to support ECE states in preparing for accession. From 2000 the EU is also intending to offer aid for agriculture and further structural funding. The applicant states have also been permitted access to Community programmes such as education and training.

The legal foundation for accession is Article O (ex 49) of the TEU. The Amsterdam Treaty added caveats for accession in Article 7 (ex F 1) so that applicants for membership must demonstrate that they respect the fundamental principles of 'liberty, democracy, respect for human rights and fundamental freedoms, and the rule of law'. Decision-making procedures vis-à-vis enlargement are straightforward. The candidate applies for membership and the Council requests an Opinion from the Commission. The Council must then decide unanimously if it wishes to open negotiations. The Commission then proposes the broad negotiating lines and the Council must agree these, again unanimously. The EU and the candidate country then agree a draft treaty of Accession which is submitted to the Council and the European Parliament. The Commission gives an Opinion on the draft treaty and the Parliament must then assent to the treaty by an absolute majority and the Council must unanimously approve the Accession Treaty. After signature by the member states and the applicant countries, the Accession Treaty must be ratified by each of the member states and the candidate state. The treaty comes into force after ratification.

EUROPEAN UNION RELATIONS WITH SOUTH-EAST EUROPE (SEE)

The former Yugoslavia and Albania were at the very margin of Union concerns prior to the 1990s, and in the post-Cold War period the European Union has been pilloried for not preventing war in the Balkans. It is arguable, however, whether any international actor could have prevented conflict in this region. More positively, the European Union has played a very substantial part in the economic redevelopment of South-East Europe and continues to be a major player and pole of attraction for all countries in the sub-region.

The five states in the region can be divided into two groups. The first is Albania and the Former Yugoslav Republic (FYR) of Macedonia with which the European Union has managed to maintain productive relationships. Croatia, Bosnia and Herzegovina, and the Federal Republic (FR) of Yugoslavia comprise the second group – with which relations continued to be problematic – with the partial exception of the unfreezing of Croatian–EU relations consequent on 2000 elections in Croatia. Within the FR of Yugoslavia, EU relations remain complicated in that it has effectively established a separate foreign policy for Montenegro and Kosovo, both legally constituent entities within the Federal Republic.

EU policy towards the sub-region has been led by *security* priorities in terms of how to prevent war, to recover from war and to rebuild after war. The pursuit of *trade* objectives has not been a high priority for the EU. Instead it is *development cooperation* which has provided the focus of European Union policy. *Interregional cooperation* has also been a secondary issue, being promoted as an instrument in support of moves towards regional stabilisation. The tentative promise of *enlargement* to include those states that fulfil EU criteria in the moves towards democracy and respect for human rights has also helped underpin policies designed to achieve stability.

Security and Defence

EU involvement in the former Yugoslavia and Albania began as the former state disintegrated from the early 1990s onwards. The EU had some initial success in negotiating military restraint on the various parties but by 1995 had to accept a leading role for the United States in resolving the conflict in Bosnia. EU foreign policy instruments proved inadequate and, by the time of the second Balkan war in Kosovo in 1999, the EU had altered its role to that of senior partner in the civilian aspects of the military effort. EU member states retained an involvement in military action but directed their efforts through NATO – not through an EU security capacity.

Between 1991 and 1992, the EU had aspired to take the lead in Western policy towards Yugoslavia – and had been supported by the United States in so doing. In 1991 the EU had succeeded in mediating a cease-fire in Slovenia and had engaged in several rounds of shuttle diplomacy between Brussels, Belgrade and other Balkan capitals in an effort to keep the peace. An arms embargo was imposed on Yugoslavia in 1991 and in September 1991 the EU convened a conference on Yugoslavia at The Hague to find ways of resolving the crisis – attended by all six republics of the then Yugoslavia. With Serbian rejection of the conclusions of the conference, Germany pressurised the EU into recognition of both Slovenia and Croatia as independent states. Despite enormous internal unease, exacerbated by the fact that an independent commission appointed by the EU to consider the recognition issue stated that only Slovenia and the former Republic of Macedonia fulfilled democratic criteria, the EU recognised Slovenia and Croatia as independent states in January 1992.

The EU next made an effort to try to stop the Bosnian conflict from deteriorating into violence. The Bosnian Serbs had rejected independence in March 1992 – after a referendum in which they had abstained but which had resulted in a vote for secession from Yugoslavia. The Council convened another conference in March 1992 and imposed sanctions again – this time on Serbia and Montenegro in June 1992. In August 1992 the Union convened yet another conference – in London – and this time in coordination with the UN. The so-called Vance-Owen plan, named after David Owen the EU appointee and Cyrus Vance the UN appointee, emerged from the deliberations of this conference but was rejected by the Bosnian Serb Assembly in April 1993. The EU imposed further sanctions on the now rump state of Yugoslavia – comprising Montenegro and Serbia. The EU convened another conference in Geneva in November 1993 – but in early 1994, after the bombing of Sarajevo market in February, EU foreign ministers moved to refer the Bosnia crisis to NATO and accepted a role for the use of force in resolving the crisis. Divisions within the EU on the scale, scope and timing of the use of force meant that the EU could still not produce a credible policy to deal with the continuing violence in Bosnia. In June 1995, Carl Bildt replaced David Owen as EU mediator but it was the United States which led the various factions into a peace agreement – brokered and initialled under US diplomat Richard Holbrooke's tutelage at Dayton, Ohio in November 1995 – and signed in Paris in December 1995.

The European Union, like every other international actor until 1995, had had little success in preventing and then stopping the war in Bosnia, although its key member states played a major role in the security sphere. It was troops from EU member states – particularly from Britain and France – which had led the UN military protection forces (UNPROFOR) when the United States government had refused to allow ground troops to become involved in Bosnia. Britain and France were also major contributors to IFOR – the UN implementation force mobilised at the conclusion of the Dayton Accords which in December 1996 was renamed as SFOR – the Stabilisation Force for Bosnia.

The European Union was also involved in the Kosovo war of March–June 1999. The Union had expressed concern about the suppression of Albanian rights by the Belgrade-based Milosevic regime since 1992 and, as the Kosovo crisis grew more violent in 1998 when Serb military and paramilitary forces clashed with the Kosovan

Liberation Army (KLA), the EU engaged in a number of actions designed to support a resolution to the conflict. In March 1998 it supported the OSCE decision to give Felipe Gonzalez a mandate on Kosovo by also nominating Mr Gonzalez as the Union's Special Representative to Kosovo. In April 1999, it again imposed sanctions on the Federal Republic of Yugoslavia – this time on the supply and sale of oil. More vigorous action was, however, left to NATO – with EU member states utilising the wider Atlantic alliance to carry out policy to enforce compliance on Milosevic. Finally, in June, the EU special envoy, President Martti Ahtisaari of Finland along with the Russian special envoy, Victor Chernomyrdin, former Prime Minister of Russia, met with President Milosevic to negotiate the terms upon which the bombing would end. This deal provided the foundation for the final agreement to end the war between NATO and the Federal Republic of Yugoslavia on 9 June 1999. EU member states continued to play a substantial security role in postwar Kosovo as Britain, France, Germany and Italy led four of the five multinational military contingents in KFOR – the UN force established in June 1999 and designed to enforce the peace.

Actors, instruments, legal bases and decision-making procedures

The European Council and the General Affairs Council made regular pronouncements on the security situation in South-East Europe. The EU used the troika arrangements and also appointed a series of special envoys and special representatives including David Owen, Carl Bildt, Felipe Gonzalez and Martti Ahtisaari. The Commission and the Parliament played secondary roles in the security aspect of policy towards South-East Europe. Member states operated in a variety of arenas including the EU, NATO, OSCE and the UN – although some priority was given to the EU as the focus for collective diplomacy. Instruments varied from the use of the diplomatic *démarche*, to the implementation of economic sanctions and the use of military force. The legal bases for EU activity in this sphere were the CFSP provisions of the Treaty on European Union. In 1998, for instance, the EU implemented five new common positions under Article 12 (ex J 2) of the TEU and five new joint actions on the same area under Article 13 (ex J 3) in respect of what it called the 'western Balkans'. Despite the often very different perspectives, decision-makers attempted to reach consensus on policy.

Trade, Development Cooperation, Interregional Cooperation and Enlargement

In 1980 the EC had signed a cooperation agreement with the former Communist state of Yugoslavia – hoping to encourage Yugoslavia to remain independent of the former Soviet Union. The EC allocated financial aid to Yugoslavia – its third financial protocol in 1990 amounting to 807 MECU. By contrast, Albania, the other 'old' state in the region, had no contacts with the EU until 1990, after which a cooperation and trade agreement was concluded in 1992. By 1999 the only two states in the region with contractual relations with the EU were Albania with its 1992 trade agreement and the former Yugoslav Republic of Macedonia with which a cooperation agreement came into force in 1998. Since the break-up of the former Yugoslavia, however, the EU's main channel of foreign policy is via the conduit of development cooperation as the new states of Bosnia and Herzegovina, Croatia, the former Yugoslav Republic of Macedonia and the Federal Republic of Yugoslavia have become dependent on outside economic aid. It is the EU and the member states that are major donors to these states and to Albania.

Post-Dayton the EU developed what it termed its 'regional approach' to reconstruction. EU objectives were to support the peace accords through creating an area of 'political stability and economic prosperity'. The former Yugoslav Republic of Macedonia and Albania received preferential treatment under this approach compared to the other three countries, as Bosnia, Croatia and Yugoslavia were all carefully scrutinised as to their compliance with the Dayton agreements. Political and economic conditionality were overt features of the approach. Access to European Union trade preferences, financial and economic assistance and contractual relations were explicitly linked to progress in democratisation and, for the three 'Dayton' states, implementation of the peace accords.

In 1999, the EU updated the approach by agreeing a 'Stabilisation and Association Process' for the countries of South-Eastern Europe. The EU promised to negotiate new Stabilisation and Association Agreements (SAA) with those states that had moved in some way towards democratisation and political and economic reform. States would be offered 'a prospect of EU integration' – the idea being that the possibility of future EU membership would act as an incentive for cooperation in peace-building in the region. In addition to the prospect of negotiating an SAA, the stabilisation process also included provisions to encourage intraregional trade and economic cooperation, democratisaton, assistance in law enforcement and political dialogue at the regional level and was also intended to encourage private financial investment. The entire process was designed to contribute to the June 1999 Stability Pact for South-Eastern Europe – an EU initiative designed to provide a mechanism for cooperation between the EU, the United States, Russia, Japan, the South-East European states themselves, and Turkey along with the international financial institutions and any other country operating in the region. In 1999, however, only the FYR of Macedonia complied with the European Union's conditions for starting negotiations for a Stabilisation and Association Agreement in that it demonstrated what the Commission termed 'a credible commitment to continue on the path of democratisation and good-neighbourly and cooperative relations within the region'.

Overall financial transfers to South-Eastern Europe between 1991 and 1999 from the EU and the member states were substantial with Bosnia the recipient of the largest amounts of assistance – 2.5 billion Euros. The next largest amounts went to Albania and Croatia at 1.5 billion Euros each. Yugoslavia – including Montenegro and Kosovo – received just over a billion Euros while the Former Yugoslav Republic of Macedonia received the smallest amount of assistance – just over half a billion Euros. From the EU itself (not including the member states) Bosnia received the largest amount of assistance – at just over 2 billion Euros, then Albania at just over 800 million Euros, Yugoslavia at just under 500 million Euros, the FYR of Macedonia at just over 400 million Euros and lastly Croatia at just over 350 million Euros.

Serbia received some humanitarian assistance – for refugees, displaced persons and vulnerable groups. The European Union also donated 30,000 tons of heavy fuel and gas to opposition-run municipalities in Serbia. This 'energy for democracy' programme was designed to demonstrate that EU hostility was directed at the Milosevic government – not the Serbian people. EU allocations amounted to 7.7 million Euros in 1998 and 505 million Euros in 1999. The 1999 amount was divided into 127 million Euros for reconstruction assistance and 378 million for humanitarian aid. Allocations were increased in 2000 – to a total of 360 million Euros – with 275 million Euros going to reconstruction assistance, 50 million Euros to humanitarian aid and 35 million Euros for 'exceptional financial assistance'.

Trade and interregional cooperation efforts may be encouraged by the 2001 arrest of ex-President Milosevic although it may not make substantial progress until the remaining political conflicts within Yugoslavia are resolved. Enlargement to include the FYR of Macedonia may be technically possible but is problematic because of Greek hostility to the idea and again because of the instability illustrated by the violent skirmishes between Albanian separatists and the Macedonian army in 2001. Enlargement to include the other states in this region is a very distant prospect. In the short term, therefore, development cooperation provides the cornerstone of EU policy and practice towards the region.

Actors, instruments, legal bases and decision-making procedures

Within the Union both the Commission and the Council have played prominent roles in terms of the pursuit of economic reconstruction. Chris Patten, the Commissioner responsible for external relations at the turn of the century, has taken a leading role. After the war, the United Nations Mission in Kosovo (UNMIK), headed by Bernard Kouchner, led the reconstruction effort – with the EU taking the lead in the economic reconstruction sector. The member states made significant financial contributions to the overall economic reconstruction effort. The EBRD also funds projects in the region – in all the states except Yugoslavia – lending some 7.5 billion Euros between 1991 and 1999. The EU works closely with the World Bank in attempts to coordinate donor activity for the decimated economies of this sub-region.

The EU has proved itself adept in both developing existing instruments and developing new initiatives designed to deal with the specific economic and political instability in the area. Bosnia and Herzegovina, Croatia and FYR of Macedonia, for instance, continue to benefit from trade preferences originally designated for the former Yugoslavia. Albania and the FYR of Macedonia are also entitled to aid from the PHARE programme. Other classical instruments utilised have been humanitarian aid provided through ECHO (to all states in this sub-region) as well as EIB loans (to Albania). In addition the EU created the OBNOVA programme in 1996. This is an EC instrument designed to provide funding in support of the Dayton peace accords and is intended to help reconstruct Bosnia and Herzegovina, Croatia, the FYR of Macedonia and Yugoslavia. The Stability and Association Agreements will provide a new means of association with the EU – designed to give partner countries 'a prospect of

EU integration'. The trade and cooperation agreements with the FYR of Macedonia and Albania are based on conventional sources – Articles 133 (ex 113) and 310 (ex 238) of the treaties establishing the European Communities.

EUROPEAN UNION RELATIONS WITH CYPRUS, MALTA AND TURKEY

At the beginning of the twenty-first century, European Union foreign policy towards Cyprus, Malta and Turkey is shaped by the question of future accession. The European Union has agreed that the next round of enlargement should include Cyprus and Malta which are both actively involved in the implementation of pre-accession strategies. Since 1997, Turkey has also been considered as a potential candidate country with a dedicated 'European strategy' agreed to help Turkey prepare for accession in 1998. *Security and defence, trade, development cooperation* and questions of *interregional cooperation* are treated in the context of EU policy on enlargement.

Historically *security* issues, in the broadest sense, have impinged on EU relations with Cyprus and Turkey to the extent that the EU has attempted some cautious political intervention in Cyprus to encourage a solution to the division of the island. It has also made diplomatic and economic interventions in Turkey in response to internal political developments. The EC, for instance, froze its relations with Turkey in 1980 as a response to military intervention in the political process and has frequently condemned human rights abuses, particularly of the Kurdish minority. The EU has consistently argued that Turkey could not be considered as a candidate for membership until respect for human rights and rule of law was more firmly established within the country. The EC/EU position on Turkey, however, has also been tempered by its understanding of Turkey as a key strategic ally – and a member of NATO. The relationship with Turkey is further complicated by the Turkish military occupation of northern Cyprus since 1974 – precipitated by the Cypriot government's declaration of union with Greece. The Greek/Turkish border within Cyprus has since 1974 been patrolled by United Nations peacekeepers and has sometimes seen tense security stand-offs – for instance in 1996 when a Greek Cypriot was killed by Turkish troops. Positive change in relations between Greece and Turkey after the devastating earthquake of August 1999 – including preliminary agreements to pursue cooperation in the areas of tourism, culture, environment and combating organised crime – offer some hope that it may be possible to secure a negotiated solution to some of the more long-standing and difficult issues in Greek–Turkish relations. This may in turn facilitate a climate of cooperation where the Cyprus 'problem' could at last be negotiated.

The EU has engaged in *trade* relations with Cyprus, Malta and Turkey under the auspices of association agreements since, respectively, 1972, 1970 and 1963. The EU remained an important trade partner for all three states – but to a varying extent. Between 1994 and 1998, for instance, the EU share of Cypriot imports increased from 55.5 per cent to 61.9 per cent while Cypriot exports to the EU remained at around 50 per cent, slightly decreasing from 52.2 per cent to 50.4 per cent. In the same period, the EU share of Malta's imports declined from just over 75 per cent to 69 per cent while the percentage of Malta's exports to the EU declined more dramatically – from 74 per cent to just under 53 per cent. Turkey on the other hand increased its import and export share to the EU in the same period – from just over 44 per cent to 52.4 per cent of imports and just under 46 per cent to 50 per cent of exports. EU relations are much more intense with Cyprus and Turkey than with Malta. The EU and Turkey established a customs union in 1995 while Cyprus and the EU expect to complete a customs union in 2002.

The EU provides *development cooperation* to all three states. Some of this comes in the form of financial assistance by way of the financial protocols attached to the association agreements. Other assistance comes in the form of humanitarian aid – for instance the 34 million Euros provided for disaster relief and rehabilitation after the 1999 earthquake in Turkey. Cyprus, Malta and Turkey participate in the Euro–Mediterranean (Euro–Med) partnership established in the wake of the Middle East peace process of the early 1990s (see Chapter 6). The EU and its 15 member states engage in *interregional cooperation*, therefore, in a formalised and institutionalised manner through the various meetings of the partnership.

It is *enlargement*, however, which provides the EU frame of reference to these three countries in the early twenty-first century. The 1963 association agreement with Turkey had included a clause that envisaged Turkish membership of the then EC although Turkey did not apply for membership until 1987. Cyprus and Malta applied to join in 1990 although Malta froze its membership application in 1996 after the Malta Labour party won the general election –

unfreezing its application after the victory of the Nationalist party in the elections of 1998.

Cyprus and Malta have been included in the enlargement negotiations along with the East European countries since 1994. The EU agreed a specific pre-accession strategy for Cyprus in December 1997 at the European Council in Luxembourg which permitted access to technical assistance and participation in certain Community programmes and projects – particularly those aimed at improving administrative capacity and in the fields of Justice and Home Affairs. The major problem remained the absence of a political solution to the Cyprus conflict and hence the lack of Turkish Cypriot participation in the negotiations. EU reports on Cyprus therefore deal only with Greek Cyprus – leading to a slight air of unreality about negotiations ostensibly designed to deal with the whole island but in fact only covering the wealthier southern Greek Cyprus. The EU hopes that the attractions of potential membership may help to encourage a settlement of the conflict but also risks importing a long-running international site of conflict within its own borders if a solution is not found prior to the deadline for enlargement negotiations.

Malta on the other hand presents few problems in terms of potential accession. It fulfils the Copenhagen political and economic criteria in that it is a functioning democracy, has an established market economy and is capable of fulfilling its obligations under the *acquis* – including possessing the capacity to cope with competitive pressure and market forces once a member of the Union. The EU began its 'screening' process of Malta in 1999 and in June 1999 the General Affairs Council agreed to include Malta in the multilateral political dialogue with the East European applicants and Cyprus.

Turkey has been a problematic case for the European Union. The EU's major ally, the United States, has encouraged Turkish efforts to join the EU because of Turkey's strategic importance in the Middle East and as a 'gateway' to the central Asian states of the former Soviet Union. The EU has been more cautious about Turkish membership – partly because of the Cyprus issue and partly because Greece, Turkey's major antagonist, has been wary of Turkish membership. In addition to these geopolitical concerns, however, there are others. Turkey is a very large state, with a population of some 63 million people whose average income in 1998 was just 32 per cent of the EU average. Countering this is the fact that Turkey, along with Norway and Switzerland, is more economically integrated with the European Union than any other state in non-EU Europe, and the EU reports that Turkey more or less fulfils the economic criteria of Copenhagen. It has many of the characteristics of a market economy and is likely to be able to cope with competitive pressures and market forces within the Union. At the turn of the century, however, in 1999, the major issue of contention was that the Union did not consider that Turkey met the Copenhagen political criteria. The EU was concerned about widespread torture, restrictions on freedom of expression, human rights and protection of minorities. It was particularly concerned that the death penalty be not carried out on Abdullah Öcalan, the Kurdish leader – sentenced to death in June 1999 by the State Security Court.

Nevertheless the EU has pursued a policy of continuing engagement and dialogue with Turkey. Since 1997 the EU has developed a specific European strategy for Turkey that included measures to intensify the customs union and implement financial cooperation, to support approximation of Turkish legislation to the *acquis* and to encourage Turkey's participation in specific Community programmes and agencies. The December 1999 European Council at Helsinki confirmed the strategy – allocating 150 million Euros to assist in implementation during the years 2000–02.

Actors, instruments, legal bases and decision-making procedures

The Council and the Commission have been the major actors in the relationship with the three states – with the Parliament assuming an activist stance on relations with Turkey. The major instruments utilised to facilitate the relationship were the financial protocols attached to the association agreements. The EU has also engaged in diplomatic efforts to support a peace settlement in Cyprus and has used diplomatic means to bring pressure on the Turkish authorities on political issues. Since the mid-1990s, however, an important instrument has been the promise of accession. Pre-accession partnerships and the EU's 'screening' process have encouraged the adoption of the *acquis*. The political and economic strategic objectives of EU foreign policy – adoption of liberal democracy and market economies – are thus fulfilled through self-adoption by the partner states. The legal bases for the association agreements with the three countries were Articles 133 (ex 113) and 310 (ex 238) of the treaties establishing the European Communities. The association agreements were accompanied by Association Councils, Association Committees and arrangements for inter-parliamentary cooperation. Decision-making in respect of Turkey has not been straightforward

– with a failure to reach unanimity by the Council in 1991 entailing the rejection of a Commission proposal to enhance and improve relations. In 1995, the Parliament used its powers of assent in respect of the customs union with Turkey to insist on attention to human rights issues. The Parliament threatened not to ratify the customs union and only reluctantly agreed to do so after some political prisoners were released and changes in Turkish legislation on terrorism took place.

THE EUROPEAN UNION FOREIGN POLICY PRIORITY

The strategic foreign policy priority for the European Union in the early twenty-first century is to build a strong, prosperous, liberal democratic and politically stable Europe. Huge strides were made towards integrating northern European countries into the Union, and political and economic efforts remain focused on incorporating most of the remaining European states in the European constriction which, by the early twenty-first century, is neither geographically divided nor split between organisations which are functionally separate from each other. The European Union of the twenty-first century, therefore, has changed to become an organisation that is more representative geographically of the continent and is much more capable in its ability to pursue diverse policy interests abroad than the European Community of the 1950s. Whether or not this is a 'good thing' or a 'bad thing' is discussed in the final chapter.

Guide to Further Reading for Chapter 8

There is now an enormous literature on EU relations with the rest of Europe. Some sub-regions have more coverage than others with Central and Eastern Europe tending to be well covered and Russia and the NIS, by contrast, not as extensively analysed. A good chapter on EU relations with the wider Europe is in Christopher Piening, *Global Europe: The European Union in World Affairs* (London: Lynne Rienner, 1997). An overview of post-Cold War European security issues which includes relevant material on OSCE, EU, WEU and the Baltic–Nordic region is W. Park and G. Wyn Rees (eds), *Rethinking Security in Post-Cold War Europe* (Harlow: Addison Wesley Longman: 1998).

On relations with the northern neighbours, two indispensable sources are Helen Wallace (ed.), *The Wider Western Europe: Reshaping the EC/EFTA Relationship* (London: Pinter/RIIA, 1992) and Lee Miles (ed.), *The European Union and the Nordic Countries* (London: Routledge, 1996). On relations with the NIS, the secondary sources are limited. Try Ole Nørgaard, 'The Post-Soviet Newly Independent States and the European Community: Prospects for Trade, Investment and Aid', in Ole Nørgaard, Thomas Pedersen and Nikolaj Petersen, *The European Community in World Politics* (London: Pinter, 1993) and Antje Herrberg, 'The European Union and Russia: Toward a New *Ostpolitik'*, in Carolyn Rhodes (ed.), *The European Union in the World Community* (London: Lynne Rienner, 1998). The best source of raw data on EU relations with the NIS is the EUROPA website of the European Commission at http://europa.eu.int/ – although this is of course not a source of critical evaluation of policies.

There are a number of accessible and systematic treatments of EU relations with East and Central European states. The most comprehensive and detailed, but unfortunately not available in paperback, is Karen E. Smith, *The Making of EU Foreign Policy* (London: Macmillan, 1999). Also useful is John Pinder, *The European Community and Eastern Europe* (London: Pinter/Royal Institute of International Affairs, 1991), Alan Mayhew, *Recreating Europe: The European Union's Policy Towards Central and Eastern Europe* (Cambridge: Cambridge University Press, 1998), Heather Grabbe and Kirsty Hughes, *Enlarging the EU Eastwards* (London: Pinter/Royal Institute of International Affairs, 1998). The Commission's view on enlargement can be found in Graham Avery and Fraser Cameron, *The Enlargement of the European Union* (Sheffield: Sheffield Academic Press, 1999). European Union policy towards East and Central Europe is also summarised in various official documents. For the quote in this chapter on trade and development cooperation see European Parliament, Directorate-General for Research, *Fact Sheets on the European Parliament and the Activities of the European Union* (Luxembourg: Office for Official Publications of the European Communities, 1994), p. 119.

EU policy towards South-East Europe has been transformed from an almost complete lack of interest prior to the break-up of Yugoslavia into an interventionary and active involvement in recent years. As a result there is little secondary literature. A good overview on the security issues is Andreas G. Kintis, 'The EU's Foreign Policy and the War in Former Yugoslavia', in Martin Holland (ed.), *Common Foreign and Security Policy* (London: Pinter, 1997). The EU website carries reports, speeches and a mass of data on EU activity in this area and can be accessed at http://europa.eu.int/comm/external_relations/see/intro/index.htm.

Two short accounts of relations with Cyprus, Malta and Turkey, the second with particular reference to enlargement, can be found in Christopher Piening, *Global Europe: The European Union in World Affairs* (London: Lynne Rienner, 1997) and Graham Avery and Fraser Cameron, *The Enlargement of the European Union* (Sheffield: Sheffield Academic Press, 1999). A view from the other side can be found in Christopher Pollacco, *Malta–EEC Relations* (Msida, Malta: Mireva, 1992). A comprehensive source on developments in respect of enlargement can be found on the EU enlargement website at http://europa.eu.int/pol/enlarg/index_en.htm.

9 Guns or Butter?

This book started out by asking if the European Union possessed a foreign policy. The last eight chapters have demonstrated that if we can get away from considering only that which is sanctified by the procedures and legalities of CFSP, we undoubtedly find that the EU has a comprehensive, extensive and sometimes remarkably effective foreign policy. It is simply banal to argue that because the EU achieves its foreign policy aims through a whole panoply of non-CFSP instruments and activities by fiat, it does not possess a foreign policy. The European Union is not of course always successful or efficient and therefore sometimes does not achieve foreign policy objectives or does not carry out policy very well. This is the same for all states – including the most powerful.

Some of the argument is necessarily about the perception or 'theory' one holds of what constitutes foreign policy (see annotated reading list at the end of the chapter for specific theorists). Theoretical issues do need to be resolved but they are nowhere near as important as the implications of the argument for the ethics and politics of the European Union. In practice, the Union can now intervene in almost any area of the world in almost any aspect of foreign policy. It has a massive armoury of instruments and activities that it can mobilise to achieve objectives abroad. Ethically, the question is should it do so? The Union, with its history of conflict with the United States, could become an increasingly independent actor in international affairs. Politically, the question is will it do so? And, given what we know about the Union's history and trajectory in foreign affairs so far, what can we say about what the future priorities of the European Union will be in its international relations? Where do we go from here?

THE THEORIES

There are very many theories of international relations and politics that could help to explain and understand the European Union's role in world affairs. Some of these theories share certain assumptions even if they differ in their methodologies, normative biases and conclusions. Clusters of theories sharing basic assumptions can be thought of as traditions of inquiry, formerly widely known as 'paradigms'. In contemporary international relations research the three most common traditions of inquiry can be categorised as Realist, Interdependence (or Liberal) or Social Constructivist. We should be careful when we are using these labels. It can be very dangerous to try to summarise complex bodies of thought because inevitably the richness, variety and sophistication of the best exponents in the field become lost in the flattening and simplifying of theories in the attempt to convey their essence. It is sometimes necessary, however, to construct 'ideal types' in order to convey the basic or fundamental elements of theoretical approaches. The ideal types used here are just this – simplified models of fundamentals of the theory – and should definitely not be interpreted as representing the range and scope of inquiry inherent in the developed theoretical traditions outlined below.

An ideal-type Realist considers the state as the most important actor in international relations and recognises international politics as inherently insecure with, in the end, the state's commitment and capability to defend itself militarily as the sign of its competence in foreign affairs. A state's priority is to defend its national security. An Interdependence theorist is also concerned with the security of states but considers that foreign policy and international relations can cover a gamut of different issues – environment, money, migration are just some examples. Interdependence theorists are also prepared to recognise that international organisations can play an important role in the international system. Trade and economic interreaction can encourage 'win–win' behaviour in the international system such that everyone can benefit from such relationships – even if not everyone and every state will benefit equally. Social Constructivists focus on states as the subject of inquiry but argue that the interests and identities of states are historically and socially constructed, partly through inter-state socialisation processes. Cultural and institutional aspects of the state's environment – international norms – both constitute and regulate the behaviour of states.

An ideal-type Realist would have some difficulties with the geo-issue-area approach offered in this book insomuch as it includes trade, development, interregional cooperation and enlargement as forming an integral part of foreign policy. Realists – so the stereotypes go – consider the military aspects of security as the primary domain of foreign policy – with geopolitical strategy forming the framework for Realist foreign policy priority setting. It is probably enough to respond to this hypothetical Realist critique by pointing out that the Realist of such stereotypes simply does not exist – except in the oversimplified transpositions of their thought into some textbooks.

Almost all the great Realist scholars have understood the importance and significance of economic goals and economic instruments as key aspects of state security policy. If state – and here European Union – security is envisioned as the protection of core values and interests and foreign policy is the approach to state security, then all the issue-areas developed in this book have at some point directly involved the protection and defence of European Union security. Union policy on enlargement towards Eastern and Central Europe, for instance, can be conceived of partially as a response to the need to consolidate geopolitical stability in the European periphery such as to maintain the security of the European heartlands. The key but perhaps not insurmountable problem for Realist scholars is the centrality of the state to their analyses. But some Realists have also not ruled out the possibility of other organisations becoming as important as the state in the future. The state for Realist theorists is, arguably, of historical significance but is not a paradigmatic universal.

An Interdependence theorist would have less difficulty with a broader understanding of foreign policy – as almost by definition the Interdependence theorists understand international organisations as playing important political as well as economic roles in the international system. In addition Interdependence theorists – with their intellectual foundations in liberal trade theories where trade and growing economic links are somehow bound to bring peace – would feel reasonably at home with the idea that foreign policy invokes a wider spectrum of issues and instruments than narrow versions of defence-based foreign policy approaches would allow. Finally, the Social Constructivists would probably have no necessary quarrel with the more inclusive approach to foreign policy offered here – although in practice the emphasis on *what states do* in their work might make for some uneasiness in the conception of the European Union as a more or less independent actor.

There are, therefore, few great theoretical obstacles to adopting the approach that the European Union has a foreign policy that it exercises throughout the world in a number of different issue-areas. A rear-guard action could come from the institutionalist ghetto of European integration analysis which concentrates on procedure at the expense of substance – form at the expense of content – in a defence of the idea that CFSP procedures as written in the treaties should limit the scope of inquiry into European Union foreign policy. Yet this is the minor exception and as most of this work is atheoretical at best and anti-theoretical at worst it can be dismissed as a serious venture in the investigation of what constitutes European Union foreign policy.

THE ETHICS

The European Union then is a serious foreign policy actor that has pursued its objectives abroad using a wide variety of instruments. It has a clear philosophy in its promotion of liberal capitalist democracy, the role of law, human rights and democratisation. The pursuit of these objectives has not been merely rhetorical but neither has it been allowed to stand in the way of its economic and security interests. Economic security priorities – particularly in respect of the stability of oil supplies – lie behind the continued efforts to maintain close relationships with states where there is grave concern about human rights violations – such as Saudi Arabia and Algeria. On the other hand the attempts made to reconstruct civil societies in the Balkans – although as much about securing stable political environments in Europe as about humanitarianism – have at least attempted to assist in the rebuilding of those societies along pluralist and democratic lines. There are in other words both positive and negative aspects of the Union's claims for ethical standing in the pursuit of its foreign policy objectives.

The European Union does not have to be a selfless political actor in order to engage in ethically acceptable foreign policy behaviour. It is outcome more than motivation that should be the criterion upon which to evaluate action in this respect. For instance, it may well suit the European Union's market-based interests to be developing a more visible role in Asia – in trade, development cooperation and in interregional fora. At the same time, however, it does no harm at all for Chris Patten to be reminding his hosts in Pyongyang – as he did in the troika visit to north Korea in 2001 – that human rights is an issue which the Europeans will be concerned with in their future dealings with north Korea.

European Union foreign policy does indeed support the interests of elites in Europe who want to promote the interests of European business abroad. It also, however, can and sometimes does support the interests of wider coalitions. In Central America in the 1980s the Community's support for a multilateral approach to peace was crucial in legitimating the inclusion of the region's left and moderate wings in the peace-building process – much against the wishes of the then United States administration. In a more contemporary example, it is because of the promise of EU and other international support for 'civil society' and 'good governance' that astute (and sometimes cynical) individuals and groups in East and Central Europe can press their own governments for improvements in accountability and transparency.

What pushes the European Union in the direction of an ethical foreign policy – even though, as for states, interests are likely to count out values every time – is the particular and unique nature of European Union foreign policy. What is structurally important about the ethics of EU foreign policy is its visibility. In an organisation of 15 or more states which are jealous of their national foreign policy-making autonomy and are constantly watching the Union for signs of overreach – it is difficult to engage in the worst types of foreign policy *realpolitik*. Such actions require secrecy and activity by small groups of people who are protected from public scrutiny – often through claims that such clandestinity is in the national interest. In addition, the necessity for the Union to be accountable to and to maintain support from 15 sets of public opinion and 15 govern-ments and Parliaments and 15 sets of national media precludes any foreign policy activity that is not underpinned by a very broad level of public consensus. It is in the end the pressure of public opinion that tends to keep European Union foreign policy activity at least relatively 'clean'. This is perhaps one reason why the Union sometimes seems to view itself as an intrinsically ethical foreign policy actor.

The European Union also benefits from the fact that it does not yet have a direct military capacity. It has had no European Union army that has been directly engaged in the bombing of foreign cities even if its member states have been sometimes in this position – for instance in the Kosovo war and the bombing of Belgrade. The Union has been directly involved in peace-keeping and peace-building – but not peace-enforcement (as war-making is sometimes termed in the early twenty-first century). As long as the Union can keep its putative military forces in the realm of supporting humanitarian work and peace-keeping, it may be able to maintain a reputation for being more ethically acceptable in its foreign policy than its member states or than its major ally the United States. Should the day come when the Union engages in more warlike activity – for instance, in a joint action which includes bombing Iraq or which introduces ground troops in any combat, maybe for instance in an exacerbated Macedonian conflict – there would be less chance of the Union being judged any differently from any state which engages in such activities. Each foreign policy action would have to be judged on the individual merits of that particular activity.

Should the EU engage in foreign policy? That all depends. If the Union is in a position to engage in a genuinely ethical foreign policy in some situations – in other words if the self-interests of the Union can coincide with the ability to improve the conditions of life for individuals globally – then these developments should be supported. Even if, at minimum, the EU could be said to be operating by the old humanitarian maxim of 'do no harm', this itself would be a step forward for the ethics of foreign policymaking everywhere.

THE POLITICS

Politically, the Union is now capable of assertive and independent behaviour abroad. In a geopolitical context where independence for the Union has always meant above all acting autonomously from the United States, a developed foreign policy capacity allows the Union, should it so wish, to at minimum provide an irritant to the United States and at maximum to appear threatening or aggressive. This is not a new feature of Union foreign politics. In the 1980s the then Community and the United States disagreed on a whole range of international security and trade issues.

The difference today is that the Union of the 2000s is a far more competent and developed entity than that of the 1980s.The Union has a global currency, the Euro, at its disposal. It has an enlarged territory that includes most of the prosperous nations of Europe and it has become a pole of political attraction in the rest of Europe to the extent that nearly every other European state wants to join. The Cold War is over and the anti-Communist ties that used to bind the United States and Western Europe so tightly are no longer so compelling. Structurally the bonds that link the Union to the United States are still mutually important – in terms of trade, investment and more or less common political philosophies. But room for conflict over markets and differing conceptions of how to promote the political good life may also make for tension.

Conversely there are some opportunities for a global division of labour between the Union and the United States. To some extent, Union intervention alongside NATO in support of the peace process in Macedonia in 2001 demonstrated the Union's easy slippage into the 'soft power' role besides the 'hard power' presence of the United States as the dominant power within the North Atlantic alliance. Crudely, if the United States can provide the 'guns' for peace-enforcement, the European Union is better placed to provide the 'butter' for reconstruction after the bombing. It is unlikely, however, that the Union would be satisfied in every political conflict abroad to take the subordinate role that this division of labour implies. This is particularly so if the new Bush administration continues with its trajectory of withdrawing from international agreements and pursuing aggressive unilateralism abroad. With the combination of a stronger Union and a US administration in 2001 that seems to have every intention to focus on Asia, not Europe, it would be unsurprising if conflict did not occur. How that conflict will be managed and resolved will provide the story of the next decade of EU/US relations.

WHERE NEXT FOR EUROPEAN UNION FOREIGN POLICY?

The Union's clear priorities for the next decade are the consolidation of political stability in Europe and the maintenance and consolidation of a prosperous and sustainable market economy that will be able to take advantage of trade and investment opportunities available to it abroad. Its security priorities include both territorial defence – even if this is recognised as more usefully dealt with in NATO – and the prevention and containment of political violence on the European periphery.

Relations with the world's largest powers – the US and Russia – will continue to frame the parameters of EU foreign policy. No state or international organisation can afford to ignore the United States, which is the only superpower in the world at the beginning of the twenty-first century. For the Union, the US is both economic competitor and political ally. The challenge for European Union foreign policymakers is how to contain conflicts with its major ally at the same time as ensuring that divergent Union political and economic interests are not given up to US agendas. Russia is still important because of its territorial presence on the edge of the European continent and because of its continuing military potential. The EU is interested in the potential of the Russian market but this is a subsidiary interest compared to that of working out a security *modus operandi* which will contain any future Russian ambitions to regain its old empire in Europe and will allay the fears of Baltic and East and Central European states of a resurgent Russia.

Policies towards the neighbouring South are led by a dual push to prevent uncontrolled migration into Europe and to provide in some ways for economic development through trade and aid support. Policies towards the distant South are more variegated – but are less urgent for the Union. Where trade can be encouraged as in the case of relations with China and Latin America the Union will do so. Where aid is a more appropriate economic response as in EU relations with the African, Caribbean and Pacific countries, the Union will continue to uphold historic commitments. In the hierarchy of commitments and priorities, relations with the distant South – apart from with those countries where trade is an important feature such as some of the east Asian states – will be subordinated to the more immediate priority of providing support to East and Central Europe.

GUNS *AND* BUTTER

The European Union is likely to become more and not less involved in foreign policy. It is likely to want to expand its security profile, and the Bush administration's lone ranger tactics abroad may provide just the impetus that the Union requires to rejuvenate the European Security and Defence Identity (ESDI), which so far has been little more than a paper concept. The Union does not need a dedicated army to promote hard power security objectives. It can perfectly well utilise the Western European Union or the individual capacities of member states. Unless the United States disagrees outright it may also call upon aspects of the NATO capability to help implement policies. It also has an array of economic instruments that it has not been shy of using in the pursuit of security objectives (sanctions, trade and aid concessions). Its ability to mobilise the 'guns' component of foreign policy may be indirect, but it is viable.

The 'butter' component of Union foreign policy needs less introduction. Trade and development cooperation provide the more or less uncontroversial mainstay of Union policies abroad. Whether expanding trade ties with the United States and Japan or rebuilding houses in Kosovo and providing fertiliser in north Korea – the Union plays, uncontrovertibly, a global economic role. That all of this engagement is part and parcel of the pursuit of a tightly knit array of foreign policy goals is perhaps less appreciated.

MAINTAINING ACCOUNTABILITY

The Union is a powerful foreign policy actor. As with any other foreign policy actor, it is public scrutiny and critique that can help to keep policymakers accountable. More needs to be done to investigate the difference between what goes on paper (the treaties and procedures) and what the Union actually does in the world (the foreign policy outcomes). Hopefully, this book takes a step in this direction.

Guide to Further Reading for Chapter 9

A useful overview of international relations theory is J. Baylis and Steve Smith (eds), *The Globalization of World Politics* (Oxford: Oxford University Press, 1997). Realism, Liberalism and Social Constructivism are well covered here. For a discussion of Realism, Liberal and Social Constructivist theories see Hazel Smith, 'Chapter 1: Why is there no International Democratic Theory?', in Hazel Smith (ed.), *Democracy and International Relations: Critical Theories/Problematic Practices* (London and New York: Macmillan and St Martin's Press, 2000).

The founding text of modern Realism can be found in Hans Morgenthau, revised by Kenneth W. Thompson, *Politics Among Nations: The Struggle for Power and Peace*, sixth edition (New York: Alfred A. Knopf, 1985). The text provides a full understanding of the relationship of economic goals as political goals for states and the use of economic instruments to achieve foreign policy goals. Even Kenneth Waltz as the archetypal 'structuralist' or 'neo-realist' accepts that broader issues can be of concern for states than merely military security – citing population growth as one. See Kenneth Waltz, *Theory of International Politics* (New York: McGraw-Hill, 1979). For a sophisticated dissertation of what political community might look like 'beyond the states system' see Hedley Bull, *The Anarchical Society: A Study of Order in World Politics* (London: Macmillan, 1985).

The classic exposition of interdependence theory is in Robert O. Keohane and Joseph S. Nye, *Power and Interdependence*, second edition (London: Scott, Foresman, Little and Brown, 1989). There are a huge variety of Social Constructivist approaches. For one of the most coherent see John Gerard Ruggie, *Constructing the World Polity* (London: Routledge, 1998).

Bibliography

Allen, David and Pijpers, Alfred (eds) *European Foreign Policy and the Arab–Israeli Conflict* (Dordrecht: Martinus Nijhoff, 1984)

Allen, David, Rummel, Reinhardt and Wessels, Wolfgang (eds) *European Political Cooperation* (London: Butterworth, 1982)

Allen, David and Smith, Michael 'Western Europe's Presence in the Contemporary International Arena', in *Review of International Studies*, Vol. 69 No. 1, 1990

Avery, Graham and Cameron, Fraser *The Enlargement of the European Union* (Sheffield: Sheffield Academic Press, 1999)

Bailey, Richard *The European Community in the World* (London: Hutchinson, 1973)

Barbé, Esther and Izquierdo, Ferran 'Present and Future of Joint Actions for the Mediterranean Region', in Holland, Martin (ed.), *Common Foreign and Security Policy* (London: Pinter, 1997)

Baylis, J. and Smith, Steve (eds) *The Globalization of World Politics* (Oxford: Oxford University Press, 1997)

Bretherton, Charlotte and Vogler, John *The European Union as a Global Actor* (London: Routledge, 1999)

Bull, Hedley *The Anarchical Society: A Study of Order in World Politics* (London: Macmillan, 1985)

Calingaert, Michael *European Integration Revisited: Progress, Prospects and US Interests* (Boulder: Westview, 1996)

Cameron, Fraser *The Foreign and Security Policy of the European Union* (Sheffield: Sheffield Academic Press, 1999)

Church, Clive H. and Phinnemore, David *European Union and European Community: A Handbook and Commentary on the Post-Maastricht Treaties* (London: Harvester Wheatsheaf, 1994)

Coffey, Peter *The EC and the United States* (London: Pinter, 1993)

Corbett, Richard, Jacobs, Francis and Shackleton, Michael *The European Parliament*, third edition (London: Cartermill, 1995)

Council of the European Communities/Commission of the European Communities *Treaty on European Union* (Luxembourg: OOPEC, 1992)

De Schoutheete, Phillipe *La Coopération Politique Européenne* (Brussels: Labor, 1980)

Edwards, Geoffrey 'Europe and the Falklands Islands Crisis 1982', in *Journal of Common Market Studies* Vol. XXII No. 4, June 1984

Edwards, Geoffrey and Regelsberger, Elfriede (eds) *Europe's Global Links: The European Community and Inter-Regional Cooperation* (London: Pinter, 1990)

European Commission *Europe and Japan: The Next Steps* Com (95) 73 final, Brussels, 08.03.1995

European Parliament, Directorate-General for Research *Fact Sheets on the European Parliament and the Activities of the European Union* (Luxembourg: Office for Official Publications of the European Communities, 1994)

Featherstone, Kevin 'The Mediterranean Challenge: Cohesion and External Preferences', in Lodge, Juliet (ed.) *The European Community and the Challenge of the Future*, first edition (London: Pinter, 1989)

Featherstone, Kevin 'The EC and the US: Managing Interdependence', in Lodge, Juliet (ed.) *The European Community and the Challenge of the Future*, second edition (London: Pinter, 1993)

Featherstone, Kevin and Ginsberg, Roy H. *The United States and the European Union in the 1990s: Partners in Transition*, second edition (New York: St Martin's Press, 1996)

Flaesch-Mougin, Catherine and Lebullenger, Joël *Les relations contractuelles de l'Union Européenne avec les pays et groupements Latino-Americains* (Rennes: Centre de Recherches Européennes de Rennes, undated but 1996)

Gambles, Ian *Prospects for West European Security Co-operation* (London: IISS/Adelphi papers 244, 1989)

Ginsberg, Roy H. *Foreign Policy Actions of the European Community: The Politics of Scale* (Boulder: Lynne Rienner, 1989)

Ginsberg, Roy. H. 'The EU's CFSP: The Politics of Procedure', in Holland, Martin (ed.) *Common Foreign and Security Policy: The Record and Reforms* (London: Pinter, 1997)

Grabbe, Heather and Hughes, Kirsty *Enlarging the EU Eastwards* (London: Pinter/RIIA, 1998)

Grant, Richard *The European Union and China: A European Strategy for the Twenty-first Century* (London: Royal Institute of International Affairs, 1995)

Grenville, J.A.S. *A World History of the 20th Century, Volume 1* (Glasgow: Fontana Press, 1986)

Grilli, Enzo R. *The European Community and the Developing Countries* (Cambridge: Cambridge University Press, 1993)

Halliday, Fred *The Making of the Second Cold War* (London: Verso, 1986)

Herrberg, Antje 'The European Union and Russia: Toward a New *Ostpolitik*', in Rhodes, Carolyn (ed.) *The European Union in the World Community* (London: Lynne Rienner, 1998)

Hewitt, Adrian 'Development Assistance Policy and the ACP', in Lodge, Juliet (ed.) *The European Community and the Challenge of the Future*, second edition (London: Pinter, 1993)

Higgott, Richard 'Shared Response to the Market Shocks', in *The World Today* Vol. 54 No. 1, January 1998

Hill, Christopher (ed.) *National Foreign Policies and European Political Cooperation* (RIIA/Allen & Unwin, 1983)

Hill, Christopher and Smith, Karen E. (eds) *European Foreign Policy: Key Documents* (London and New York: Routledge in association with the Secretariat of the European Parliament, 2000)

Hinsley, F.H. *Power and the Pursuit of Peace* (Cambridge: Cambridge University Press, 1988)

Hogan, Michael J. *The Marshall Plan: America, Britain and the Reconstruction of Western Europe, 1947–1952* (Cambridge: Cambridge University Press, 1987)

Holland, Martin *The European Community and South Africa: European Political Cooperation Under Strain* (London: Pinter, 1988)

Holland, Martin *European Community Integration* (New York: St Martin's Press, 1993)

Holland, Martin *European Union Common Foreign Policy: From EPC to CFSP Joint Action and South Africa* (London: Macmillan, 1995)

Holland, Martin 'The Joint Action on South Africa: A Successful Experiment?', in Holland, Martin (ed.) *Common Foreign and Security Policy: The Record and Reforms* (London: Pinter, 1997)

Holmes, Peter and Smith, Alasdair 'The EC, the USA and Japan: The Trilateral Relationship in World Context', in Ugur, Mehmet (ed.) *Policy Issues in the European Union* (London: Greenwich University, 1995)

Hurwitz, Leon *The European Community and the Management of International Cooperation* (Westport, Connecticut: Greenwood, 1987)

Ifestos, Panayiotis *European Political Cooperation: Towards a Framework of Supra-national Diplomacy?* (Aldershot: Avebury, 1987)

International Institute of Strategic Studies *Adelphi* papers (London: International Institute of Strategic Studies, various dates)

International Institute of Strategic Studies *Strategic Survey* (London: International Institute of Strategic Studies, various dates, annual publication)

Keohane, Robert O. and Nye, Joseph S. *Power and Interdependence*, second edition (London: Scott, Foresman, Little and Brown, 1989)

Kintis, Andreas G. 'The EU's Foreign Policy and the War in Former Yugoslavia', in Holland, Martin (ed.) *Common Foreign and Security Policy* (London: Pinter, 1997)

Laffan, Brigid *Integration and Cooperation in Europe* (London and New York: Routledge, 1992)

Lodge, Juliet (ed.) *The European Community and the Challenge of the Future*, second edition (London: Pinter, 1993)

Lowe, David 'Keynote Article: The Development Policy of the European Union and the Mid-Term Review of the Lomé Partnership', in Nugent, Neill (ed.) *The European Union 1995: Annual Review of Activities* (Oxford: Blackwell, 1996)

Mayhew, Alan *Recreating Europe: The European Union's Policy towards Central and Eastern Europe* (Cambridge: Cambridge University Press, 1998)

Miles, Lee (ed.) *The European Union and the Nordic Countries* (London: Routledge, 1996)

Mols, Manfred 'Cooperation with ASEAN: A Success Story', in Edwards, Geoffrey and Regelsberger, Elfriede (eds) *Europe's Global Links: The European Community and Inter-Regional Cooperation* (London: Pinter, 1990)

Moravcsik, Andrew 'Negotiating the Single European Act', in Keohane, Robert O. and Hoffmann, Stanley *The New European Community: Decisionmaking and Institutional Change* (Boulder: Westview, 1991)

Morgenthau, Hans revised by Thompson, Kenneth W. *Politics among Nations: The Struggle for Power and Peace*, sixth edition (New York: Alfred A. Knopf, 1985)

Neville-Jones, Pauline 'Dayton, IFOR and Alliance Relations in Bosnia', in *Survival*, Vol. 38 No. 4, Winter 1996–97

Nicoll, William and Salmon, Trevor C. *Understanding the European Communities* (London: Philip Allan, 1990)

Nørgaard, Ole 'The Post-Soviet Newly Independent States and the European Community: Prospects for Trade, Investment and Aid', in Nørgaard, Ole, Pedersen, Thomas and Petersen, Nikolaj *The European Community in World Politics* (London: Pinter, 1993)

Nørgaard, Ole, Pedersen, Thomas and Peterson, Nikolaj (eds) *The European Community in World Politics* (London: Pinter, 1993)

Nugent, Neill *The Government and Politics of the European Union*, fourth edition (London: Macmillan, 1999)

Nuttall, Simon *European Political Cooperation* (Oxford: Clarendon, 1992)

Office for Official Publications of the European Communities (OOPEC) *Treaties Establishing the European Communities*, abridged edition (Luxembourg: OOPEC, 1987)

Official Publications of the European Community, *Bulletin* of the European Union (Luxembourg: Office for Official Publications of the European Communities, published monthly)

Østergaard, Clemens Stubbe 'From Strategic Triangle to Economic Tripolarity: Japan's Responses to European Integration', in Nørgaard, Ole, Pedersen, Thomas and Petersen, Nikolaj (eds) *The European Community in World Politics* (London: Pinter, 1993).

Park, William *Defending the West: A History of NATO* (Brighton: Wheatsheaf, 1986)

Park, W. and Rees, G. Wyn (eds) *Rethinking Security in Post-Cold War Europe* (Harlow: Addison Wesley Longman: 1998)

Pedersen, Jørgen Dige 'The EC and the Developing Countries: Still Partners?', in Nørgaard, Ole, Pedersen, Thomas and Petersen, Nikolaj (eds) *The European Community in World Politics* (London: Pinter, 1993)

Peterson, John *Europe and America: The Prospects for Partnership* (London: Routledge, 1996)

Peterson, John and Sjursen, Helene (eds) *A Common Foreign Policy for Europe? Competing Visions of the CFSP* (London: Routledge, 1998)

Piening, Christopher *Global Europe: The European Union in World Affairs* (Boulder: Lynne Rienner, 1997)

Pijpers, Alfred, Regelsberger, Elfriede and Wessels, Wolfgang in collaboration with Edwards, Geoffrey (eds) *European Political Cooperation in the 1980s: A Common Foreign Policy for Western Europe?* (Dordrecht: Martinus Nijhoff/TEPSA, 1988)

Pinder, John *The European Community and Eastern Europe* (London: Pinter/RIIA, 1991)

Pollacco, Christopher *Malta–EEC Relations* (Msida, Malta: Mireva, 1992)

Rhodes, Carolyn (ed.) *The European Union in the World Community* (Boulder: Lynne Rienner, 1998)

Ruggie, John Gerard *Constructing the World Polity* (London: Routledge, 1998)

Rummel, Reinhardt (ed.) *Toward Political Union: Planning a Common Foreign and Security Policy in the European Community* (Nomos: Baden-Baden, 1992)

Sengupta, Jayshree 'The Effect of Project 1992 on the ASEAN', in Sideri, Sandro and Sengupta, Jayshree (eds) *The 1992 Single European Market and the Third World* (London: Frank Cass, 1992)

Shakona, Yousif Maloud Mohammed 'The Arab Regional Organizations' Relations with the European Community' (University of Kent: unpublished doctoral thesis, 1996)

Shultz, George P. *Turmoil and Triumph: My Years as Secretary of State* (New York: Charles Scribner's Sons, 1993)

Smith, Hazel 'European Community Policy towards Central America in the 1980s' (London School of Economics, doctoral thesis, 1993)

Smith, Hazel *European Union Foreign Policy and Central America* (London: Macmillan, 1995)

Smith, Hazel 'Actually Existing Foreign Policy – or Not? The European Union and Latin America', in Peterson, John and Sjursen, Helene (eds) *A Common Foreign Policy for Europe?* (London: Routledge, 1998)

Smith, Hazel (ed.) *Democracy and International Relations: Critical Theories/Problematic Practices* (London and New York: Macmillan and St Martin's Press, 2000)

Smith, Karen *The Making of EU Foreign Policy: The Case of Eastern Europe* (London: Macmillan, 1999)

Sperling, James and Kirchner, Emil *Recasting the European Order: Security Architectures and Economic Cooperation* (Manchester: Manchester University Press, 1997)

Stevens, Christopher 'Trade with Developing Countries', in Wallace, Helen (ed.) *The Wider Western Europe: Reshaping the EC/EFTA Relationship* (London: Pinter/RIIA, 1992)

Wallace, Helen and Wallace, William (eds) *Policy-Making in the European Union*, fourth edition (Oxford: Oxford University Press, 2000)

Waltz, Kenneth *Theory of International Politics* (New York: McGraw-Hill, 1979)

Weigall, David and Stirk, Peter (eds) *The Origins and Development of the European Community* (Leicester and London: Leicester University Press, 1992)

Weil, Gordon L. *A Foreign Policy for Europe* (Bruges: College of Europe, 1970)

Whitman, Richard 'Towards a Zone of Stability and Security in the Mediterranean? The EU and the Development of an EMEA', paper presented to UACES research conference, University of Birmingham, September 1995

Winn, Neil 'European Crisis Management in the 1980s', paper prepared for the annual conference of the British International Studies Association (BISA), York, December 1994

Woolcock, Stephen *Market Access Issues in EC–US Relations: Trading Partners or Trading Blows?* (London: RIIA/Pinter, 1991)

Zielonka, Jan (ed.) *Paradoxes of European Foreign Policy* (The Hague/London/Boston: Kluwer Law International, 1998)

WEBSITES

http://www.europa.eu.int/comm/dgs_en.htm
www.euromed.net/eu/iraq_en.htm
http://europa.eu.int/pol/enlarg/index_en.htm.

Index

Compiled by Auriol Griffith-Jones